THE DEVELOPMENT OF WORLD TRADE ORGANIZATION LAW

The Development of World Trade Organization Law

Examining Change in International Law

GREGORY MESSENGER

OXFORD
UNIVERSITY PRESS

OXFORD
UNIVERSITY PRESS

Great Clarendon Street, Oxford, OX2 6DP,
United Kingdom

Oxford University Press is a department of the University of Oxford.
It furthers the University's objective of excellence in research, scholarship,
and education by publishing worldwide. Oxford is a registered trade mark of
Oxford University Press in the UK and in certain other countries

First Edition published in 2016

Published in the United States of America by Oxford University Press
198 Madison Avenue, New York, NY 10016, United States of America

British Library Cataloguing in Publication Data
Data available

Library of Congress Control Number: 2015957149

ISBN 978–0–19–871646–4

Preface

This book aims to give an account of how the law of the World Trade Organization develops. This task is complicated by a number of factors: WTO law is not an island, whether in relation to general international law or to domestic legal systems; the substance and influence of WTO law extends far beyond its membership and, to further cloud matters, those involved in developing WTO law take numerous forms from judicial bodies to multinational corporations. Their roles are integral to understanding how WTO law functions as part of a fluid and dynamic system, continually changing and adapting.

Looking under the surface of WTO law, to the multiplicities of influences and actors involved, raises challenges to how we distinguish the relevant from the incidental and the fundamental from the superfluous. This book looks outside of traditional legal scholarship to confront this challenge, borrowing from philosophy and international relations theory. In doing so, it offers an approach that opens the examination of WTO law to a range of influences, acknowledging the role that law plays in further interests, constraining behaviour and constituting identities.

As part of a broad nexus of interlocking jurisdictions and interests, the WTO provides a particularly interesting example of how international law develops in a globalized age. The WTO is, on the one hand, a traditional and principally inter-State organization, on the other, a site of radical institutional development where both public and private global actors interact. It is an institution with near-universal membership that has to coexist with increasing numbers of regional and bilateral trade organizations, taking the analysis of WTO law and the WTO system beyond fragmentation debates and into an acknowledgement of multiple competing networks and jurisdictions that can be characterized as neither helping nor hindering the WTO but rather contributing to the development of its law.

The use of causal language as the principal explanatory tool for this book allows a wider examination of how WTO law develops as part of a globalized process. This is of particular importance now, as international law expands in both scope and reach and lawyers become increasingly important in helping to identify the relevant rights and duties of those concerned. There is a danger that in focussing on identifying the applicable law in a specific case, the broader questions over the development of law are set aside. The challenges posed by globalization to the traditional model of international law are frequently examined, however, this is increasingly left to scholars working in international relations. While offering insightful and interesting conclusions, there is an important place for legal scholars to engage with the way in which the law develops. Appreciative of law's difference from other norms and mindful of the importance of the legal rules *as they stand*, legal scholarship can offer insights into the changing nature of international regulation. This book is one such attempt, identifying a range of different influences on the development of law: the instrumental influence of law used to stimulate its development, the systemic influence of law constraining and enabling those within a system, and the constitutive influence of law creating identities and interests. The approach used is not social-scientific but instead one more suited to the skills of legal scholars based on pragmatic reasoning and analytical explanation. As such, it offers scholars of both law and international relations a challenge to the division of labour thus far adopted: to legal scholars it questions the utility of focussing on normative hierarchy and restricting analysis to rules rather than actors; to international relations scholars, it asserts the need to engage with legal systems as real and distinct social structures, which require different methodological approaches to those often used in the social sciences.

While the book does not seek to offer a predictive model of legal development through the WTO, it does offer certain insights that can be of interest not only to scholars but also to practitioners. A key theme that runs throughout is the unpredictability of attempts by globalized actors to encourage the development of WTO law in their favour. Whether through raising claims or creating institutions, the results are often unexpected. This is not to say, however, that no pattern can be discerned: indeed, the argument made here is that we can understand the development of law best once we accept the multiple ways in which law changes, stimulated by actors but not dependent upon them.

While this book does not set out a path to follow, it does identify certain trends in the success of such behaviour thus far. Beyond the WTO, it offers insights into how international organizations or institutions evolve and develop in light of the behaviour of globalized actors. In the face of international deadlock in negotiations (not only in trade), this book offers some examples of how an area of international law can develop in fascinating ways, often without anything as clear-cut as new international agreement. More importantly, it is hoped that it offers a possible analytical framework which may be of use in these non-WTO areas of international law.

Acknowledgements

A number of people and institutions have helped with the development and completion of this book. It is loosely based on my doctoral thesis, defended in December 2013 for which I was fortunate to have received funding from the Arts and Humanities Research Council. It would not have been possible to begin, proceed, or complete the thesis without the guidance of my supervisor, Dan Sarooshi. His clear analysis, encouragement, and patience have been indispensable and I consider myself extremely fortunate to have received such support and friendship during the doctorate and since. I am also indebted to my examiners, Dapo Akande and Mary Footer who provided rigorous and detailed comments in the *viva* and later. Their dedication helped to crystallize a number of ideas in the period since, particularly in turning the thesis into this book.

I have been extremely fortunate to have been supported by the Queen's College first as a graduate student, and later as a Junior Research Fellow. Queen's offered me a place not only to work on the book and pursue other projects, but also to do so in a truly multi-disciplinary and vibrant environment. I am also thankful for being able to be part of the international law communities at Oxford and Durham which offered exciting spaces in which to engage with international lawyers of almost all conceivable stripes. I am grateful to the Liverpool Law School and my new colleagues, especially Amandine Garde, for their support and encouragement in getting over the final hurdles to completion.

Any project is the result of discussions with a number of people and this book is no different. I have benefitted from conversations with and comments from friends and colleagues over the years, helping develop the ideas in the thesis and then from the thesis to the book. I am especially grateful to Jean d'Aspremont, Gleider Hernández, Lawrence Hill-Cawthorne, Frank Soodeen, Patricia Jimenez Kwast, Andrew Lang, Aiofe O'Donoghue, Martins Paparinskis, Michail Risvas, Fiona Smith, Robert Schütze, Antonios Tzanokopoulos, Stefan Talmon, Vaughan Lowe, and Calum Musto. I am particularly indebted to Raquel Barradas de Freitas who let me question her about any number of jurisprudential issues, and only ever responded with thoughtful observations and kindness.

I am thankful to John Louth and his team at Oxford University Press, in particular, Merel Alstein, Anthony Hinton, and Emma Endean. They have been both professional and patient with a frankly neurotic first-time author. I am grateful to them for their help in the process, as well as to the anonymous reviewers who provided a large number of constructive and insightful comments. I am also thankful to the production team, in particular Geetha Parakkat for her help in shepherding the book to publication.

This book could not have been completed without a close personal support network. I am grateful to Paul Earlie for his emotional support and affection, insight, and gentle reminders to be clear about what it is I mean. I am thankful for the support of my family, who have have offered both encouragement and the most loving space in which to enjoy each other's company, an hour around the kitchen table making up for any number of hours at a desk.

It is hard to express the debt I owe my parents, Chris and Ana Mari, for everything that they have done for me. Without their selfless and unflinching support in every conceivable form, I would not have the privilege of being able to pursue my vocation, let alone complete this work. This book is dedicated to them.

Table of Contents

Tables of Cases

1. INTERNATIONAL

A. GATT/WTO

1. GATT reports

2. WTO Panel Reports

B. International Court of Justice

C. Other

2. EU AND DOMESTIC

A. EU

B. USA

Table of Instruments

1. TREATIES

A. GATT/WTO

B. EU

C. Other international agreements

2. LEGISLATION

A. EU

1. Directives

2. Regulations

B. US

3. OTHER DOCUMENTS

A. GATT

B. WTO

C. EU

1

Introduction

A. Introduction

How does international law develop and how do we examine, specifically, the development of World Trade Organization (WTO) law? This book seeks to answer this question, offering an approach to examine the development of international law over time. It aims to offer an explanation of how WTO law has developed but also present insights into what these explanations tell us about how international law functions. A recurring theme of this book is the acknowledgement of the underlying complexity in how legal systems function at numerous levels. Complexity here is not presented as an impossible obstacle that cannot be overcome but rather as offering opportunities to acknowledge the multi-faceted and nuanced ways in which international law develops. This complexity finds voice not only in the object of our examination, the law itself, but also through the related concepts we use to examine the law. One such term, and the focus of this book, is 'development'.

This chapter introduces the foundations of the book. First (in Section B), it identifies the challenges we face in understanding how law develops over time, the relationship between the passage of time and law, and the tensions that underpin it. This part draws out these problems which sets the context for the remainder of the book as a study of how international law develops at the WTO. In Section C, the use of the WTO as a model for exploring such issues in international law is explained, identifying the characteristics of the WTO that offer so much potential to pursue broader investigation within its confines. Finally, Section D outlines the structure of the remainder of the book.

B. Legal Development and the 'Course of International Law'

We refer to the development of law often, though the idea of what development means in this context is often overlooked.[1] Where it is examined, it is as part of

[1] For example RY Jennings, 'The Judiciary, International and National, and the Development of International Law', (1996) 45 *International and Comparative Law Quarterly* 1–12.

another debate, customarily relating to judicial discretion or activism (depending on one's political outlook) rather than for its own sake. The term is nonetheless commonplace, and its analysis opens insights into how we understand the way in which law functions.

1. 'Progressive Development' and international law

Perhaps the most obvious reference to development of law in international law is the notion of 'progressive development'. Under the United Nations system, the 'progressive development' of international law is tasked to the General Assembly[2] and subsequently pursued by the International Law Commission.[3] Under the Charter, the wording indicates a distinction between 'progressive development' and 'codification' thus suggesting that progressive development cannot be mere codification.[4] Article 15 of the ILC Statute provides some guidance:

> In the following articles the expression 'progressive development of international law' is used for convenience as meaning the preparation of draft conventions on subjects which have not yet been regulated by international law or in regard to which the law has not yet been sufficiently developed in the practice of States.[5]

Here we have an account of development where rules are clarified and gaps are filled,[6] as opposed to codification which is understood as a process of 'formulation and systemization of rules in international law where there already has been extensive State practice, precedent and doctrine'.[7] Some accounts acknowledge that these are not two distinct categories but rather a matter of degree,[8] with both 'development'[9] and 'codification' playing a quasi-legislative role.[10] Indeed, Lauterpacht's bold claim, distinguishing the concept of codification in international law from that in domestic law, was that 'the task of codifying international law, if it is to mean anything, must be primarily one of bringing about an agreed body of rules rather than introducing systematic order and precision into legal rules already covered by customary or conventional agreement of states'.[11]

[2] Article 13(1)(a) Charter of the United Nations ('UN Charter') (26 June 1945) 59 Stat 1031; TS 993; 3 Bevans 1153.

[3] Statute of the International Law Commission ('ILC Statute') adopted by the General Assembly in resolution 174 (II) of 21 November 1947, as amended by resolutions 485 (V) of 12 December 1950, 984 (X) of 3 December 1955, 985 (X) of 3 December 1955 and 36/39 of 18 November 1981.

[4] Article 13(1)(a) UN Charter.

[5] Article 15 ILC Statute.

[6] Of this view: PC Jessup, 'Development of International Law by the United Nations', (1945) 39 *American Journal of International Law* 745, 755.

[7] Ibid.

[8] H Lauterpacht, 'Codification and Development of International Law', (1955) 49 *American Journal of International Law* 16.

[9] G Finch, 'The Progressive Development of International Law', (1947) 41 *American Journal of International Law* 611, depicting 'development' as a quasi-legislative process where particular issues (for example maintenance of peace) are prioritized.

[10] H Lauterpacht, 'Codification' n. 8, 29, describing the 'legislative function of developing and improving the law'.

[11] Ibid., 22.

Continuing: 'It follows from the preceding observations that, unlike codification in other fields, codification of international law must be substantially legislative in nature.'[12]

Aside from these early debates over the meaning of progressive development and codification in international law, the term 'development' has not received substantial treatment, with its use fitting into a range of different though related positions. For some, development is linked to institutional rather than normative advances in international law.[13] For many, however, the principal focus has been the concept of development as a specifically judicial form of developing the law, and how it relates to the appropriate exercise of powers by judicial bodies, at both international[14] and domestic levels.[15]

2. The development of international law and change

Today our usage of development is considered unproblematic: we customarily mean a form of legal activity between law-making and law-applying, traditionally used as part of the discourse regarding the appropriate role of judicial bodies. Yet law develops in a number of ways and through a number of influences, not only through judicial or indeed 'legislative' means, and not only by tribunals or States but by a range of actors across jurisdictional boundaries.[16] This complicates matters for a concept that is often used parasitically, given meaning on the basis of another on-going debate.

At a more fundamental level the concept of development contains a further layer of complexity. The development of law contains within it an implicit acknowledgement of change. For something to develop, it must change from one or many things into another. Development is, in its widest sense, the name we give to our explanation of change over time.

Change is a central part of the human experience: it requires an acknowledgement of both a changing world and our own change in relation to it. Change inspires optimism but also a deep disquiet and insecurity as we look to a world in seeming perpetual change.[17] In response to our anxiety we seek to identify

[12] Ibid., 29.

[13] T Meron, 'War Crimes in Yugoslavia and the Development of International Law', (1994) 88 *American Journal of International Law* 76.

[14] C Weeramantry, 'Constitutional and Institutional Developments: The Function of the International Court of Justice in the Development of International Law', (1997) 10 *Leiden Journal of International Law* 309.

[15] A Tzanakopoulos and CJ Tams, 'Introduction: Domestic Courts as Agents of Development of International Law', (2013) 26 *Leiden Journal of International Law* 531, 538.

[16] See A Lang, *World Trade Law After Neoliberalism: Reimaging the Global Economic Order* (Oxford, Oxford University Press 2011) 159–61; A Roberts and S Sivakumaran, 'Lawmaking by Nonstate Actors: Engaging Armed Groups in the Creation of International Humanitarian Law', (2012) 37(1) *Yale Journal of International Law* 107, 111–25.

[17] Captured in Heraclitus's theory of flux: '"everything gives way and nothing stands fast" and, likening the things that are to the flowing of a river, he says "you cannot step into the same river twice."' Plato *Cratylus* 402a in J Cooper (ed.), *Plato: Complete Works* (Indianapolis; Cambridge, Hackett 1997) 120.

continuity, stability, and similarities in what we examine. Thus, we describe the changed thing in such a way as to identify its history or antecedents; by sharing something in common with what went before this change is more easily understood and accepted.[18] In doing so, we explain the change more readily, seeking explanation as 'the desire for explanation seems to be satisfied only by the discovery that what appears to be new and different was there all the time'.[19]

For those interested in the study of law, this existential disquiet aroused by development as change is buttressed by a functional tension: like all law, international law must be certain yet fluid, precise yet open to modification.[20]

This tension between the need for stability and change creates numerous challenges for those concerned with the effective functioning of a legal system.[21] A treaty comes into force and at that point constitutes an obligation for the parties to it.[22] A rule of customary international law crystalizes and thus constitutes an obligation for those who have not objected to its formation.[23] These rules continue to apply long after they are first created, the world changes, circumstances change, subjects change, and thus the law must adapt to this reality so as to continue to find support, legitimation, and fulfil its purpose. The adaptation of the law, its development, requires mechanisms that permit the law to change in a way that maintains its authority.[24]

In his 2013 Hague Lectures, James Crawford identified the continual nature of change in law, subtitling them 'The Course of International Law' and thus capturing the sense of both an educational course as well as an inherent sense of movement and change over time. Echoing the insights of McDougal and Higgins amongst others, international law, in his account, was to be understood as a continual process of claim and counter-claim, adapting over time to the demands made of it by States.[25]

Similarly, in using the term 'development' in *The Development of International Law by the International Court*, Lauterpacht incorporated an acknowledgement of

[18] The philosophical underpinnings of such claims reach back to the earliest pre-Socratic debates regarding the nature of the universe, specifically in the Ionian school. For a concise analysis: WKC Guthrie, *The Greek Philosophers* (London, Methuen 1950) 22–42. The consequences of such debates are widely felt, presenting a number of challenges to questions of free will, summed up in the deeply ambivalent statement in Ecclesiastes 1.9: 'What has been is what will be, and what has been done is what will be done and there is nothing new under the sun.'

[19] L Stebbing, *A Modern Introduction to Logic* (2nd edn, London, Methuen 1933) 404.

[20] F Berman, 'What Does "Change" Mean? International Law vs. the International Legal System', (2003) 8 *Austrian Review of International and European Law* 11, 11.

[21] R Pound, *Interpretations of Legal History* (Cambridge, Cambridge University Press 1930) 1–2.

[22] Article 26, Vienna Convention on the Law of Treaties ('VCLT') (23 May 1969) 1155 UNTS 331; 8 ILM 679 (1969).

[23] *Anglo-Norwegian Fisheries* (*United Kingdom v Norway*) [1951] ICJ Rep 116, 131.

[24] See, M McDougal et al., *Studies in World Public Order* (New Haven, Yale University Press 1960) 10–11 and 170–2; J Raz, *The Authority of Law: Essays on Law and Morality* (Oxford, Oxford University Press 1979) 28–33.

[25] J Crawford, 'Chance, Order, Change: The Course of International Law', (2013) 365 *Recueil des Cours de l'Académie de Droit International* paras 1–2. In this sense, the judicial development of law is principally responsive: G Hernandez, *The International Court of Justice and the Judicial Function* (Oxford, Oxford University Press 2014) 185.

law as part of a dynamic and continual process requiring an acceptance of change as a central feature of our object of description.[26] Here Lauterpacht gave a clear and pragmatic account of the challenges faced by accommodating the passage of time within a legal system. While the role of the International Court[27] in developing international law was uncontroversial (provided it exercised this power with caution), he referred to the theoretical debates over judicial law-making as 'animated, but highly unreal'.[28] Nonetheless, Lauterpacht was aware of the challenges facing judicial involvement in developing the law, stating that though:

> A system of law expressly sanctioning judicial legislation would be a contradiction in terms ... At the same time, the fact remains that judicial law-making is a permanent feature of administration of justice in every society. The reconciliation, in this respect, between fact and legal theory is brought about by means of the fiction that the enunciation of the new rule is no more than an application of an existing legal principle or an interpretation of an existing text. In the international sphere the problem is complicated, on the one hand, by the requirement of caution and restraint called for by the sovereignty of States and by the voluntary and, therefore, precarious nature of the jurisdiction of international tribunals. It is intensified, on the other hand, by the strong inducements to supplement and remedy the deficiencies and inconsistencies of an imperfect system of law.[29]

The complications identified by Lauterpacht have changed little since. Indeed, they have grown in the face of the increasing institutionalization of the international legal order. Though some of the 'deficiencies' in international law have been resolved in some areas (notably the WTO), the demand to supplement the rules and procedures of the system is great, as is the extant importance of jurisdictional consent.

International law now regulates a staggering array of human activity from human rights protection to space missions, from environmental protection to the use of force. The detail of these international rules has increased, necessitating the involvement of domestic and regional institutions to incorporate rules into their own systems as well as the development of new international institutions to ensure compliance and facilitate further rule-making. The role of judicial bodies in the development of international law continues to stimulate debate, as increasingly does the role of secondary rule-making bodies. Traditional accounts of legal development solely through the decisions of judicial bodies and treaty change are no longer adequate to furnish complete explanations for how international law develops.[30]

[26] Echoed in other titles, for example, C J Tams and J Sloan (eds), *The Development of International Law by the International Court of Justice* (Oxford, Oxford University Press 2013).

[27] The collective term used by Lauterpacht to refer to the International Court of Justice and Permanent Court of International Justice. H Lauterpacht, *The Development of International Law by the International Court* (Cambridge, Cambridge University Press 2010 reissue, first published 1954) 3.

[28] H Lauterpacht, *Development*, n. 27, 21.

[29] Ibid., 155.

[30] See for example, the debate in: A Lang and J Scott, 'The Hidden World of WTO Governance', (2009) 20 *European Journal of International Law* 575; A Lang and J Scott, 'The Hidden World of WTO Governance: A Rejoinder to Richard H. Steinberg', (2010) 20 *European Journal of International Law* 1073.

One consequence of the institutional and substantive changes in international law is the increase in the number of participants involved in the development of international law in both the judicial and 'legislative' contexts.[31] These participants or actors range from States to transnational corporations and civil society organizations. The variety of actors and the augmented reach of international law (and its attendant institutions) have increased the number of potential interactions between domestic, regional, and international law in a variety of forms. Having a multitude of actors and institutions engaged in the creation, interpretation, and application of international law clutters our view of what may have once seemed a clear picture, international law as a system created and maintained by States based on consent. Instead, often covered by the leitmotif of globalization, we are in a time of intensive global interactions including (and in many ways dependent on) a complex legal framework of competing and interacting jurisdictional influences.[32]

3. Time and the development of international law

The greatest challenge to examining the development of law does not come from the increased number of actors in international relations or the increasing frequency of interactions to which they are parties. These changes make the examination and analysis of international law more difficult, but they are not the underlying difficulty in reconciling the way we describe the law with the way we experience the passage of time.

Specifically, the difficulty is this: accounts of what international law is are based on law as expressed through decisions (judicial or quasi-legislative) at specific points in time. This has distracted us from appreciating that law develops continually and that snapshots (the judgment, the treaty, the formulation of custom) are not adequate to explain how law develops. The changes in law that constitute its process of development are subtle and continuous while accounts of the development of law over time based around static moments are problematic, based on the assumption that law can be determined at a set point in time until a later moment of interpretation, declaration, or modification.[33]

In instances where custom develops or interpretation in light of practice changes, the premise is that there exists a moment, a specific point in time which marks this

[31] 'Legislative' in the sense of primary rule-making that is not judicial in nature. Lauterpacht was quite comfortable with this terminology, though some might prefer a more cautious approach: S Talmon, 'The Security Council as World Legislature', (2005) 99 *American Journal of International Law* 175.

[32] A Hurrell, *On Global Order: Power, Values, and the Constitution of International Society* (Oxford, Oxford University Press 2007) 199.

[33] The study of 'legalization' (understood as the 'dynamic process through which law changes and develops') is a notable exception: J Dunnoff and M Pollack (eds), *Interdisciplinary Perspectives on International Law and International Relations: The State of the Art* (Cambridge, Cambridge University Press 2013) 34. See also, Abbott et al., 'The Concept of Legalization', (2000) 54(3) *International Organization* 401 and the accompanying volume.

transition from the law that was and the law that now is.[34] To explain the development of law in this manner is to explain the development of law from *a* to *b* to *c*, rather than as part of a continuum where discrete moments are inseparable from those that go before and after them.[35] Such static accounts simplify the role of the interpreter (in whichever capacity) as static in time, enjoying a stable relationship with the subject of interpretation.[36]

At a superficial level, this presupposes a 'correct' interpretation at a specific point in time (for example, a judgment) though the history of legal scholarship and practice is replete with examples of seemingly clear judgments being reappraised and redefined, their 'true' meaning illuminated and then applied.[37] More importantly, however, is the way in which the conception of law as static points in time distorts our accounts of what the law is. This is clearer if we take a recent example, the *Peru v Chile* maritime dispute.[38]

The case concerned the delimitation of the maritime boundary between Peru and Chile. Peru denied that the boundary had ever been fixed, claiming that all previous arrangements had been provisional or in the interest of maintaining neighbourly relations, and thus the boundary should now be fixed using the equidistance principle. For its part, Chile claimed that a maritime boundary had been fixed along the parallel of latitude since 1952, evidenced by a number of agreements and subsequent practice.

The Court's analysis was entirely orthodox: it identified the key moments in the history of Chile–Peru relations vis-à-vis their maritime zones, as identified (through the process of litigating the case) by the parties to the dispute.[39] Specifically, it pointed to the unilateral proclamations made by Chile, Ecuador, and Peru in 1947 claiming a 200 nautical mile extension of certain maritime rights, the 1952 Santiago Declaration between Chile, Ecuador, and Peru which claimed exclusive rights over the maritime zone as well as the seabed and subsoil, and the 1954 Special Maritime Frontier Zone Agreement which used the parallel as a dividing line, the purpose of which was to reduce friction from issues arising from local fishing vessels inadvertently crossing into the waters of neighbouring States.

[34] This raises serious conceptual challenges, especially in the case of customary international law, over when an act is a breach of, or a change in, the customary rule. For a novel analysis: B Lepard, *Customary International Law: A New Theory with Practical Applications* (Cambridge, Cambridge University Press 2010) 277–84.

[35] This image is informed by Bergson's critique of understanding time as a series of instances rather than a continual relationship between one's perception of past and present. H Bergson, *An Introduction to Metaphysics* (London, Macmillan 1913), in particular at 10–11. See also, AD Lindsay, *The Philosophy of Bergson* (London, JM Dent & Sons 1911) 94: 'Consciousness cannot be regarded as a series of momentary states: for all consciousness is consciousness of time and hence of change.'

[36] For sensitive accounts of such a challenge: R Dworkin, 'How Law is Like Literature', in *A Matter of Principle* (Oxford, Oxford University Press 1986) 146–77, at 158; I Venzke, *How Interpretation Makes International Law: On Semantic Change and Normative Twists* (Oxford, Oxford University Press 2012) 46–9; T Endicott, *Vagueness in the Law* (Oxford, Oxford University Press 2000) 9–15.

[37] For example, the reappraisal of the *Lotus case* in the joint separate opinion of Judges Higgins, Koojimans, and Buergenthal, *Arrest Warrant of 11 April 2000 (Democratic Republic of the Congo v Belgium)* (Judgment) [2002] ICJ Rep 3, para. 51.

[38] *Maritime Dispute (Peru v Chile)* (Judgment) [2014] ICJ Rep 3.

[39] Ibid., para. 24.

The Court was clear that neither the 1947 proclamations nor the 1952 Santiago Declaration delimited the boundary between Chile and Peru. It did, however, consider that the 1954 Agreement demonstrated that a boundary had been agreed, though not in that specific instrument.[40] This is not surprising, the nature of events and our experience of them is such that we cannot distinguish specific discrete moments in time, rather they are part of a continuum, distinguished in our minds only because we give them retrospective importance.[41] The Court found itself in this position, returning to the continual practice of Peru and Chile in the intervening years, looking to, *inter alia*, the behaviour of fishing vessels to determine the terms of the agreement (for which there was no clear specific moment in time).[42]

The Court, however, found itself trapped by the way in which we speak of law: it thus constructed the maritime boundary through specific milestones, with 'practice' filling in the gaps. The conclusion of the Court on this point is not the key issue, rather the way in which it sought to construct a moment of agreement. The Court sought to use static moments, encased in text, yet these moments are not static, and the legal obligations involved did not develop at specific points in time but rather fluidly over time (as its search through fishing practices acknowledged). By prioritizing fixed points in time the Court constructed facts based on static events encased in text which in turn impacts on others whose experiences and factual situation is not understood through the same 1947–1952–1954 linearity. This is not an abstract problem: ways in which the Court set out the facts of the Peru–Chile dispute could well have an impact on other cases, including the pending *Bolivia v Chile* dispute, as the territorial overlap in both cases is significant.[43] The authoritative claim of the Court as to the facts and their subsequent legal consequences set the ground for later participants to engage with the same subject matter. It is not that the legal rights of a third party may have been affected which is relevant, it is rather that the way in which the world thinks of the facts in this instance is distorted by the presentation of a narrative built on a linear construction of history and the law.[44]

To examine the development of international law requires an acknowledgement of these complexities: the trying conceptual foundations of dynamic change, the multiplicity of sources, and diversity of actors. It is in the face of these challenges that this book turns to causal language: the relationship between causal concepts and how we understand the world is profound and, for our purposes, indispensable. By turning to causal language we can find ways to incorporate

[40] Ibid., paras 90–2.

[41] To think of a moment in time is a conscious effort, as soon as we think of the moment immediately before or after we know that there is no line dividing them. A static point in time in our recollection then is a snapshot: 'Immobility [in the sense of the image of a static point in time] is but a picture (in the photographic sense of the word) taken of reality by our mind.' H Bergson, *Écrits et paroles*, translated in L Kolakowski, *Bergson* (Oxford, Oxford University Press 1985) 12–13.

[42] *Peru v Chile*, n. 38, paras 104–11.

[43] *Obligation to Negotiate Access to the Pacific Ocean* (*Bolivia v Chile*).

[44] It should be noted that boundary disputes are highly emotive, relating in a direct way to some of the fundamental conceptions of Statehood through territoriality.

our understanding of how law develops in a dynamic fashion, taking on board the challenges identified in examining how international law changes over time. Chapter 2 develops this approach, tracing the merits of using causal language to clarify the way in which we can understand how law develops in light of a multiplicity of influences. Importantly, it also reframes common accounts of how international law functions by identifying the implicit causal nature of these explanations. A reconceptualization of how we understand causes in our explanation of legal development offers a range of tools to help us in our quest to make sense of the temporal and interactional challenges of international law's development in a globalized age.

C. The World Trade Organization as a Bellwether

The WTO is a fascinating object of study, yet while widely hailed early on by those in legal and political fields, for many it appears to have failed to live up to its promise. At a political level there has been near-deadlock in negotiations over further large-scale liberalization for over a decade, while legally, the novelty of the impressive dispute settlement system has worn off and many disputes revolve around what many might consider technical matters of interest only to specialists.

Why then choose the WTO as an object of study to examine how we understand the development of international law? Put simply, the WTO is the international law laboratory par excellence. Challenges faced by international law today, whether relating to substantive obligations, institutional challenges, procedural matters, or interpretative debates, are all present within the WTO. Issues which are considered potential or theoretical in other areas of international law are present and pressing at the WTO. Questions arise over the actions of sub-State bodies,[45] whether WTO law regulates acts of the executive which do not claim binding force,[46] the acts of seemingly private bodies within the domestic sphere,[47] or private bodies at the international level.[48] These debates arise in diverse areas of international law, yet at the WTO we are offered the opportunity to examine them with a comparatively complete factual record[49]

[45] Provincial milk marketing boards in Canada, for example: *Canada—Measures Affecting the Importation of Milk and the Exportation of Dairy Products*, Report of the Appellate Body (13 October 1999) WT/DS103-113/AB/R.

[46] *Japan—Measures Affecting Consumer Photographic Film and Paper*, Panel Report (31 March 1998) WT/DS44/R, para. 10.49.

[47] In the case of State-owned commercial banks, for example: *United States—Definitive Anti-Dumping and Countervailing Duties on Certain Products from China*, Report of the Appellate Body (11 March 2011) WT/DS379/AB/R.

[48] See the debates arising at the WTO from the influence of private standard setting bodies: Note by the Secretariat, 'Private Standards and the SPS Agreement' (24 January 2007) G/SPS/GEN/746.

[49] Rare, perhaps, though relevant: for example, the debates in *Oil Platforms* (*Islamic Republic of Iran v United States of America*) (Judgment) [2003] ICJ Rep 161, especially the Separate Opinion of Judge Owada, paras 41–52.

and without prior complications relating to jurisdictional issues or rule identification.[50]

The traditional criticisms of international law are, to a larger part than in any other area of international law,[51] rectified at the WTO: it includes a detailed set of obligations (the covered agreements), an effective institutional structure for the development and interpretation of these obligations as well as to ensure their compliance.[52] Together these improvements have led to increasing influence of international law (in the form of WTO law) between the members and within their territory.[53]

Beyond these formal institutional and normative developments, there also exist important informal institutional structures of the WTO, engaging with transnational regulators, other international organizations, civil society and interest groups, all under the aegis of 'trade' relations yet sensitive to the pervasive nature of trade as a motivator for regulation.[54]

The institutional framework of the WTO, both formal and informal, and its (comparatively) detailed set of rules make it a particularly attractive site to a wide set of actors whether States of varying levels of economic strength, non-governmental organizations, multinational enterprises, or transnational regulators. Though nominally restricted to States and customs unions,[55] the members of the WTO play a principal rather than exclusive role in the institution.

It is for all of these reasons that we see in the WTO concerns or points of interest across international law playing out here. The examples examined in this book are illustrative; even within this limited selection we can identify questions of how law engages with questions of intergenerational equity and how conceptions of fairness can be accommodated within processes of law-making and interpretation, democratic legitimacy and governance (including debates over standard of review), the relationship between public and private actors at the international plane, and

[50] See, the noted debates regarding applicable law in *Military and Paramilitary Activities in and against Nicaragua* (*Nicaragua v United States of America*) (Merits) [1986] ICJ Rep 14.

[51] The obvious exception is the law of the European Union (EU) which constitutes a form of regional international law: ILC, 'Fragmentation of International Law: Difficulties Arising from the Diversification and Expansion of International Law' (13 April 2006) A/CN4/L682, paras 46–222. Nonetheless, the near uniform claims of its *sui generis* nature make it an unhelpfully contentious example.

[52] Through a range of institutional structures, not only formal dispute settlement procedures: M Footer, 'Some Theoretical and Legal Perspectives on WTO Compliance', (2007) 38 *Netherlands Yearbook of International Law* 61.

[53] Debates regarding the direct effect of WTO obligations within the EU notwithstanding: H Ruiz Fabri, 'Is There a Case—Legally and Politically—for Direct Effect of WTO Obligations?', (2014) 25(1) *European Journal of International Law* 151.

[54] J Steffek, 'Awkward Partners: NGOs and Social Movements at the WTO' and S McGuire, 'What Happened to the Influence of Business? Corporations and Organized Labour in the WTO,' in A Narlikar, M Dauton, and R Stern (eds), *The Oxford Handbook on the World Trade Organization* (Oxford, Oxford University Press 2012), M Krajewski, 'Legitimising Global Governance Through Transnational Parliamentarisation: How Far Have We Come? How Much Further Must We Go?', in T Cottier and M Elsig (eds), *Governing the World Trade Organization: Past, Present and Beyond Doha* (Cambridge, Cambridge University Press 2011).

[55] Article XII.1, Agreement Establishing the World Trade Organization ('WTO Agreement') (15 April 1994) 1867 UNTS 154; (1994) 33 ILM 1144.

the ability of international law to accommodate a variety of State forms within a uniform set of rules.[56]

D. Structure of the Book

This book is structured as follows. Chapter 2 sets out the book's principal claims: specifically, it identifies international law as part of a global process (B) and the international legal system as both complex and complicated (C). These sections expand upon the observations made in this chapter, on law's fraught relationship with the passage of time and the challenges faced by international law's place as part of an intricate web crossing jurisdictional boundaries. Chapter 2 continues by turning to causal language in order to clarify and reframe the challenges presented by the development of international law (D). Specifically, three common explanatory approaches to describing the way in which law functions (formalism, functionalism, and idealism) are reappraised as expressing different types of cause on the development of law. By setting out a conception of 'cause' built on classical insights to causation, this chapter opens the possibility of understanding the law's development in causal terms.

Having identified the causal influences at play in the development of international law, Chapter 3 examines them in the specific context of international trade regulation at the WTO. It analyses the constitutive (B), instrumental (C), and systemic (D) influences of law at the WTO. In doing so, it draws on a range of materials to identify commonalities across seemingly competing theories of legal development, suggesting that legal accounts can explain most clearly how actors develop the law across the globe, influenced by the law they seek to develop.

Chapters 4, 5, and 6 narrow the examination to specific areas of trade regulation, each offering different insights and lessons for the development of law more generally. Chapter 4 examines the seemingly simple example of WTO law developing through the use of domestic models of legislation and impelled by specifically domestic concerns by examining the law on safeguard measures. The relationship between the expectations of those encouraging this legal development and the unexpected outcomes is the substance of this chapter. Chapter 5 moves from examining legal development through domestic influences (and its surprising results) to understanding the development of international law through inter-institutional contestations. Specifically it examines the challenges presented by competing methodologies for resolving disputes in the case of sanitary and phytosanitary (SPS) measures. The relationship between key concepts within SPS regulation and the institutions involved in their interpretation at the WTO are illuminated, demonstrating the importance of institutional identities and the underlying epistemological conflicts between them. Chapter 6 moves to the challenge of regulating areas of action which challenge fundamental distinctions in trade

[56] Chapters 4, 5, and 6 respectively.

regulation, here specifically, conceptions of public and private authority. Using the regulation of subsidies as an example, this chapter examines the development of WTO law in this area through processes of contestation relating to the appropriate scope of governmental action and their oversight at the WTO. Each chapter examines a different dimension of a globalized legal process: from a US–WTO dynamic, to a (partial) EU–US dynamic, and finally to China's role in contesting fundamental concepts under the WTO law.

The final chapter (Chapter 7) offers insights taken from the preceding analysis. Principally, it draws attention to the need to understand law as a multi-causal construct, one that can only be fully understood through causal language. Drawing lessons from the specifics of WTO law, this chapter looks to international law more broadly, seeking to open avenues of possible further investigation into the development of international law in a globalized world.

2

International Law in a Globalized World

A. Introduction

When discussing the current state of international law, or international relations more broadly, it is customary to refer to the exceptional time in which we live.[1] In particular we draw attention to the cultural, political, and economic processes of globalization as a distinguishing feature of our age and as the pre-eminent phenomenon through which we reappraise the perennial debates in international law scholarship: fragmentation, legitimacy, effectiveness, and authority.[2] Indeed, for the examination of how international law develops over time, and most particularly in international economic affairs, engaging with the concept of globalization would appear to be essential.

The more sceptical reader might draw attention to previous periods in history of international economic and cultural interdependence, of heterogeneous communities of actors (transnational and otherwise), and institution building.[3] A critical reader might identify the vagueness of the concept and its ability to mean a number of things to a number of people, 'anything from the Internet to a hamburger. All too often … a polite euphemism for the continuing Americanisation of consumer tastes and cultural practices'.[4] It is a deeply contested concept, in part a result of its mixed provenance from various disciplines and conceptual frameworks.[5]

Nonetheless, there is merit in acknowledging the importance of 'globalization' in its reified form; not only because it has become a core part of our discourse and thus worthy of engagement but also because it speaks to a phenomenon, not a new one necessarily, but one which is currently experienced with an intensity which is distinct from previous periods of history.

[1] P Lamy, *The Geneva Consensus: Making Trade Work For All* (Cambridge, Cambridge University Press 2013) 1–18.

[2] For example, M Kumm, 'The Legitimacy of International Law: A Constitutionalist Framework of Analysis', (2004) 15(5) *European Journal of International Law* 907; N Roughan, *Authorities: Conflicts, Cooperation, and Transnational Legal Theory* (Oxford, Oxford University Press 2013).

[3] For a concise account: M Steger, *Globalization: A Very Short Introduction* (3rd edn, Oxford, Oxford University Press 2013) 17–36.

[4] S Strange, *The Retreat of the State* (Cambridge, Cambridge University Press 1996) xiii.

[5] I Clark, *Globalization and International Relations Theory* (Oxford, Oxford University Press 1999) 34.

How then are we to clarify what we mean by globalization and what this means for understanding international law today? We might narrow the discussion by focussing on a specific aspect of globalization, its economic dimension, for example.[6] However, globalization includes cultural and social aspects which have direct relevance for our legal discussions as they impact upon our understanding of the law and how it is applied or altered.

More fruitfully, we can identify key features of globalization, such as interdependence or interconnectedness,[7] or the pre-eminence of movement (whether of people, capital, goods, or ideas).[8] Here, however, the focus is given to the primacy of interaction. This is especially pertinent as the central characteristic as one of globalization's primary features in its current form is its dependence on new technologies. These technologies do not require individuals to physically move to be able to play an engaged role in a transnational community or engage with others across jurisdictional boundaries.[9] Thus, by focussing on interactions, when we refer to globalization we refer not to something new per se but specifically to the high intensity of interactions between actors across the globe.[10] Such interactions may be economic, cultural, or political, while the actors involved range from individuals to the institutions they create.

As a descriptive account, there are limitations, however. The phenomenon of globalization is not truly global, or at least, the intensity of these interactions is not uniform. Levels of interconnectedness, integration into international systems of trade and finance, capacity for free movement of people, all vary between States. To offer a view of the world as 'globalized' is to offer an account of how we understand the world, premised on fundamentally liberal assumptions prioritizing the individual. In offering accounts of how international law develops today, however, globalization serves as a more accurate description of how global processes (including international law) function as compared to the traditional alternative: the Westphalian State system.[11] Indeed, one of the strengths of globalization as an

[6] R Gilpin, *Global Political Economy* (Princeton, Princeton University Press 2001) 364.

[7] D Held, A McGrew, D Goldblatt, and J Perraton (eds), *Global Transformations, Politics, Economics and Culture* (Cambridge, Polity Press 1999) 2, 'the widening, deepening and speeding up of worldwide interconnectedness in all aspects of contemporary social life, from the cultural to the criminal, the financial to the spiritual.'

[8] For example, 'the mass movement of persons, capital, ideas and information—summed up as "globalization"', J Crawford, 'Chance, Order, Change: The Course of International Law', (2013) 365 *Recueil des Cours de l'Académie de Droit International* para. 122.

[9] S Strange n. 4, 7–9; P Bobbitt, *The Shield of Achilles: War, Peace and the Course of History* (London, Penguin 2002) 725. Beyond the more traditional examples, we might note that over 140 million people engage in truly transnational activities in the form of co-operative and competitive electronic entertainment: <http://www.statista.com/statistics/261262/number-of-online-gamers-worldwide-by-region> while the second largest exercise in popular voting (second only to the Indian general election) is the Eurovision song contest where individuals vote from the Pacific coast of Russia to the Atlantic shores of Morocco.

[10] A 'trend' rather than a discrete phenomenon: R Keohane, *Power and Governance in a Partially Globalized World* (London, Routledge 2002) 15.

[11] Accepting the globalization ideal over the Westphalian ideal has the effect of further entrenching globalization discourse in our understanding of international law. This is unavoidable though it serves as a meta-example of the constitutive influences discussed later in this chapter: D.4(c).

account of global processes is its ability to assimilate the principles of an international legal system of sovereign States. Globalization as a concept does not reject the primary role of States in international law: it merely claims that they do not play the *only* role in international law. States remain central actors in every field of international law and fundamental to understanding how it is that international law develops.[12]

By putting globalization at the centre of the analysis of international law, we can illustrate the complexities and nuances of how international law develops. Instead of examining the effect of globalization on international law, or international law's effect on globalization, we instead understand globalization as a continuum of global processes of varying intensity of which international law is one.

This chapter makes two inter-related claims: first, international law is a global process, and understanding it as such offers numerous advantages to make sense of the development of international law; second, that in opening our analysis in this fashion we are presented with a profoundly complex and complicated picture, a picture that can be understood most clearly in causal terms. The causal move is essential as it reframes common competing accounts of how international law develops into a holistic model that accepts the different ways in which different influences impact upon the development of law.

B. International Law as a Global Process

International law develops in light of influences from across jurisdictional boundaries. While the international legal system may be understood in formal terms as a single legal system,[13] in practice international law is created and developed through numerous interactions at a number of levels of governance and between actors in both private and public spheres.[14]

This is particularly the case in international trade; WTO law is inspired by domestic and regional trade law just as domestic and regional systems are required to comply with WTO rules.[15] Complementing this bidirectional relationship is

[12] A Hurrell, *On Global Order: Power, Values, and the Constitution of International Society* (Oxford, Oxford University Press 2007) 26.

[13] *Ahmadou Sadio Diallo (Republic Of Guinea v Democratic Republic of the Congo) Compensation,* (Judgment) [2012] ICJ Rep 324, declaration of Judge Greenwood, para. 8: 'International law is not a series of fragmented specialist and self-contained bodies of law, each of which functions in isolation from the others; it is a single, unified system of law and each international court can, and should, draw on the jurisprudence of other international courts and tribunals, even though it is not bound necessarily to come to the same conclusions.' See also, *United States—Standards of Reformulated and Conventional Gasoline*, Report of the Appellate Body (20 May 1996) WT/DS2/AB/R, DSR 1996:I, 16.

[14] Identifying the challenge between these two propositions: B Simma, 'Of Planets and the Universe: Self-Contained Regimes in International Law', (2006) 17 *European Journal of International Law* 483, 484.

[15] For example, twenty-three out of twenty-six of the original GATT 1947 provisions were largely based on US proposals: D Sarooshi, 'Sovereignty, Economic Autonomy, the United States, and the International Trading System', (2004) 15(4) *European Journal of International Law* 651, fn 74.

the network of institutions that have developed at the WTO (and beyond) that serve as both forums for the membership as well as autonomous actors in their own right. The result is a complex network of domestic, regional, and international influences on the development of WTO law that go beyond the disciplines found in the covered agreements or the interpretations given by panels and the Appellate Body.

In international trade, the primary concern of trade agreements was once the reduction of tariffs and other border measures.[16] Today, the international trade regime centred at the WTO is concerned with both tariff and non-tariff barriers to trade in goods and services as well as aspects of the regulation of intellectual property rights.[17] At the regional level, the number of trade agreements has increased dramatically over the past three decades,[18] deepening the level of trade liberalization between those States beyond their obligations at the WTO. For some States, their commitments at both the international and regional levels in the regulation of international trade have led to the creation of domestic mechanisms for the enforcement of international and regional trade-related rights and obligations.[19] States that do not have comparable domestic regimes are still required to maintain conformity of their domestic laws, regulations, and administrative procedures with their obligations under the covered agreements,[20] as are international organizations that are also members of the WTO such as the European Union.

The regulation of international trade is particularly susceptible to a global analysis as the norms from which obligations stem at the international, regional, and domestic levels are incorporated and transferred from one level to another.[21] Increasing numbers of obligations under WTO law require members to enact specific internal mechanisms to comply with those obligations.[22] The obligations

[16] P Mavroidis, *The General Agreement on Tariffs and Trade: A Commentary* (Oxford, Oxford University Press 2009) 7–8.

[17] See Agreement Establishing the World Trade Organization ('WTO Agreement') (15 April 1994) 1867 UNTS 154; (1994) 33 ILM 1144 and its Annexes.

[18] See *The WTO and Preferential Trade Agreements: From Co-existence to Coherence* (World Trade Report 2011).

[19] For example: in the United States of America, the *Uruguay Round Agreements Act of 1994* (Pub L 103–465, 108 Stat 4809) and *Statement of Administrative Action* (H.Doc 103–316 (I), at 1032–33) set out the framework for the incorporation of obligations under the WTO covered agreements into US law; while in the European Union, *Council Regulation (EC) No 260/2009 of 26 February 2009 on the common rules for imports* [2009] OJ L84/1 sets out the generally applicable rules in line with obligations under the WTO covered agreements. Both US and EU law is supplemented with further specific provisions for other aspects of obligations under the WTO (e.g. calculating anti-dumping margins etc).

[20] Article XVI(4) WTO Agreement, Art. 26 Vienna Convention on the Law of Treaties ('VCLT') (23 May 1969) 1155 UNTS 331; 8 ILM 679.

[21] The phenomenon of multi-sourced equivalent norms: T Broude and Y Shany (eds), *Multi-Sourced Equivalent Norms in International Law* (Oxford, Hart Publishing 2011). See also the ongoing work of the International Law Association Study Group on Principles on the Engagement of Domestic Courts with International Law.

[22] For example, Art. X General Agreement on Tariffs and Trade (1994) Multilateral Agreements on Trade in Goods ('GATT') 1867 UNTS 187; Art. III General Agreement on Trade in Services ('GATS') 1869 UNTS 183; and Art. 63 Agreement on Trade-Related Aspects of Intellectual Property Rights ('TRIPS') 1869 UNTS 299 all require the publication of laws and regulations that may impact the trade in those areas, while under the Annex B.3 Agreement on the Application of

under the covered agreements are incorporated as members introduce new legislation or administrative procedures to comply with their WTO commitments. While the internal obligations are not international in nature (the distinction between international and domestic law stands), they are coterminous with the WTO obligation.[23] Conversely, the use of domestic provisions in new WTO provisions has a similar effect, blurring the usefulness of maintaining the distinction between WTO law and other relevant systems of law in the final analysis. There are areas of activity that will be subject to numerous overlapping jurisdictions; health regulations enacted by Member States of the European Union is a clear example where domestic law, EU law, and WTO law are all relevant.[24] Though as a matter of positive law the obligations can be separated (and are by judicial or quasi-judicial bodies), the process of 'judicial dialogue'[25] whereby the judiciaries of different jurisdictions engage with each other's decisions or acts is well documented, even where the judicial bodies do not explicitly make reference to the other jurisdiction in question.[26]

The nature of trade regulation in the global economy thus requires a broader approach to understand its development. Rather than examining only legal rules and principles under the covered agreements or the domestic law of States as a matter of their own law, we must examine the different levels of interactions between different jurisdictions. Gregory Shaffer gives a vivid account of this in the context of privacy standards in the EU and US. He states:

> [S]ingle jurisdictional analysis fails to account for the dynamics of regulatory change in a globalizing economy. What happens in one jurisdiction can affect not only the playing field in other jurisdictions, but also the players' perceptions of their stakes ... We live in a world where it is less and less accurate to think solely in terms of national regulation and national institutions. In one sense, the EU Directive is an exogenous force in internal U.S. conflicts over the regulation of privacy protection, shifting the stakes of U.S. political

Sanitary and Phytosanitary Measures ('SPS') 1867 UNTS and Art. 10 Agreement on Technical Barriers to Trade ('TBT') 1868 UNTS 120, members are also required to set up 'enquiry points' for traders.

[23] 'Coterminous' is used to describe those rights and duties that members have incorporated into their own legal systems to comply with the covered agreements. These may be incorporations by reference to the covered agreements themselves, verbatim repetition of the relevant provisions of the covered agreements in a domestic legal instrument or alternatively may be worded differently but held to be compliant (by the member) with their obligations under the covered agreements. While they constitute separate legal obligations (domestic and not international), their substance is such that they necessarily imply consequences for the member at the WTO level where they are not WTO compliant.

[24] Though the relationship between potential overlapping domestic and EU obligations is in theory settled (through Case 6/64 *Costa v ENEL* [1964] ECR 585 to Declaration No 17 concerning primacy, annexed to the Lisbon Treaty [2010] OJ C83/344), in practice the situation is potentially more complicated (cf., s. 18 European Union Act 2011 and *Brunner v The European Union Treaty*, Case 2134/92, 1 *Common Market Law Review* 57 (1994)).

[25] For example, A Tzanakopoulos, 'Judicial Dialogue in Multi-level Governance: The Impact of the Solange Argument', in O Fauchald and A Nollkaemper (eds), *The Practice of International and National Courts and the (De-)fragmentation of International Law* (Oxford, Hart Publishing 2012).

[26] M Bronckers, 'From "Direct Effect" to "Muted Dialogue": Recent Developments in the European Courts' Case Law on the WTO and Beyond', (2008) 11(4) *Journal of International Economic Law* 885.

and economic actors. On the other hand, it is misleading simply to segregate the foreign from the domestic, the external from the internal. In importing and exporting goods and services, countries can also import standards and procedures. In a globalizing economy characterized by high numbers of transactions, widely dispersed stakes, and competing national, regional, and transnational jurisdictional authorities, the allocation of decision-making among alternative institutions (be they markets, legislatures, or courts) at alternative levels of social organization (be they sub-states, states, regions, or international regimes) becomes even more complex.[27]

Shaffer identifies both the benefits of a multi-jurisdictional account and its core challenge: the complexity of global process accounts. The use of causal language as an explanatory tool to clarify the interactions of law in a complex and complicated system is introduced later, though the key point to identify here is the importance of process accounts that acknowledge influences across jurisdictions.

A caveat is required at this stage: while it is argued that we should examine international law as part of a process in which domestic law plays a significant role, this book does not aim to set out a fully functioning model of how domestic law and international law at the WTO relate to each other at a formal level (i.e. as a matter of positive law). It does not make a normative case for the primacy of one system over another nor does it suggest rules for conflict avoidance or resolution where an inconsistency appears (if we accept that such an inconsistency can exist).[28] It will be argued that process accounts offer a useful, though incomplete, analytical approach to examining how law develops in light of multi-jurisdictional influences.

1. The key characteristics of process-based accounts

While process-based accounts need not accept a multi-jurisdictional analysis of the law, they often do.[29] Some of the key characteristics of process-based accounts of law are examined here, identifying the advantages that such accounts may have in examining the development of international law taking into account the influence of different legal systems and influences.

The desire to break down the barriers between domestic legal systems and public international law is not new. Phillip Jessup coined the term 'transnational law' in 1956[30]

[27] G Shaffer, 'Globalization and Social Protection: The Impact of EU and International Rules in the Ratcheting Up of U.S. Privacy Standards', (2000) 25 *Yale Journal of International Law* 1, 38.

[28] Important though these issues are, the vast body of literature arising from decisions concerning conflicting supremacy claims in international law (such as the *Kadi* saga) is a testament to this.

[29] In some cases, the relationship between multi-jurisdictional examination and process accounts are necessarily related: H Steiner, 'Constructing and Developing Transnational Law: The Contribution of Detlev Vagts', in PHF Bekker, R Dolzer, and M Waibel (eds), *Making Transnational Law Work in the Global Economy: Essays in Honour of Detlev Vagts* (Cambridge, Cambridge University Press 2010) 12–14.

[30] P Jessup, *Transnational Law* (New Haven, Yale University Press 1956) 2: 'I shall use, instead of "international law", the term "transnational law" to include all law which regulates actions or events that transcend national frontiers. Both public and private international law are included, as are other rules which do not wholly fit into such standard categories.'

while Myers McDougal proposed understanding law as a global social process, founding the New Haven School in the 1960s.[31] Recently, a number of approaches have become particularly influential: the Global Administrative Law project at NYU, for example, or the International Public Authority project.[32] Others still approach the shifts in governance and law in the international community through a lens of 'constitutionalism'.[33] The literature in these different approaches is vast and the views posited divergent. Some tend towards a unifying theory of a fragmented international legal order while others encourage the continuing development of a 'heterarchical' relationship between discrete legal orders or systems.[34] Where these theories or schools coincide is their desire to describe (and in some cases support) a world view that accepts the interdependence and globalization of politics, trade, and law as its starting point.

Hand in hand with broader based examinations of how international law develops (which include in one way or another acknowledgement of other legal systems and influences) are process-based accounts of law. Such accounts of law have had a lasting impact on how international lawyers perceive and interpret international law.[35] One principal approach which has married multi-jurisdictional analysis and process-based accounts is the concept of 'transnational legal process'.[36]

There is no settled theory of transnational legal process or an accepted list of definitions for the terminology used.[37] Instead, it is an approach to understand the way law functions and develops in a globalized world.

[31] M McDougal & Associates, *Studies in World Public Order* (New Haven, Yale University Press 1960) 10–11: 'Systems of public order are embedded in a larger context of world events which is the entire process of the globe. We speak of "process" because there is an interaction, or "social" because living beings are the active participants, of "world" because the expanding circles of interaction among men ultimately reach the remotest inhabitants of the globe.'

[32] B Kingsbury et al., 'The Emergence of Global Administrative Law', (2005) 68 *Law and Contemporary Problems* 15; B Kingsbury, 'The Concept of "Law" in Global Administrative Law', (2009) 20(1) *European Journal of International Law* 23; A von Bogdandy, R Wolfrum, J von Bernstorff, P Dann, and M Goldmann (eds), *The Exercise of Public Authority by International Institutions: Advancing International Institutional Law* (London, Springer 2010).

[33] M Kumm, 'The Legitimacy of International Law: A Constitutionalist Framework of Analysis', (2004) 15 *European Journal of International Law* 907; EU Petersmann, 'The WTO Constitution and Human Rights', (2000) 3(1) *Journal of International Economic Law* 19; D Cass, 'The "Constitutionalization" of International Trade Law: Judicial Norm-Generation as an Engine of Constitutional Development in International Trade', (2001) 12(1) *European Journal of International Law* 39; A O'Donoghue, *Constitutionalism in Global Constitutionalisation* (Cambridge, Cambridge University Press 2014).

[34] N Krisch, *Beyond Constitutionalism: The Pluralist Structure of Postnational Law* (Oxford, Oxford University Press 2010).

[35] J Crawford, 'Chance, Order, Change' n. 8, para. 2.

[36] H Koh, 'Transnational Legal Process', (1996) 75 *Nebraska Law Review* 181. See also, 'Symposium' in *Yale Journal of International Law* (2007). Other notable work in the 'law as process' approach is: R Higgins, *Problems and Process: International Law and How We Use It* (Oxford, Clarendon Press 1996); R Higgins, 'Policy Considerations and the International Judicial Process', (1968) 17 *International and Comparative Law Quarterly* 58.

[37] For an examination of different approaches to transnational law: C Scott, '"Transnational Law" as a Proto-Concept: Three Conceptions', (2009) 10(7) *German Law Journal* 859.

Jessup's original definition of transnational law was simply any law that regulated cross-border activity.[38] Essentially an amalgam of public and private law, domestic and international law: transnational law is whatever law might apply to a cross-border situation or activity regardless of its source. Harold Koh expands on Jessup's definition, introducing the movement of norms as a key factor. He argues:

> Perhaps the best operational definition of transnational law, using computer-age imagery, is: (1) law that is 'downloaded' from international to domestic law: for example, an international law concept that is domesticated or internalized into municipal law, such as the international human rights norm against disappearance, now recognized as domestic law in most municipal systems; (2) law that is 'uploaded, then downloaded': for example, a rule that originates in a domestic legal system, such as the guarantee of a free trial under the concept of due process of law in Western legal systems, which then becomes part of international law, as in the Universal Declaration of Human Rights and the International Covenant on Civil and Political Rights, and from there becomes internalized into nearly every legal system in the world; and (3) law that is borrowed or 'horizontally transplanted' from one national system to another: for example, the 'unclean hands' doctrine, which migrated from the British law of equity to many other legal systems.[39]

This description of transnational law resonates with the development of international trade law. Some members of the WTO 'download' their obligations under the covered agreements into their own law by virtue of incorporation.[40] In the case of some States this follows from having 'uploaded' their own domestic law into certain covered agreements in the first place.[41] This is particularly the case with the US and the GATT but also to a lesser extent certain EU Member States, Canada, and Australia.[42] There are even incidents of 'horizontal transplants' as certain practices are either implicitly or explicitly incorporated into the legal systems of the Member States bypassing the WTO. An example of this is the practice of States in relation to the conclusion of preferential trade agreements that may or may not be in compliance with Art. XXIV GATT.[43]

[38] P Jessup, *Transnational Law* n. 30.

[39] H Koh, 'Why Transnational Law Matters', (2006) 24 *Penn State International Law Review* 745, 745–6.

[40] For example, Council Regulation (EC) No 260/2009.

[41] For example, provisions of the Agreement on Safeguards ('Safeguards Agreement') 1869 UNTS 154, which are based on US legislation (ss. 201–2 of the Trade Act 1974 [Pub L 93-618, 88 Stat 1978]). See Chapter 4 for a fuller discussion.

[42] The prevalence of developed 'Western' States is not an accident. With the exception of Japan, the GATT and later the WTO has, until the twenty-first century, been disproportionally influenced by Western States. This does not necessitate a connection between 'transnational' and 'Western', however, as it is possible to factor the influence of emerging economies into a transnational model as suggested by Onuma: 'This transcivilizational perspective can supplement and rectify the two prevalent perspectives in the twentieth century [international and transnational] by paying more attention to non-State-centric, non-modernistic or non-West-centric aspects of human ideas and activities which could have an important bearing on international law.' Y Onuma, 'A Transcivilizational Perspective on International Law', (2010) 342 *Recueil des Cours de l'Académie de Droit International* 95.

[43] Though seemingly norms of behaviour rather than legal norms, they may contribute to subsequent practice under Art. 31(3)(b) VCLT or established practice under Art. 2(1)(j) Vienna Convention on the Law of Treaties between States and International Organizations or between International Organizations (21 March 1986) UN Doc.A/CONF.129/15.

Koh's account of transnational law offers a way to consider the interactions between ideologically or thematically connected legal norms, irrespective of whether their source is domestic or international. The focus on the movement of legal norms across jurisdictions rather than an examination of a broader 'global' legal regime is of particular use. Without making supremacy claims, it focuses on the fluid and dynamic processes of legal development across different jurisdictions. This is one of the key advantages of transnational legal process: notably its acceptance of a web of interacting rights, duties, and principles at the domestic and international levels that can be manipulated by interested actors. A wider acceptance of the actors involved in transnational legal process offers another advantage when examining the development of WTO law: while States are still the primary actors in international law they are not the only actors and a genuinely convincing account of the development of WTO law must accept the roles played by others.

2. The actors engaged in law as a global process

States are not the only relevant actors within the development of international law. Indeed, depending on the level of one's analysis, it is debatable whether they ever have been, even at the international level.[44] The role of transnational actors other than States engaging in networks within international organizations such as the WTO are central to the development of international law. At the domestic or regional level, non-State transnational actors can have a key role and engage directly with the development of areas of law. However, as a matter of international law, certain key activities such as the conclusion of treaties or raising claims in international tribunals are still the primary domain of States or, increasingly, international organizations.[45] As a matter of law, the State enjoys full legal personality[46] though as a matter of fact, the State can be understood as both an actor in its own right as well as 'a representative institution constantly subject to capture and recapture, construction and reconstruction by coalitions of social actors'.[47]

The distinction between the normative claim and the descriptive claim is relevant: while it is important to examine the role of non-State actors, at the international level, this is often at its most pertinent where they act through the legal

[44] 'Level' in the Waltzian sense of individual, national, and international: K Waltz, *Man, the State, and War: A Theoretical Analysis* (2nd edn, New York, Columbia University Press 2001). On the inaccuracies of the Westphalian narrative: S Krasner, 'Compromising Westphalia', (1995–96) 20(3) *International Security* 115; A Osiander, 'Sovereignty, International Relations, and the Westphalian Myth', (2001) 55(2) *International Organization* 251.

[45] In the case of the International Court of Justice, exclusively that of States: Art. 34, Statute of the International Court of Justice (ICJ Statute) (26 June 1945) 3 Bevans 1179; 59 Stat 1055; 33 UNTS No 993.

[46] I Brownlie, *Principles of Public International Law* (7th edn, Oxford, Oxford University Press 2008) 69.

[47] A Moravcsik, 'Taking Preferences Seriously: A Liberal Theory of International Politics', (1997) 51(4) *International Organization* 513, 518.

personality of the State.[48] This is not State-centrism but rather an acceptance of the realities of international law. Transnational legal process as used here is a descriptive and analytical tool, not a normative claim. We can find echoes of this position in the work of Alexander Wendt, stating:

> It should be emphasized that 'state-centrism' in this sense does not preclude the possibility that non-state actors, whether domestic or transnational, have important even decisive, effects on the frequency and/or manner in which states engage in organized violence. 'State-centrism' does not mean that the causal chain . . . stops with states, or even that states are the 'most important' links in that chain, whatever that might mean. Particularly with the spread of liberalism in the twentieth century this is clearly not the case, since liberal states are heavily constrained by non-state actors in both civil society and the economy. The point is merely that states are still the primary medium through which the effects of other actors on the regulation of violence are channelled into the world system. It may be that non-state actors are becoming more important than states as initiators of change, but system change ultimately happens *through* states. In that sense states still are at the center of the international system, and as such it makes no more sense to criticize a theory or international politics as 'state-centric' than it does to criticize a theory of forests for being 'tree-centric.'[49]

The role of non-State transnational actors is particularly important at the WTO as its institutional structure serves as a nexus for actors to stimulate developments in the WTO system as well as the legal systems of the WTO's membership (e.g. through the large numbers of committees or technical assistance programmes).[50] It has been pointed out that it is an unfortunate side-effect of early economic theories that people view States as 'traders' at all, when with few exceptions private economic actors trade, not their States.[51] However, the behaviour of individuals is still often under the aegis of the State, at times acting through its legal personality or where not, such as in the case of lobby groups, acting through some form of legal framework (weak though it may be).[52]

[48] International investment law is an unusual exception to this where many bilateral investment treaties provide for investor-State arbitration. For example, Art. 24 US Model Bilateral Investment Treaty 2012. Inidividual rights in this instance are nonetheless dependent on State grant, much as they are in human rights treaties which permit the raising of claims by individuals.

[49] A Wendt, *Social Theory of International Politics* (Cambridge, Cambridge University Press 1999) 9.

[50] For country-specific examples of public–private partnerships in raising disputes: G Shaffer and R Meléndez-Ortiz, *Dispute Settlement at the WTO: The Developing Country Experience* (Cambridge, Cambridge University Press 2010).

[51] M Trebilcock and R Howse, *The Regulation of International Trade* (3rd edn, London, Routledge 2007) 3–4: 'An unfortunate semantic legacy of Ricardo's demonstration of the gains from international trade, perpetuated in the terminology of much subsequent trade literature and debate is that in international trade countries are trading with each other. This, of course, is rarely the case. As in purely domestic exchanges, private economic actors (albeit located in different countries) are trading with each other.'

[52] For example, in the US, the Lobbying Disclosure Act 1995 [Pub L 104-65, 109 Stat 691], as amended by the Honest Leadership and Open Governance Act 2007 [Pub L 110-81, 121 Stat 735], which requires lobbyists to register with the Clerk of the House of Representatives and Secretary of the Senate. See also the EU's largely voluntary (at this stage) European Transparency Initiative: Communication from the Commission, 'A Framework for Relations with Interest Representatives (Register and Code of Conduct)', Brussels 27/5/2008, COM (2008) 323 Final.

Besides private actors, the institutions of the WTO itself constitute separate actors as well as forums. Just as the State is both actor and forum, the dispute settlement system (for example) offers a space for actors to engage with each other but is also home to panels and the Appellate Body, themselves important actors in their own right. In privileging the State and international organizations as principal actors, the structure of international law encourages others to create and work through the bodies of States and international organizations. In this way, while actors come in a wide range of forms, at the international level they often act 'as' or 'through' the institutions with which they engage.

The ability of actors to act through different institutions can create confusion: when does the institution the actor engages through (such as a State) constitute a separate actor? The most single defining feature of globalized actors is that they identify as that actor. Actors commonly hold numerous separate identities (individual and collective): an individual will be a member of a family, region, nation, religious denomination, sexual orientation, and political affiliation.[53] Transnational actors engage across these groups, sometimes as part of an interest group, at others as part of an institution. While the State is pre-eminent in international law and is given considerable focus, accepting the influence of other actors requires them to be factored into the analysis of how law develops at the WTO.[54]

In light of the forgoing claims we can see that process-based accounts in the transnational vein offer numerous advantages. First, they examine different levels of legal rights, duties, and principles in an examination of the development of an area of law, accepting the role of different levels of legal regulation in a globalized economic system as necessary to understanding the process of creating, applying, and interpreting law at the WTO.

Similarly, process accounts identify the central role that globalized actors play in the development of international law. Transnational legal process accounts examine the process of change in law-making, law-applying, and law-interpreting at international and domestic levels by focussing on the role of transnational actors as they stimulate interactions across jurisdictions, initiating proceedings before domestic and international courts, or lobbying for legislative or administrative outcomes at the domestic and international levels. For Koh, how transnational law is used and by whom is central to his understanding of transnational legal process:

> Transnational legal process describes the theory and practice of how public and private actors—nation-states, international organizations, multinational enterprises, non-governmental organizations, and private individuals—interact in a variety of public and private, domestic and international fora to make, interpret, enforce, and ultimately internalize rules of transnational law.[55]

[53] The identity of an actor is, in part, constituted through the legal environment in which they exist: below at D.4(c); Chapter 3.B.

[54] This adds to the complexity of such an analysis, the resolution for which is the use of causal language: below at D(2).

[55] H Koh, 'Transnational Legal Process' n. 36, 183–4.

In this account, the behaviour of transnational actors is what defines the process of creating, interpreting, and applying transnational law. This is an image that some find compelling: actors using law for a specific purpose.[56]

While actors may use the law to encourage certain outcomes we know that this process is not certain: internal conflicts between the values, norms, rules, and principles within a system can produce results that some actors might not anticipate. Such accounts, which prioritize the importance of law as an autonomous logical structure, understand a legal system as a body of rules influencing those within the system, subordinated to the rule in question. In short, the law itself constitutes a separate influence on its development.[57]

Clearly, neither of these accounts are complete as the objective of those that apply or interpret the law may influence the outcomes expected, as may the structural biases of the regime.[58] In order to resolve this challenge, Gregory Shaffer explains this circularity of influences through the concept of recursivity. This refers to the circular influence of law on actors and actors on law.[59] Borrowing from the work of Halliday and Carruthers, this is a model that is not fixed at a single point in time but describes continual cycles of change and influence from one jurisdiction to another.[60] It depicts cycles of legal influence and change that are continually active at domestic and international levels between two poles: 'law in practice' on the one side and 'law on the books' on the other.[61]

Recursivity encourages viewing legal change as a 'two-way street' rather than the influence of one legal instrument or legal system on another. The advantage of recursivity is its inclusiveness in determining what the triggers or influences of change may be. Rather than focussing solely on actors (though they play a key role), recursivity also takes into account the constituting role of legal concepts, structural biases, and the importance of power relationships, as well as the form of the legal obligation per se (whether it is a soft law instrument, treaty provision, or custom) and the attendant consequences of that form.[62] This is particularly important at the WTO where increasing attention is being given to the influence of committees, working groups, and trade policy review mechanisms on the development of law at the WTO, expanding the scope of analysis from the covered agreements and the reports of the DSB alone.[63]

[56] As we will examine later, this is especially present in functionalist accounts of the law: below at D(1).

[57] As we will examine later, this is especially present in formalist accounts of the law: below at D(1).

[58] M Koskenniemi, 'The Politics of International Law—20 Years Later', (2009) 20(1) *European Journal of International Law* 7, 9ff.

[59] G Shaffer, 'Transnational Legal Ordering and State Change', in G Shaffer (ed.), *Transnational Legal Ordering and State Change* (Cambridge, Cambridge University Press 2012) 13–14.

[60] T Halliday and B Carruthers, 'The Recursivity of Law: Global Norm Making and National Law Making in the Globalization of Corporate Insolvency Regimes', (2007) 112(4) *American Journal of Sociology* 1135.

[61] Ibid., 1146. [62] Ibid., 1142–3.

[63] See A Lang, *World Trade Law After Neoliberalism: Re-Imagining the Global Economic Order* (Oxford, Oxford University Press 2011) 161–9.

Process-based accounts in the transnational legal process mode thus offer a number of advantages: transnational legal process is open to both domestic and international influences on the development of a legal regime; it is a fluid and dynamic model that views the development of law as influenced by actors using the law for their benefit; and understands the recursive process of law as a system and the constituting influence of legal concepts.

3. The limitations of understanding law as a global process

In spite of the advantages identified, there are limitations with process-based accounts, especially those in the transnational vein. The first is the attendant claim that transnational legal process offers an account for compliance of international rules through a process of internalization of norms.[64] This is a contested claim that is unnecessary for the acceptance of how transnational legal process functions, though it has distracted the debate in this field nonetheless.[65]

Similarly, the claim that there is a new type of law, 'transnational law', as a normative category rather than a mere descriptive tool is also problematic.[66] The current divisions between jurisdictions and the legal rights and duties therein are maintained as a useful and accurate depiction of the legal realities of the international trading regime. Indeed, maintaining a legal pluralist view of the international system supports the core tenets of a transnational view: that actors are not limited to the systems in which they are subjects but rather engage at different levels of governance and regulation in order to pursue their objectives. Indeed the legal differences between systems explain the trans-jurisdictional movement of actors.

The final limitation is that if we are to incorporate domestic and international legal influences and also accept that these influences are both actor-driven and systemically influenced, we are left with a profoundly complex and complicated subject of analysis.

The most common attempts to resolve these difficulties have been to apply social-scientific methods and positivist models.[67] Positivism here is used to refer not to legal positivism (a theory for determining the validity of legal rules)[68] but to positivism in the philosophy of science: broadly speaking, 'those approaches that (1) believe in a "scientific method" that is applicable across sciences,

[64] H Koh, 'Why Do Nations Obey International Law?', (1997) 106 *Yale Law Journal* 2626.

[65] For example, A Guzman, 'A Compliance-Based Theory of International Law', (2002) 90 *California Law Review* 1823, 1836.

[66] So called 'transnational legal substance': H Koh, 'The Globalization of Freedom', (2001) 26 *Yale Journal of International Law* 305; H Koh, 'Why Transnational Law Matters', (2005–06) 24 *Pennsylvania State International Law Review* 745.

[67] For example: A Guzman, *How International Law Works: A Rational Choice Theory* (Oxford, Oxford University Press 2008); M Pollack and G Shaffer, *When Cooperation Fails: The International Law and Politics of Genetically Modified Foods* (Oxford, Oxford University Press 2009); W Schwartz and A Sykes, 'The Economic Structure of Renegotiation and Dispute Resolution in the World Trade Organization', (2002) 31 *Journal of Legal Studies* 179.

[68] J Gardner, 'Legal Positivism: 5½ Myths', (2001) 46(1) *American Journal of Jurisprudence* 199, 227.

(2) assume naturalism, (3) assume empiricism, (4) believe in value-neutrality of scientific method, and (5) emphasise the importance of instrumental (predictive) knowledge.'[69]

As the rest of this chapter examines, the scientific inclination is problematic: examining and explaining the development of law is not a scientific process (in the positivist sense) but a discursive one. There are profound limitations with transposing the methodology of science to the examination of legal developments. The following section expands on the concerns with empirical approaches though acknowledges the motivation for such attempts, notably the desire to provide an explanatory rationale for an otherwise bewildering and confusing system.

C. International Law as a Complex and Complicated System

The international legal system is both complicated and complex.[70] It is complicated in the sense that it contains a multiplicity of institutions and actors[71] from across jurisdictional boundaries.[72] It is complex in the sense that these institutions and actors adapt to the legal system, both changing in response to it as well as altering the legal system itself.[73]

International law develops within this system, changing as part of a dynamic process responding to, and influencing, the institutions and actors with which it engages who provide the momentum for its development. As law in turn influences actors, we are left with a problematic subject of study: a system that develops in the face of a range of different influences in different ways.[74]

Developing thus, in light of a plurality of influences, from numerous institutions and actors within a legal system and other, inter-related, influential legal systems (both regional and domestic), examining the development of international law presents a considerable challenge.[75] This is ever more so the case once we acknowledge the conceptually fraught nature of how law develops over time.[76]

[69] M Kurki, *Causation in International Relations: Reclaiming Causal Analysis* (Cambridge, Cambridge University Press 2008) 61–2.

[70] On the distinction between complicated and complex systems: S Gunitsky, 'Complexity and Theories of Change in International Politics', (2013) 5 *International Theory* 1, 35.

[71] These range from States to transnational corporations and civil society organizations. See A Boyle and C Chinkin, *The Making of International Law* (Oxford, Oxford University Press 2007) 41–97.

[72] That is to say, actors engaged in the international legal system also often engage in domestic or regional legal systems.

[73] 'Co-adaptive.' S Gunitsky, n. 70, 46.

[74] Ibid., 43.

[75] On recent developments in acknowledging the complexity of the international legal system (or its regimes): J Pauwelyn, 'At the Edge of Chaos? Foreign Investment Law as a Complex Adaptive System, How It Emerged and How It Can Be Reformed', (2014) 29(2) *International Centre for Settlement of Investment Disputes Review* 372; M Varella, *Internationalization of Law: Globalization, International Law and Complexity* (London, Springer 2014); S Puig, 'International Regime Complexity and Economic Law Enforcement', (2014) 17(3) *Journal of International Economic Law* 491.

[76] Identified in Chapter 1.B(3).

How do we make sense of this process? The three tactics are customarily used by legal scholars: the first, is to exclude the 'extraneous' influences on the development of international law, most commonly those perceived of as 'political', and leave their analysis to scholars in other disciplines;[77] the second is to hold to the distinction between legal systems as a matter of positive law and reject legal influences that do not enjoy a formal relationship with the international legal system.[78] The third is to incorporate the methodology of other disciplines to provide insights for the examination at hand ('law and ...' approaches). Each response speaks to a desire to make the complexities of international law's development intelligible and manageable, to explain the world, and thus make sense of it. Yet, there are challenges to understanding the development of international law through the use of these options. The following section identifies these difficulties, paving the way for the use of causal language as an alternative.

1. Methodological challenges to examining law as a complex system

If we accept that international law is part of a global process, one that bears the hallmark of a complex and complicated system, we are left with a quandary: how do we examine law in this context?

Though much analysis has focussed on the identification of *lex lata* within a legal positivist tradition,[79] those seeking to examine how international law develops more broadly have frequently turned to the social sciences: international relations scholarship,[80] political science research,[81] or empirical work more generally (including economic analysis).[82]

[77] Symptomatic of an insecurity vis-à-vis domestic law. See M Koskenniemi, 'The Fate of Public International Law: Between Technique and Politics', (2007) *Modern Law Review* 1: 'Compared with the sophisticated techniques of domestic law, international law seemed primitive, abstract and above all political, too political.'

[78] There are subtle variations on this theme that nonetheless produce productive outcomes, see: J Pauwelyn, 'Is It International Law or Not, and Does It Even Matter?', in J Pauwelyn, R Wessel, and J Wouters (eds), *Informal International Lawmaking* (Oxford, Oxford University Press 2012) 125–61, at 126 drawing the distinction between legal normativity and 'legal imperativity.'

[79] J Alvarez, *International Organizations as Law-makers* (Oxford, Oxford University Press 2005) 46–7. The paradigmatic example often given: L Oppenheim, 'The Science of International Law: Its Tasks and Method', (1908) 2 *American Journal of International Law* 313.

[80] For a brief overview of some approaches: AM Slaughter and SR Ratner, 'Symposium on Method in International Law', (1999) 93 *American Journal of International Law* 291; AM Slaughter, 'International Law and International Relations Theory', (2000) 285 *Recueil des Cours de l'Académie de Droit International* 235; J Dunnoff and M Pollack (eds), *Interdisciplinary Perspectives on International Law and International Relations: The State of the Art* (Cambridge, Cambridge University Press 2013).

[81] E Hafner-Burton, D Victor, and Y Lupu, 'Political Science on International Law: The State of the Field', (2012) 106(1) *American Journal of International Law* 47.

[82] For an overview, G Shaffer and T Ginsburg, 'The Empirical Turn in International Legal Scholarship', (2012) 106 *American Journal of International Law* 1.

While legal scholarship has often focussed on either the rule-making process as conducted by either legislative or quasi-legislative bodies, or the interpretative role that judicial or quasi-judicial bodies have on how the law is applied,[83] social-scientific scholarship has engaged more openly with the influence of other 'non-legal' factors in the development of international law and its effect on the material world.[84]

In spite of these insights, a methodological bifurcation for examining how international law develops over time continues to exist: on one hand legal analysis for the determination of the positive rule, identifying the development of law through static moments (decisions, either legislative or judicial);[85] and on the other hand, implicitly empirical analysis to examine law in the material world.[86] It is for this reason that for some it appears that we are 'playing a different game'.[87]

While social-scientific approaches to how international law affects the material world produce numerous insights, it is argued here that their implicit empiricist underpinnings are inappropriate for examining the development of international law *qua* law. In acknowledging the benefits of such approaches though within a legal response, the aim is to suggest a constructive nexus between disciplines, rather than simple critique.[88]

Though social-scientific studies aid in the study of international law's material impact,[89] two claims are made here as to why the law itself cannot be subjected to empirical examination in this fashion. First, law cannot be observed in the way necessary for empirical analysis and, second, law develops through facts that have a particular legal meaning, and it is their relevance in a legal context that explains how law changes.

On the first claim, key factors are not available to us in determining what the law is and how it changes: empirical approaches focus on the importance of examining 'observables' (those things which can be viewed, studied and, most importantly,

[83] A strong tradition that continues today: A Clapham (ed.), *Brierly's Law of Nations* (7th edn, Oxford, Oxford University Press 2012); J Crawford (ed.), *Brownlie's Principles of International Law* (8th edn, Oxford, Oxford University Press 2012).

[84] For example, K Sikkink, *The Justice Cascade: How Human Rights Prosecutions are Changing World Politics* (New York, WW Norton & Co 2011).

[85] Some nonetheless offering particular insights into how law is understood, for example, I Venzke, *How Interpretation Makes International Law: On Semantic Change and Normative Twists* (Oxford, Oxford University Press 2012).

[86] Empiricism here understood broadly as the epistemological tradition derived principally from the work of David Hume. Its necessary components are examined at nn 89–96 and accompanying text.

[87] J Goldsmith and A Vermeule, 'Empirical Methodology and Legal Scholarship', (2002) 69(1) *University of Chicago Law Review* 153.

[88] The call for legal responses to the influence of globalization on the international legal order is made most clearly in A Halpin and V Roeben (eds), *Theorising the Global Legal Order* (Oxford, Hart Publishing 2009) 1–2.

[89] 'If we want to know how the world is changing—and how our legal rules shape and should respond to that change—empirical studies are simply unavoidable.' B Simmons and A Breidenbach, 'The Empirical Turn in International Economic Law', (2011) 20 *Minnesota Journal of International Law* 198.

measured in some manner)[90] and require the possibility of repeating conditions in order to test hypotheses.[91]

The ability to quantify and exclude variables, repeating experiments with controlled variations is the *sine qua non* of the empiricist's method. However, the development of law is not conducive to such an exercise.[92] The international legal system is complex, responding to and adapting to the behaviour of actors and institutions which constitute them, making repetition highly problematic. Further, the nature of law is such that it does not permit observation in the manner necessary for empirical analysis. Its real yet immaterial nature,[93] responsive to differing expectations and needs of social orders[94] make its 'scientific' classification fundamentally problematic.

What is more, the types of facts that relate to the functioning of legal processes, such as interpretative approaches, differ from the types of facts found in empirical enquiry; while the act of interpretation can be influenced by observation (theories or opinions of the interpreter, for example) the nature of objectively knowable facts within the world cannot.[95] This presents problems for an empirical examination of how the law develops, where observables are not clear or quantifiable and where 'regularity' is difficult to conceptualize (and more difficult to provide) given changing facts and circumstances to each incident of legal interaction or change.[96]

The second challenge to understanding the development of international law *qua* law is that law develops singularly through facts that have a legal meaning.[97] Though any number of material and ideational forces impact on the law (and law certainly affects the material world), it is only by framing such influences in legal ways that they have an effect on the development of law. Power presents the most obvious example: power asymmetries have a considerable impact on law, however, it is only by framing the power asymmetry within a legal context (authority of the legislator, for example) that the power takes legal effect. Legal reasons for action,

[90] Note, for example, Simmons and Breidenbach n. 89, 199–200: 'by "empirical" we mean a systematic examination of observable phenomena from which the researcher explicitly seeks to draw broader conclusions about the way the world—or some part of it—works.'

[91] 'Regularity determinism.' D Hume, *A Treatise of Human Nature* (L Selby-Bigg ed.) (Oxford, Clarendon Press 1975) 130. See also, M Kurki, *Causation in International Relations* n. 69, 58.

[92] Note, the challenges raised by Brian Tamanaha in 'The Folly of the "Social-Scientific" Concept of Legal Pluralism', (1993) 20 *Journal of Law and Society* 192.

[93] N MacCormick, *Institutions of Law: An Essay in Legal Theory* (Oxford, Oxford University Press 2007) 292–3.

[94] '... law is thoroughly a cultural construct ... Law is whatever we attach the label law to.' (Though acknowledging that there is an ideal of law that may well be universal at fn. 135): B Tamanaha, 'An Analytical Map of Social Scientific Approaches to the Concept of Law', (1995) 15(4) *Oxford Journal of Legal Studies* 501, 535.

[95] Legal scholarship is replete with examples where the perspective of the interpreter (and the impossibility of escaping it) is key. See S Fish, *Is There a Text in This Class? The Authority of Interpretative Communities* (Cambridge, MA, Harvard University Press 1980).

[96] Quentin Skinner shares similar concerns within the philosophy of history, as an implicitly empirical approach 'assumes a necessary uniformity of relationship between antecedents and event, and so ignores the conditional form of many of the explanations given even in the natural sciences.' Q Skinner, 'The Limits of Historical Explanations', (1966) *The Journal of the Royal Institute of Philosophy* vol. XLI, nos. 157, 199, 200.

[97] H Kelsen, *General Theory of Law and State* (Cambridge MA, Harvard University Press 1945) 178.

whether by law-makers or interpreters, are necessary for the law to be *law* and not the mere exercise of 'naked power'.[98]

This is not say that other 'non-legal' influences are not important. Indeed, to deny the effect of such influences on the development of law would be to restrict oneself to such a degree that what is offered is only a partial account of how law develops, precisely the concern that equally leads to a rejection of the kind of legal accounts discussed below. Social-scientific studies provide numerous insights into the different types of influence, though if they are to aid us they have to be reframed as influences on legally relevant facts.[99]

If we are to reject implicitly empirical approaches to the examination of how international law develops, can we not use the traditional tools of legal scholarship? The concern here relates to the earlier discussion on understanding the development of international law as intimately connected with understanding the change in law over time, as a progressive and continual process. In spite of the necessarily fluid nature of law, its claim to stability has influenced the way in which legal scholarship engages with it: law is identified at fixed points in time, suggesting a finality, a certainty as to what the law is at any one point in time (even though we may debate its future 're'-interpretation).

Accounts that prioritize the determination of a specific rule prioritize a specific moment in time: the result of such a static appreciation of how time is understood in relation to legal change fetishizes the moment at which the change is understood, and the text in which it is allegedly crystallized. Not only does this not correspond to our understanding of how facts change and thus international law develops (that is, subtly and progressively over time) but it also encourages a fixation on judicial decisions as central to our appreciation of legal change.[100] To be clear, the legal import of judicial decisions is not be questioned, rather the way in which they are used as static symbols of what is a more nuanced process.[101]

How then are we to progress? The purpose thus far has not been to pick holes in methodological or epistemological approaches to the law's development in different disciplines. Rather, the aim has been to delineate and identify where these approaches aid us. Indeed, in the following section it is suggested that the ways in which both law and international relations describe the functioning of international law offer many of the answers we are looking for. What is proposed is to reframe these accounts in terms of causal influences.

What follows is an examination based on identifying causes and offering explanations, without focussing on the predictive accuracy of accounts. An advantage

[98] M McDougal et al., *Studies in World Public Order* n. 31, 10–11 and 170–2.

[99] That is, influences that base their claim for legitimacy in legal terms.

[100] Judicial decisions are clearly important, the point here is that they are not the only way in which law changes, and fixating on them distracts from other relevant expressions of how law develops. Note the role of other law-making processes such as standard setting: M Geboye Desta, 'GATT/WTO Law and International Standards: An Example of Soft Law Instruments Hardening Up?', in A Bjorklund and A Reinisch, *International Investment Law and Soft Law* (Cheltenham, Edward Elgar 2012) 148.

[101] The development of law as an extension or *durée*, rather than a series of specific moments: Chapter 1.B(3).

of rejecting an empirical method for examining the development of international law removes the need to focus on generalizable outcomes and predictions.[102] Instead, the examination becomes explanatory, a way of understanding why law develops in the way that it does. Causal language is often explanatory in aim,[103] it aids in making sense of the complex and complicated international legal system and its development through a plurality of influences.

This broadens the analysis of how international law develops, positing the role of actors as the driving force behind the development of international law yet not in control of it. The complex interplay between the influence of actors on the law and the influence of law on actors is reappraised, viewing the development of international law as a response to actions, norms, and ideas, across jurisdictions, simultaneously.

D. Explaining the Development of International Law

Different types of explanation contain within them a set of correlative assumptions. In the case of legal explanation, different accounts of the nature of law contain within them assumptions about how it functions. In the following section, three accounts of the law are sketched. These are not meant to offer a comprehensive account of all views, they are necessarily broad-brush strokes, and include numerous positions within each that would customarily disagree. However, the utility arises in each category's shared assumptions over how law affects those within its system, rather than identifying disciplinary boundaries *per se*.

1. Three explanations: Functionalism, formalism, and idealism

A recurring theme in this book is the importance of taking a plural approach to examining the development of international law. In part this is a response, and attempt to reconcile, the approaches taken elsewhere where one conception of how law functions is identified. The common narratives or lenses for examining the law are the most obvious example. It is not that these accounts are incorrect per se, rather that they do not furnish complete explanations. Amongst them we can broadly distinguish functionalist, formalist, and idealist lenses to understand how law develops. Though these are to a degree caricatures, the assumptions which underpin their use are important as they prioritize certain types of response to legal developments.

[102] The position taken here is singularist with regard to causes, excluding the necessary relationship between causal relations and laws. That X is a cause of Y does not mean that all X-like things invariably cause Y-like effects. Thus, there is no necessarily predictive claim made by describing a relation in causal terms. See GEM Anscombe, *Causality and Determination* (Cambridge, Cambridge University Press 1971).

[103] Though not always: there are non-causal explanations and causes that are not explanatory: Lipton, 'Causation and Explanation', in H Beebee, C Hitchock, and P Menzies (eds), *The Oxford Handbook of Causation* (Oxford, Oxford University Press 2012), at 619–31.

The first, functionalist accounts, are those premised on an instrumental view of law, understanding law as something we use to advance our own individual or collective interest.[104] In this account, actors use the law to cause a change (and thus stimulate its development). The actors involved may initiate legal proceedings within a national or regional court on the basis of rights or duties under international law in the hope that such rights or duties will be 'internalized' into his or her own domestic legal system.[105] This could be the case with obligations under treaties[106] or rules of customary international law.[107] Conversely, a State or an international organization may challenge a provision of domestic law of another State at an international tribunal where its success under domestic or regional courts would be in doubt.[108] States can encourage the creation of a new treaty obligation[109] or contribute to the creation of a new rule of customary international law in order to pursue certain objectives.[110] The underlying rationale is that law can be used to realize objectives whether through initiating litigation, creating new rules, or encouraging favourable interpretations.[111] Functionalist accounts of the law see it as an instrument to change the rules and principles that govern the legal system and, in turn, the behaviour of actors within it.[112]

The common criticism of such approaches is that law is not merely an expression of the will of interested actors or a tool to be used without appreciation of the nuances of law's nature.[113] It is clear that the creation of new rules do not always fix the problems they may have sought to resolve, and such a view of the law and how it functions misunderstands its fundamental structure as a body of rules and norms.[114]

[104] Instrumentalism (and formalism) are used in a similar though different manner to their use in P Bourdieu, 'The Force of Law: Towards a Sociology of the Juridical Field', (1987) 38 *Hastings Law Journal* 814.

[105] H Koh, 'Transnational Legal Process After September 11th', (2004) 22 *Berkeley Journal of International Law* 337, 339.

[106] For example, *Medellín v Texas* 552 US 491 (2008) as an attempt to enforce the treaty-based obligations of the US under the Vienna Convention on Consular Relations ('VCCR') (24 April 1963) 596 UNTS 261 in domestic courts following a determination by the ICJ of the US's breach of obligations under the VCCR in *Case Concerning Avena and Other Mexican Nationals (Mexico v United States of America)* (Judgment) [2004] ICJ Rep 12.

[107] For example, *Filártiga v Peña-Irala* 630 F 2d 876 (2nd Cir 1980) and *Sosa v Alvarez-Machain* 542 US 692 (2004) where claims under customary international law were raised in US courts though with considerable limitations, increased by *Kiobel v Royal Dutch Petroleum* 133 S.Ct. 1659 (2013).

[108] For example, *United States—Anti-Dumping Act of 1916*, Report of the Appellate Body (28 August 2000) WT/DS/136/AB/R, 16–29.

[109] Whether by amendment procedures under existing treaties or by the conclusion of a new treaty.

[110] For example, the impact of the 1945 Truman Proclamation on the development of the customary rules of the law of the sea, recounted vividly in V Lowe, *International Law* (Oxford, Oxford University Press 2007) 36ff.

[111] On the influence of functionalism in how international organizations are understood (and see themselves): J Klabbers, 'The Emergence of Functionalism in International Institutional Law: Colonial Aspirations', (2014) 25(3) *European Journal of International Law* 645.

[112] Some expressions of functionalism coincide with aspects of realism: H Morganthau, 'Positivism, Functionalism, and International Law', (1940) 34(2) *American Journal of International Law* 260, 274.

[113] Or indeed that such accounts prioritize certain objectives as more legitimate than others. This is a common criticism of legal process accounts as a result of a perceived relationship between the New Haven School and US foreign policy objectives: A Orford, 'Scientific Reason and the Discipline of International Law', (2014) 25(2) *European Journal of International Law* 369, 381.

[114] N Krisch, 'International Law in Times of Hegemony: Unequal Power and the Shaping of the International Legal Order', (2005) 16(3) *European Journal of International Law* 369, 407.

This is the formalist account, one which views law as a set of rules and the identification of law as a logical process, determined not by the expectations of those that created the law (in whatever capacity) but through the identification of legitimate legal reasons.[115] Though the meaning of formalism varies wildly, it is used here in its widest sense, which is to say not only as a theory for identifying rules[116] but also relating to the application of rules.[117] While formalism is often related to positivism, this is not a necessary connection, indeed formalism potentially encompasses a great many positions which are not positivist: it is this broadness in the term's use that makes it appealing for its use here.[118] The purpose is to provide in very general terms a perspective. To this end, we can note that formalist accounts:

> claim that (1) the law is 'rationally' determinate, i.e., the class of legitimate legal reasons available for a judge to offer in support of his decision justifies one and only one outcome either in all cases or in some significant and contested range of cases (e.g., cases that reach the stage of appellate review); and (2) adjudication is thus 'autonomous' from other kinds of reasoning, that is, the judge can reach the required decision without recourse to non-legal normative considerations of morality or political philosophy.[119]

These accounts respond to the instrumentalization of functionalist accounts, centring on the role of formal sources as encouraging objectivity (and thus countering claims of politicization in built in functionalist approaches).[120] Such accounts, however, are also open to the criticism of offering deterministic or mechanistic conceptions of the law, concerned that the arbiters of this set of rules, the judges, follow a thread of reasoning to its correct conclusion,[121] underplaying the legal or linguistic indeterminacy in law.[122] While formalist accounts acknowledge the importance of 'taking law seriously' (i.e. appreciating the importance of the formal identification of sources of law), their wider application is subjected to the criticism that they fail to engage with the world as it is and prefer abstract categories over true forms.[123]

115 Though formalism is often used pejoratively, this need not be the case. See in particular, F Schauer, 'Formalism', (1988) 97(4) *Yale Law Journal* 509.

116 In the sense used by J d'Aspremont, *Formalism and the Sources of International Law: A Theory of Ascertainment of Legal Rules* (Oxford, Oxford University Press 2011) 15.

117 For example, D Kennedy, 'Legal Formality', (1973) 2 *Journal of Legal Studies* 351, 355; HLA Hart, *The Concept of Law* (2nd edn, Oxford, Oxford University Press 1994) 124–36.

118 On the relation between formalism and positivism: J Kammerhofer, 'International Legal Positivism', in F Hoffmann and A Orford (eds), *Oxford Handbook of International Legal Theory* (Oxford, Oxford University Press 2016, forthcoming).

119 B Leiter, 'Legal Formalism and Legal Realism: What is the Issue?', (2010) 16 *Legal Theory* 111. Leiter's focus is on the US aspects of the formalism debate, yet for our purposes his definition still identifies the key characteristics of interest.

120 M Koskenniemi, *From Apology to Utopia: The Structure of International Legal Argument* (Cambridge, Cambridge University Press 2005 reissue) 189.

121 J d'Aspremont, *Formalism and the Sources of International Law* n. 116, 86.

122 A Lang, *World Trade Law After Neoliberalism* n. 63, 164 and T Endicott, *Vagueness in Law* (Oxford, Oxford University Press 2000) 7ff respectively.

123 H Laski, *Studies in Law and Politics* (London, Allen & Unwin 1932, 1969 reprint) 243: 'The problem of the juristic philosopher, in short, is the difficult one of validating his purely formal analysis of categories for the actual world about us.'

A third approach, a retort to the conflict between 'law as rules' and 'law as instrument' is one that is sensitive to the role that law plays in constituting our society and ourselves. This way of looking at the law prioritizes the importance of ideas and identities in some way constituted by concepts and discourses that 'travel' through the law.[124] Just as formalist and functionalist approaches contain within their broad set of assumptions a wide range of view points, so idealist approaches are equally varied.[125] What they share, however, is a sensitivity to the role that ideas play (whether social values, psychological constructions, or other forms of non-material social fact) on the law and how it is understood. The (comparatively) late involvement of such approaches in international relations scholarship,[126] and to international law, has placed this third approach not in direct competition with the other two but instead as an alternative in what is otherwise a caricatured opposition between formalism and functionalism.[127]

When law is viewed fundamentally as a social construction, with a central role in creating and encouraging identities and shared meanings for society and individuals,[128] such approaches focus on the role of law as a constituting force, offering powerful alternatives to functionalist or formalist accounts of how the law is understood, applied, and transmitted.[129] Where these claims offer especially productive insights is in how they are sensitive to the nature of change in law, most notably through changed meanings, thus offering an escape from the 'static time' trap that is implicit in both functionalist and formalist accounts of the law.[130]

[124] This position is deeply influenced by constructivism, 'the view that the manner in which the material world shapes and is shaped by human action and interaction depends on dynamic normative and epistemic interpretations of the material world.' E Adler, 'Seizing the Middle Ground: Constructivism in World Politics', (1997) 3 *European Journal of International Relations* 319, 322.

[125] Note 'idealist' is used here in reference to ideational influences (similar to Lang's usage, n. 63) and not as used elsewhere, for example, M Koskenniemi, *From Apology to Utopia* n. 120, 209.

[126] In the international relations context, while the seminal texts in realism and liberalism date from the 1940s (e.g. H Morgenthau's *Politics Among Nations* (Knopf, first published in 1948)), constructivism was not widely appreciated until the 1980s (e.g. F Kratochwil's, *Rules, Norms and Decisions: On the Conditions of Practical and Legal Reasoning in International Relations and Domestic Affairs* (Cambridge, Cambridge University Press 1989)).

[127] Identifying shifts and overlaps in different ways of conceptualizing the law: A Lang, *World Trade Law After Neoliberalism* n. 63, 221–72.

[128] In Philip Allott's words: '(1) Law carries the structures and systems of society through time. (2) Law inserts the common interest of society into the behaviour of society members. (3) Law establishes possible futures for society, in accordance with society's theories, values and purposes.' P Allott, 'The Concept of International Law', (1999) 10 *European Journal of International Law* 31. See also, P Allott, *Eunomia: A New World Order For a New World* (Oxford, Oxford University Press 1990) 3–8.

[129] On the benefits of combining insights from constructivism with other theoretical approaches: CO Meyer and E Strickmann, 'Solidifying Constructivism: How Material and Ideational Factors Interact in European Defence', (2011) 49(1) *Journal of Common Market Studies* 61.

[130] Note the progressive nature of the process, with meaning and content in a continual relationship: 'as the meaning of the rule changes, the rule itself changes.' P Legrand, 'What "Legal Transplants?"', in D Nelken and J Feest (eds), *Adapting Legal Culture* (Oxford, Hart Publishing 2001) 55, 61.

2. Reframing the discussion: The turn to causal language

Each of the above approaches encompasses a number of assumptions about the nature of law and how it works.[131] It is not that one is correct and another misguided, but that they each speak to an insight born of our experience and perception of law. The issue is rather the emphasis that each approach places on differing types of influence. Though not explicit, these descriptive accounts are causal: each identifies a different way in which law functions rather than *the* way in which law develops. This is where the turn to causal language can aid us in understanding how international law develops.

To explain the development of international law, we must acknowledge that different causes cause things in different ways, and this necessitates a broader conception of cause that is then used within legal scholarship, moving away from accounts that prioritize post-Humean empahses on mechanistic causes.

Causal language is concerned with making sense of the world. In the Aristotelian tradition, a causal discussion is routed in an attempt to understand the world: 'men do not think they know a thing till they have grasped the "why" of it (*which is to grasp its primary cause*).'[132] More specifically, it is concerned with helping us make sense of a complex world and events that, at first sight, may appear beyond our comprehension. When we say that *x* happens because of *y*, we are telling a story: it is a narrative explanation that connects a cause with an effect.

To understand the development of international law requires having a clear approach to the causes involved in such a process. Why does a State alter its domestic law on the marketing of certain goods in the face of a panel or Appellate Body decision?[133] Why do committees at the WTO alter their behaviour, at times in unexpected ways?[134] These sorts of questions cannot be tackled unless we have a clear idea of what caused these situations and how.[135]

More recently, Hidemi Suganami has championed the importance of causal language in creating convincing narratives of social, legal, and historical events.[136] While there are a host of approaches to the examination of causal relationships

[131] This section is deeply indebted to the work of Milja Kurki, particularly, *Causation in International Relations* n. 69 which identifies both the challenges but also the opportunities offered by causal language.

[132] Aristotle, *Physics,* II (3) in J Barnes (ed.), *Complete Works of Aristotle Volume 1: Revised Oxford Translation* (Princeton, Princeton University Press 1984) 332. Emphasis added.

[133] For example, the sale of certain beef products in Korea: *Korea—Measures Affecting Imports of Fresh, Chilled and Frozen Beef,* Report of the Appellate Body (10 January 2001) WT/DS161/AB/R and WT/DS169/AB/R, 5.

[134] For example, the inability of the Committee on Regional Trade Agreements ('CRTA') to produce a report on the Art. XXIV GATT consistency of any RTA since its creation in February 1996.

[135] This is at the root of Aristotle's criticism of earlier approaches to causation, that they 'do not define the kind of motion they are talking about.' WKC Guthrie, *A History of Greek Philosophy: Volume I* (Cambridge, Cambridge University Press 1962) 451.

[136] Though he is certainly not the first: for a comprehensive account of historical explanation as a narrative exercise see, WB Gallie, *Philosophy and the Historical Understanding* (London, Chatto & Windus 1964).

in the social sciences,[137] the work of Suganami is particularly helpful in focussing on examining causal relationships as a tool to render a situation or event intelligible.[138] Just as Aristotle stated that the purpose of understanding causes was a method for understanding 'why', so Suganami examines causation as a narrative tool: one which helps us understand the world by explaining the connections between events and results.[139]

Where Suganami digresses is his refusal to engage with the true cause of something. Suganami's approach is ontologically flat, accepting the premise that it is not possible to understand the genuine cause of something. Instead, he views causes as a way to make sense of a result. Thus, for Suganami there are no true causes, only those that offer convincing narratives.[140] While his scepticism of true causes is rejected here, the motivations behind his push for a narrative perspective are not: Suganami's position on the narrative purpose of causal language can be seen as part of his rejection of scientific methodologies used in the social sciences.

The narrative approach seeded in Aristotle's work and cultivated by Suganami, serves to avoid the empiricist approaches identified earlier. It also allows us to examine the development of law as a continuum, rather than a series of discrete legal decisions, more in keeping with the progressive nature of law's development over time. Instead, the narrative approach here permits a more appropriate method: an interpretative methodology that accepts the importance of socio-historical and legal influences on the relationship between jurisdictions and the behaviour of States and other actors. We might consider this:

> the approach to theorizing that derives from philosophy, history, and law, and that is characterized above all by explicit reliance upon the exercise of judgment and by the assumptions that if we confine our-selves to strict standards of verification and proof there is very little of significance that can be said about international relations.[141]

Rather than focussing on Newtonian or 'billiard-ball' causes that are prioritized in empiricist analyses,[142] here the discussion revolves around a greater variety of causes, familiar in classical typologies of cause.[143] Though some of these categories

[137] M Kurki, *Causation in International Relations* n. 69, outlining the general strands of theory that conceptualize cause and effect within the social sciences (and indeed before their conception).

[138] H Suganami, 'Agents, Structures, Narratives', (1999) *European Journal of International Relations* 365, 372.

[139] In doing so, rejecting empirical models of causation: M Kurki, *Causation in International Relations* n. 69, 168–70.

[140] H Suganami, *On the Causes of War* (Oxford, Oxford University Press 1996) and H Suganami, 'Agents, Structures, Narratives' n. 137, 370, M Kurki, *Causation in International Relations* n. 69, 159.

[141] H Bull, 'International Theory: The Case for a Classical Approach', (1966) 18(3) *World Politics* 361–77.

[142] The influence of mechanistic understanding of causes as pre-eminent is deeply ingrained in the modern conception of cause, considered preferable to viewing objects as having 'little souls' as Descartes' criticism of final causes ran: D Clarke, *Descartes: A Biography* (Cambridge, Cambridge University Press 2006) 246.

[143] Principally the Aristotelian categories of final, formal, material, and efficient causes: Aristotle, *Metaphysics* V.II, J Barnes (ed.), *Complete Works of Aristotle Volume II: Revised Oxford Translation* (Princeton, Princeton University Press 1985) 1600.

of cause may seem broad, and some might prefer the use of terms such as 'influence' or 'necessary precondition', it is argued that concepts such as 'influence' are inherently causal in nature. The way we use the term 'cause' varies, suggesting more than a single meaning.[144] This is acknowledged here, using a broader and more satisfactory application of the term 'cause'.

Aristotle's own example of a bronze statue is illustrative. First, the bronze is a cause of the statue, as it is an 'intrinsic feature from which something is produced'. Second, the idea of what the statue is to be is a cause of it (the idea of it which exists defining its nature). Third, the sculptor who creates the statue from the bronze is a cause of it as the 'primary principle of change or stasis'. The last type of cause is the 'cause as end', which is the purpose of the thing; in the case of the statue this might be the desire to place it in a church or its role as an ornament in the market place. In Aristotelian terminology these are the material, formal, efficient, and final causes respectively.

It has been said that the four types of cause are too broad for the term 'cause' in English; a cause for Aristotle must be necessary though it need not be sufficient, whereas in English for something to be a cause of something else it must be both necessary and sufficient.[145] David Ross cautions against translating the Greek term *αἴτιον* as cause 'for the several *αἴτια* are not causes in the sense of furnishing complete explanations of natural processes. It is only the union of them all that furnishes a complete explanation, and severally they are merely necessary conditions of natural processes.'[146]

This critique could serve to pair down Aristotle's categories that may be too broad for any useful application in legal analysis. However, the debates within legal philosophy on the definition of legal causation have rested on either sufficiency *or* necessity.[147] The idea that a cause must be both necessary and sufficient for a resulting effect to occur cannot be correct. This is particularly the case when the subject of the study (as in the case of influences between jurisdictions) is a fluid and complex system with a vast number of variables and no meaningful baseline from which to work from as a control. Such a strict interpretation of 'cause' would undermine any meaningful examination of the development of legal regimes in international trade by restricting those influences or events that we might call a cause. Most importantly, Ross' critique has weight when we seek to determine *the* cause of something, not *a* cause. Indeed, the question is primarily one of remoteness of cause, a factor which is inherently factored into narrative accounts through the demand to produce convincing explanations.

[144] On the difficulties in understanding the concept of causation: P Godfrey-Smith, 'Causal Pluralism', in H Beebee, C Hitchock, and P Menzies (eds), *The Oxford Handbook of Causation* (Oxford, Oxford University Press 2012) 326–37.

[145] D Ross, *Aristotle* (6th edn, London, Routledge 1995) 75.

[146] D Ross, *Aristotle Physics* (Oxford, Oxford University Press 1936) 35–6.

[147] The NESS approach ('necessary element of a set of conditions jointly sufficient for the result') does not require the cause to be both fully necessary and sufficient but that instead it be necessary and contribute toward sufficiency with other factors. See HLA Hart and T Honoré, *Causation in the Law* (2nd edn, Oxford, Clarendon Press 1985).

A related though separate problem with an Aristotelian approach in the way suggested is the potential multiplicity of causes. An examination of what Aristotle views as causes can lead to an important question; for Aristotle, what does not qualify as a cause?[148] One way to resolve the problem with such a broad definition of cause has been to create a hierarchy within Aristotle's four causes. In the Aquinan view, the purpose of something (final cause) is promoted as the most important cause, thus placing the role of God at the apex of all manner of understanding cause.[149] Another option is the approach of the early empiricists, stressing the role of an act or action (the sculptor himself, or act of sculpting) as the pre-eminent cause. The prioritization of types of cause is one way of narrowing Aristotle's casual categories, however, it is not the only one. Once again, when we return to the explanatory role causes and the purpose of causal language as creating convincing narratives. Focussing on a narrative approach does not mean that 'anything goes'. Indeed, Suganami argues:

> This [a narrative approach], however, does not mean that any representation is just as acceptable as any other. While there is nothing in the objective world that tells us to represent it in any particular way, there is still room for intersubjective agreement as to the relative merits of one type of (normatively embedded) depiction compared to another.[150]

If we accept this understanding of causation, we still have to understand how to place law within it. Might we consider law a 'mechanistic process' (to use Suganami's terminology) or the instrument of specific actors? This question can be reformulated: is law a cause (i.e. part of the mechanistic process of the functioning of the international legal order), or is law an instrument used by specific actors? We have seen how the role of law does not appear to conveniently fit into either of these categories. Legal systems do not function like clockwork, mechanistically progressing and producing results irrespective of any other form of influence. Nor is the law a simple instrument, to be used by an actor without any other variable influencing its development. The tension between these two approaches to the causal nature of law is an important one as each approach has its uses. By reframing these approaches in causal terms we can also see how the opposition is misleading: law is both an instrument and a system, what differs is the way in which it causes an effect.

When discussing Aristotle's categories of cause they were held to have the advantage of being broad and permitting a dynamic model which accepts different types of cause and their different types of influence or effect. While Suganami built on Aristotle's core understanding of causation as an explanatory tool (the

[148] A more specific formulation of this criticism would be that the account given so far does not distinguish between conditions and causes.

[149] T Aquinas, *Summa Theologiae* (B Davies & B Leftow eds) (Cambridge, Cambridge University Press 2006) 24–7. More traditionally, Aquinas also built on Aristotle's position that the first efficient cause must always be the divine.

[150] H Suganami, 'Agents, Structures, Narratives', n. 137, 380. Rejecting the existence of radical indeterminacy theses which would lead to a similar conclusion: T Endicott, *Vagueness in Law* (Oxford, Oxford University Press 2000) 29.

way in which we understand the world is explained through causal language), his approach is limited when applied to the development of law: his categories of cause do not fit clearly with the nature of legal influences and he avoids making any 'true' claim of the world or how it functions. Milja Kurki, however, helps to resolve some of these issues by re-working Aristotle's categories and applying them in such a way that convincing narratives can be drawn from a series of events in international affairs.

Kurki re-interprets Aristotle's types of cause in line with the complexities of the international system. For Kurki, types of cause are divided into two groups: the intrinsic causes that are expressed as social structures and the extrinsic causes that are expressed by the motivations and behaviour of actors.

One of the key advantages to the Aristotelian categories is the ability to have different types of cause which function in different ways, she identifies how:

> These four Aristotelian causes cause in different ways. Crucially, they do not just 'move' things: they also 'constitute' or 'condition' things . . . An intrinsic cause is that which is within the thing being caused, that which continues to be present in a thing through constituting it. An extrinsic cause is that which is not within the being, but which lends and influence or activity to the producing of something.[151]

Kurki understands the role of the actor and its objectives as being extrinsic causes: the actor and its acts are the causes 'by which' something happens, while its objective explains its motivation ('for the sake of'). Though moving the analysis forward, and offering insights as to conceptualizing causes in complex systems, there are gaps. Kurki's concern is with the international system as a whole, not the development of law per se. It is not only a matter of scope, but also of object of analysis. While law is bound with conceptions of cause, it is not yet clear how it causes effects, and what the consequences of these effects are. Building on the discussions thus far, the following section reappraises the use of causal language with specific application to the development of law.

3. Law as a cause and the causes of law

What then does it mean to say that law is the cause of something? Can law be an autonomous cause of anything, or must it be contingent upon another influence? These questions go to the heart of how we understand the development of international law. To say, for example, that a relationship exists between the law within two separate legal systems implies that there are effects felt in one area of law which originate in another (i.e. the result of a cause). Equally, the influence of one judgment on another: whether binding or persuasive, implies a causal relationship between the two. The concept of cause underpins much legal analysis[152] and yet the focus has not been on the relationship between bodies of law or legal

[151] M Kurki, *Causation in International Relations* n. 69, 220.
[152] Notably, HLA Hart and T Honoré, *Causation in the Law* n. 147.

decisions.[153] While we do not necessarily refer to cause or effect these concepts are at the heart of the examination of law as a system.[154]

Take the example of laws of different legal systems influencing each other. It is common to visualize the influence of one legal obligation or principle on another in terms of the interaction of two rule-sets.[155] To say that legal obligations under international law influence domestic law creates a broad selection of potential causes.[156]

For example, under world trade law members are required to provide for the possibility of judicial review of decisions that impose countervailing duties on subsidized goods.[157] Here we might find a number of causes of the influence of international law on domestic law, each with a different effect. The binding nature of the SCM Agreement is a cause of the influence on domestic law as States adapt their internal law to bring it into conformity with their international obligation. However, more specifically, is it the obligation as worded in Art. XVI:4 WTO Agreement,[158] the general obligation of *pacta sunt servanda* as codified by Art. 26 Vienna Convention on the Law of Treaties, or rather the original accession to the WTO by a member which caused the change in its domestic law? Perhaps the influence of the dispute settlement system within the WTO system is an element, or a number of these influences at the same time. We might say that the transfer of information between representatives at the WTO level influences the development of the domestic law as representatives return to their home States and develop or apply WTO related legal provisions.[159] Creating a framework for distinguishing causes and how these causes effect the law is necessary to clarify this range of possible causes and their effects. We need to be able to distinguish between the different types of cause and how they work. A pluralist approach to causation is useful in this regard as it acknowledges a range of causes with different sources and effects.

This approach has two core elements: the first, as discussed above, is its focus on the explanatory uses of narratives created by causal language which is of particular use where there are a range of complex interactions between jurisdictions

153 It should be noted that this book is concerned with causes and effects within the world of social facts and not causation as a way of determining legal responsibility.

154 Some studies do engage with the language of causation though do not fully identify what is meant by 'cause' in the context used, for example, S Marks, 'Human Rights and Root Causes', (2011) 74(1) *Modern Law Review* 57.

155 The concerns of considerable literature examining cases such as Case C-402/05 P *Kadi & Al Barakaat International Foundation v Council, Commission & United Kingdom* [2008] ECR I-6351, or the *R* (*Factortame Ltd*) *v Secretary of State for Transport* litigation.

156 Different causes, each causing its effect in a different way: Aristotle, *Metaphysics V.II*, J Barnes (ed.), *Complete Works of Aristotle Volume II: Revised Oxford Translation* (Princeton, Princeton University Press 1985) 1600.

157 Article 23 Agreement on Subsidies and Countervailing Measures (15 April 1994) LT/UR/A-1A/9 ('SCM Agreement') <http://docsonline.wto.org>.

158 'Each Member shall ensure the conformity of its laws, regulations and administrative procedures with its obligations as provided in the annexed Agreements.'

159 A Lang and J Scott, 'The Hidden World of WTO Governance', (2009) 20(3) *European Journal of International Law* 575.

and amongst globalized actors. The second element is its creation of a typology of different types of causes with different types of influence (effect). This builds on Aristotle's key insight in the examination of causation: the acceptance of a range of different types of cause that cause things in different ways. This is different to approaches that explicitly or implicitly are empirical in nature, rooted in the Humean tradition of observables and a 'mechanistic' view of causes and effects where causes are understood in terms of 'pushing and/or pulling'. Furthermore, Aristotle's causes not only cause things in different ways but also influence each other: for example, the man that walks to be healthy is healthy because he walks. His desire to cause good health makes him walk, while his good health is a cause of his ability to walk when he wishes.[160]

In determining how to understand law as a 'cause' in the development of a legal regime, the first conceptual exercise is to view law as being part of, broadly speaking, two different approaches. The first is to examine the role of law as an autonomous cause in the development of a legal regime, while the second is to use an actor as the cause who uses law to create some sort of effect within a specific body of law. The first approach ('law as cause') is the more common within legal writing for a multitude of reasons, not least the desire not to stray into areas that are more commonly dealt with in international relations scholarship (i.e. individuals' or groups of individuals' behaviour within a State determining or influencing that State's behaviour). Furthermore, legal theory on causation has been focussed more keenly on the concept of cause as a way to attribute responsibility for harm, a distinct and more specific approach to cause than that sought for here.[161]

While the 'law as cause' approach is valuable, it is also limited. It is only one half of the picture, excluding the important role of human action (whether through individuals or groups) on the development of law. It is necessary to include within the analysis an examination of the actors that may use the law to effect change in a legal regime. In this sense, the different approaches are not separate but instead complementary.

It is necessary to focus on the role of globalized actors as a key factor in the causal relationship alongside the recognized role of law. This approach both helps to identify types of cause of change in a legal regime but also the type of influence the cause has.

The division into the different types of cause is useful as this typology of causes serves to distinguish between different types of cause and how they cause things. We can thus marry the advantages of process-based accounts with the explanatory merits of causal language. The result is the typology presented in the following sections: the role of law as a system, the use of law as an instrument, and the place of law as a creator of identities and interests.

[160] Aristotle, *Metaphysics V.II*, J Barnes (ed.), *Complete Works of Aristotle Volume II: Revised Oxford Translation* (Princeton, Princeton University Press 1985) 1600.

[161] For example, HLA Hart and T Honoré, *Causation in the Law* n. 147; L Green, 'The Causal Relation Issue in Negligence Law', (1962) 60 *Michigan Law Review* 543; G Calabresi, 'Concerning Cause and the Law of Torts', (1975) 43 *University of Chicago Law Review* 69.

4. Three explanations revisited: Causal influences

What does a pluralist causal account add to an examination of the development of a legal system? The principal benefit is that we no longer restrict ourselves to thinking about causes as a single category of event. Instead, different causes are understood in different ways: some constrain, others stimulate, yet others constitute. This opens the analysis so as to ensure that we do not place too great an emphasis on one type influence over another in offering explanatory accounts. Take the example of an Appellate Body report that develops the law in a certain area. The cause of the change in the law is not only the act of the Appellate Body as a legitimately authorized interpreter. A causal explanation questions not only who changed the law but how and why. We seek to know why the Appellate Body interpreted in that manner: what restricted or encouraged their behaviour? What rules guided their decision-making? What conceptual framework did they use to come to that decision? To provide a convincing explanation of the development of the law, we have to examine the different types of cause that influenced the law. Insights from a range of approaches to international law help us in this quest, though the influences must be reframed in legal terms for them to affect the law as law. These are the three types of cause that are used to explain the development of the law: the constraining or enabling influence of law as a system, the use of law as an instrument, and the constitutive influence of law influencing the identities and interests of actors.

a. Systemic causes: Constraining and enabling

The first is the systemic influence of law, the role of law as a system of rules.[162] If we want to understand the development of international law it is not enough to say that the law relating to access to trade-related information changed because, for example, a WTO member garnered enough support for a new Ministerial Decision on reducing red tape.[163] To understand why international law changed we need to know what rules applied to the member as it agreed to the Decision: was it limited or enabled to act in the way that it did because of the rules applying to it under international law or under its own legal system? The how and why of the behaviour of actors is connected to the system of rules in which they exist and act.

We can see a relationship between the formalist accounts identified earlier and the way in which systemic causes function. Formalist accounts are premised not only on assumptions relating to the identification of rules but also on the expectation that systems of rules affect behaviour in a determined fashion.[164] To identify rules through the exercise of formal reasoning is to view law as exercising a constraining or enabling influence on the participants of that legal system.

[162] Though sharing some characteristics, this term is not used identically to HLA Hart in *The Concept of Law* n. 117.

[163] Agreement on Trade Facilitation, Ministerial Decision of 7 December 2013, WT/MIN(13)/38, WT/L/913.

[164] M Koskenniemi, *From Apology to Utopia* n. 120, 189–209.

Counter-intuitively, an advantage of this categorization is the focus on the strength of the constraining or enabling influence rather than only the legal status of the rule.[165] Though formalist accounts prioritize the distinction between law and non-law, rephrased in causal language, the systemic influence understands the legal nature of the norm as part of a scale, not of normativity but of causal strength.[166] The acknowledgement of the legal importance of the status of an obligation does not close our eyes to its potential impact. Where the obligations are more likely to illicit compliance by those bound by them, the stronger the constraining or enabling force at work.[167]

While compliance may help determine how effective international law is, it cannot determine the legal status of the obligation.[168] Imperfect compliance need not (necessarily) affect the validity of the legal obligation.[169] Rather than treating normativity in relative terms, instead the priority is the influence on causal strength.

The strength of the constraining or enabling influence of the legal regime on those within it can thus be viewed as dependent on both the normative nature of the rule (i.e. if we wish to make a binary choice: is it law or not) and a sliding scale dependent on the legitimacy of the rule.[170] As the conditions for legitimacy and law-making are often similar, we might expect laws to incline towards greater instinctive legitimacy than other types of rule.[171] An examination of systemic causes not only understands the law's influence as a form of control (restraining) but also its capacity to enable actors, empower them to act in certain ways and pursue objectives in what would otherwise be non-legal ways (rights of standing, for example).

Systems do not function without impetus: actors are central to stimulating the development of the law, whether restrained or enabled by the system in which they find themselves. This is the second influence, the effect of law when used to advance an individual or collective interest.

165 J d'Aspremont, *Formalism and the Sources of International Law* n. 115, 29–34.

166 J Goldstein and L Martin, 'Legalization, Trade Liberalization and Domestic Politics: A Cautionary Note', (2000) 54(3) *International Organization* 603, 620.

167 This has the advantage of sidestepping questions of relative normativity in international law as the focus is upon the descriptive effect of the rule not necessarily its status: though if one wishes to maintain a strict distinction (which is the preferred approach here), this does not present any difficulty.

168 R Howse and R Teitel, 'Beyond Compliance: Rethinking Why International Law Really Matters', *Public Law and Legal Theory Research Paper Series*, NYU School of Law, Working Paper No.10-08.

169 T Franck, *The Power of Legitimacy Among Nations* (Oxford, Oxford University Press 1990) 43–4.

170 Ibid., 41ff.

171 At the WTO, for example, it is claimed that 'non-discrimination, transparency and procedural fairness' are 'fundamental principles' of the institution: P Lamy, 'Developmental and Trade Significance, Changing Context and Future Prospects', speech given on 11 February 2010 in Geneva <http://www.wto.org/english/news_e/sppl_e/sppl147_e.htm>. The veracity of such a claim is clearly subject to question: M Elsig, 'The World Trade Organization's Legitimacy Crisis: What Does the Beast Look Like?', (2007) 41 *Journal of World Trade* 1.

b. Instrumental causes: Seeking outcomes

The earlier account of functionalist conceptions of the law identified the way in which law was understood through the aims and objectives of specific actors. The expectations of such accounts are that the law can be used for a specific end. At a general level this might be the promotion of certain values, but it might well equally be a very specific objective in mind without seeming systemic importance. This account is premised on an understanding of the law as something to be used, a tool for the pursuit of objectives. The way in which law functions in this capacity is instrumentally, stimulating contestations and requiring changes in behaviour.

As actors use the law they stimulate its development, often operating across jurisdictional boundaries as they pursue their objectives. While their behaviour in each legal system is examined separately, their objectives take into account the legal world as a whole. By using the law as an instrument, actors change the rules and principles that govern the legal system in question.

An instrumental use of the law can take many forms. At a general level, we may view law in instrumental terms: that is, fulfilling a specific function, commonly the creation or maintenance of social order.[172] At a more specific level, however, specific actors engage with law in instrumental terms, as they pursue their own objectives. The way in which they conceive of these objectives, and how they think about their relationship to their legal system is in part constituted through the law. This is the third and final influence: constitutive causes.

c. Constitutive causes: The influence of law on identities and interests

Actors use law to pursue their objectives at domestic, regional, and international levels while law constrains and enables their behaviour. Tied to these two influences of change in the law, there is a third cause: the role of law as it creates and conditions the identities and interests of those actors.

The creation of societies or associations on any level necessitates some form of law as the ties that bind the individual to society.[173] Part of this social function is to create and encourage identities and shared meanings for society. The result is the contribution of law in influencing the interests of actors. The focus on the role of law as a constituting force offers alternatives to solely instrumental or systemic accounts of how law develops.[174]

[172] On the pervasiveness of such a view: B Tamanaha, 'An Analytical Map of Social Scientific Approaches to the Concept of Law', (1995) 15(4) *Oxford Journal of Legal Studies* 501, 513–15.

[173] Hume, for example, denied the conception of any 'pre-social' state for mankind as he is inherently social: D Hume, *A Treatise of Human Nature* (L Selby-Bigg (ed.)) (Oxford, Clarendon Press 1975) 493ff. Similarly, Aristotle, *Politics*, I.3, 1253b1–1260b8.

[174] On the benefits of combining insights from constructivism with other theoretical approaches: C Meyer and E Strickmann, 'Solidifying Constructivism: How Material and Ideational Factors Interact in European Defence', (2011) 49(1) *Journal of Common Market Studies* 61.

As groups of actors (people or States) coalesce to form societies they form rules with which to govern those societies. Thus Fitzmaurice states that *ubi societas ibi ius*:

is more than a mere statement of a fact. The case is one not merely *of post* but of *propter hoc*. It is not simply that where society is found, law is found, but that it must be so found—that law is a necessary condition of the existence of a society as such—which is to say a necessary condition of any systematized form of inter-relationships.[175]

While the *necessary* relationship between law and social ordering is contentious,[176] we might make a weaker claim: all societies require social norms to permit their existence, and in the Western liberal tradition, this norm takes the form of law.[177] The increasing use of legal discourses to question issues in international law (see for example, the centrality of debates over the legality of the 2003 invasion of Iraq), and the increasing primacy of legal requirements to determine the most fundamental categories within international relations (most notably Statehood) demonstrate the fundamental importance of law in how the international community understands itself.[178]

If we accept that there exists a necessary bond between law and society (in our current model at least) the constitutive nature of law is clearer. In Koskenniemi's words, law 'reflects the social context' but also the 'normative views about that context. In other words, law implies an interpretation of what society is like now and what should be done in order to make it better'.[179] To interpret the current and ideal state of society through its law is to create or encourage the objectives or interests or the society's members.

Examining the constitutive role of law on the identities and interests of actors helps explain the development of international law insofar as it helps answer deeper questions of the behaviour of those catalysing legal change.

d. *Bringing together different causes and their differing effects*

By bringing together these different types of influence or cause, we can examine how international law develops by reference to the behaviour of actors as they pursue their objectives, constrained and conditioned as they are in the ways described above. Rather than oscillating between viewing international law as an instrument of States and as a system of rules applicable to them,[180] in accepting the three

[175] G Fitzmaurice, 'The General Principles of International Law Considered From the Standpoint of the Rule of Law', (1957) 92 *Recueil des Cours de l'Académie de Droit International* 38. Cf. G Tunkin, *Theory of International Law* (Cambridge MA, Harvard University Press 1974), positing the 'unfoundedness of the bourgeois concept of ubi societas ibi jus' at 237.

[176] For an analysis of the challenges faced by such an assertion: B Tamanaha, n. 171, 501.

[177] Ibid., 531–5.

[178] The overlap with internal State legality is felt especially in the recognition of new States. See J Vidmar, *Democratic Statehood in International Law* (Oxford, Hart Publishing 2013).

[179] M Koskenniemi, *From Apology to Utopia* n. 119, 474.

[180] A Orford, 'Constituting Order', in J Crawford and M Koskenniemi (eds), *The Cambridge Companion to International Law* (Cambridge, Cambridge University Press 2012) 271, 287.

different types of cause that cause things *in different ways* many of the ideological divisions that separate the literature are no longer relevant.[181] It is not that a process account of the instrumental use of law is inaccurate or that a constructivist account of the role of ideas is sufficient. Rather, each cause is part of the analysis and each type of influence corresponds to a different *way* in which law develops. Further, each cause identifies a legal influence on the law, whether through stimulating challenges, restricting the behaviour of actors, or motivating their behaviour in certain relevant ways.

If we look at all three causes of change in a legal system we can see how they each answer a different question about why the law has changed in the way that it has. Who or what changes the law? Actors stimulate changes but how do they change the law? Their method is constrained and enabled by the rules and norms of the system in which they are acting. Why do they behave in this way? The law that mediates their relationship to society and others constitutes their conception of themselves and their objectives. As will become clear in the subsequent chapters (in particular Chapters 4, 5, and 6), accounts that seek to explain the development of WTO law often overemphasize one type of causal influence, whether systemic, instrumental, or constitutive thus presenting an incomplete picture.

The following chapter examines the normative and institutional framework of the WTO (and where relevant domestic legal systems) as a site of globalized legal development. In doing so, it appraises the role of the three causal influences identified in this chapter and how they find expression at the WTO.

[181] Cf. the requirement to choose between rule-based and process-based accounts: J d'Aspremont, *Formalism and the Sources of International Law* n. 116, 13.

3

The WTO as a Site of Globalized Legal Development

A. Introduction

The previous chapters have identified the conceptual and practical difficulties with examining how WTO law (and international law more generally) develops. The numerous competing influences of different actors traversing jurisdictional boundaries as they pursue their goals, and the systems they create presents a difficult subject of study. Hence the turn to causal language, reframing common explanatory approaches to legal development in causal terms.

Thus far the discussion has been somewhat abstract, questioning how we understand international law's development over time. This chapter applies the insights from Chapters 1 and 2 to the specifics of the WTO. As identified in Chapter 1, the WTO is the ideal laboratory for the study of international law in this regard; its normative and institutional aspects embody globalized legal processes, while the subject matter under its jurisdiction is necessarily broad and linked to countless areas of human behaviour.[1]

This chapter takes the three causal influences identified in Chapter 2 and applies them to the specifics of WTO law, giving a more detailed illustration of how they function in world trade. It acknowledges a deeper, explanatory understanding of causes, accepting that the purpose of causal language is to understand why something happens. It marries this with the position that law develops through specifically *legal* influences, thus legitimizing its change over time.[2]

The effect of the three causal influences on the normative and institutional structures of the WTO are examined here: the constitutive effect of law on international trade (B), the instrumental effect of law at the WTO (C), and the systemic effect of law on globalized actors at the WTO (D). Each causal influence explains part of the picture, one way in which the law develops. It is only when viewed together, however, that a complete picture can be drawn.

[1] Chapter 1.C. [2] Chapter 2.C and D.

B. The Constitutive Effect of Law in International Trade

Globalized actors use law to pursue their objectives at domestic, regional, and international levels while law constrains and enables their behaviour as they do so.[3] The influence of the trans-jurisdictional activity of actors and the restrictions the law places on them fail to explain *why* it is that these actors seek to pursue their interests in this way and how the law is central both to their method and objectives. This is the starting point in examining the development of WTO law: identifying the constitutive influence of law on international trade.

Aside from understanding WTO law on its own terms (that is, as a quasi-autonomous body of rules within the international legal system) much attention has been paid to the interests of actors involved in trade policy and the impact they have on the law.[4] More recently, increasing attention has been paid to the role of ideas in WTO law; the way in which shared understandings and knowledge structures influence the content and application of WTO law.[5] This section reframes these differing strands by placing law at the centre of the debate, stressing its role as a mechanism for constituting the identities, and thus interests, of globalized actors.

This section argues that the interests of actors are understood *through* their identities, and that law plays a powerful central role in constituting the identities of actors. It identifies the constitutive effect of law on the identities of (1) individuals engaged in trade and (2) the institutions related to trade, while (3) identifies the role that law plays in structuring the central relationship in international trade—the distinction between public and private. As a result, (4) argues that law's constitutive effect in these three areas encourages globalized actors to develop world trade law in an manner consistent with their own values.

1. Law's influence on individuals in international trade

Key elements of actors' identities in trade are constituted by law, whether domestic or international. At the most general level, corporate legal personality is constituted by domestic law, while international legal personality is constituted by international law. The influence of law goes further than this overarching level of generality, as important as it may be.

For example, a shoe manufacturer who wishes to export their wares to a neighbouring State is dependent on being able to claim a right over the shoes that they

[3] Chapter 2.D(4).

[4] For example, JH Jackson, 'The Great 1994 Sovereignty Debate: United States Acceptance and Implementation of the Uruguay Round Results', (1997) 36 *Columbia Journal of Transnational Law* 157; R Brewster, 'Rule-Based Dispute Resolution in International Trade Law', (2006) 92(2) *Virginia Law Review* 251; G Shaffer and J Trachtman, 'Interpretation and Institutional Choice at the WTO', (2012) 52(1) *Virginia Journal of International Law* 103.

[5] Most notably: A Lang, *World Trade Law After Neoliberalism: Re-Imagining the Global Economic Order* (Oxford, Oxford University Press 2011); and S Cho, *The Social Foundations of World Trade: Norms, Community and Constitution* (Cambridge, Cambridge University Press 2014).

manufacture. Not only that, they must also be able to rely on legal institutions that identify them as an 'owner' competent to sell the shoes made in his factory while those that were the proximate creators of the shoes are identified as 'workers' and as such do not enjoy rights over the manufactured goods.[6] Thus, the shoe manufacturer's very identity as a 'trader' is dependent on a set of legal institutions that permit them to act as they do and pursue that which they wish (in this case, profit), as well as rely upon the law to enforce their rights against those who do not share this understanding of property rights.

The contentious inclusion of intellectual property rights within the WTO is a particularly telling example.[7] Here, not only is the recognition of intellectual property rights as 'private rights' incorporated into the WTO,[8] but also that in this case TRIPS requires the introduction of criminal sanctions for violations of 'wilful trademark counterfeiting or copyright piracy on a commercial scale'.[9] Such a development was unique in international IP protection, which had hitherto not required criminal sanctions for violations of IP rights.[10] In this case, the TRIPS grants IP rights holders the ability to have their rights recognized in the domestic legal systems of the membership, thus extending their characterization as rights holders.

Beyond the direct involvement of law in constituting specific identities, law indirectly plays a constitutive role through the values held by individuals and subsequently, their interests. The argument here is that law is value-laden, and that law serves to mediate between individuals' values and the shared values of a community.[11]

In an examination of law's involvement with those engaged in trade, the division between interests and identities is misleading.[12] Identity requires value judgments to be able to assess the world around us, including institutions of law. Identity is thus 'shot with value through and through' as it aids us in determining what is worthwhile.[13] Interests are determined later, in light of values: concepts such as

[6] For a comprehensive analysis of the coercive role of the State in the maintenance of property rights: R Hale, 'Coercion and Distribution in a Supposedly Non-Coercive State', (1923) 38(3) *Political Science Quarterly* 470.

[7] On the debates: J Bhagwati, *In Defense of Globalization* (Oxford, Oxford University Press 2007) 182–5; J Stiglitz, *Globalization and its Discontents* (London, Penguin 2002) 7–8; A Panagariya, 'TRIPs and the WTO: An Uneasy Marriage', in K Maskus (ed.), *The WTO, Intellectual Property Rights and the Knowledge Economy* (Cheltenham, Edward Elgar 2004).

[8] Fourth recital to the preamble, Agreement on Trade-Related Aspects of Intellectual Property Rights (15 April 1994) LT/UR/A-1C/IP/1 <http://docsonline.wto.org> ('TRIPS').

[9] Article 61 TRIPS.

[10] See *China—Measures Affecting the Protection and Enforcement of Intellectual Property Rights*, Report of the Panel, WT/DS362/R (26 January 2009) para. 7.529.

[11] Law is not the only mediator, religion may play a similar role, however, law is unique as the 'authoritative voice of a political community', J Raz, *Between Authority and Interpretation* (Oxford, Oxford University Press 2009) 99–102.

[12] cf., the distinction between 'value' actors and 'interest' actors: K Abbott and D Snidal, 'Values and Interests: International Legalization in the Fight Against Corruption', (2002) XXXI *Journal of Legal Studies* 141, 145–50.

[13] In Raz's terms, 'self-understanding': J Raz, n. 11, 111.

cost and benefit are dependent upon prior value judgements of what is worthwhile.[14] It is the law's relationship to values that anchors its ability to constitute key elements of actors' identities.

Legal processes are social ones: at all points, values play their role as law is made, applied, and interpreted.[15] The values of a society help determine the objectives of the legislators, the frame of reference of administrative agents or the imperatives of judges. The prioritization of certain values will influence not only what is to be the subject of legal regulation or deregulation but also the way in which these topics are to be approached. The introduction of new legislation, the application of that legislation by administrative bodies, the review of the legislation by judicial bodies—at each of these points the influence of society's values, and the view of what shape society ought to take, is brought to bear.[16]

For example, one can take 'fairness' as a starting point, a socially-determined value that has multiple facets. One actor may view fairness in terms that prioritize intergenerational equity: this is to say that current generations ought to consider the consequences to future generations in their decision-making processes.[17] The proceeding norm within the context of the WTO system, which focuses on the role of development as a tool for peace and prosperity,[18] might be that States should not use the overarching aims of the covered agreements to ignore their environmental obligations to future generations. One formulation of the specific resultant rule can be found within the exceptions of Art. XX GATT, specifically Art. XX(b) and Art. XX(g).[19] Thus a value suggests a norm that, in turn, crystallizes into a specific legal obligation under the GATT. This is not to say that this is the only interpretation, but rather that within systems such as the WTO, terms are continually contested and respond to the behaviour of actors.[20] Indeed, it is of interest that the original conception of Art. XX(g) was

[14] There are parallels with the reasoning used here and Lang's framing of material factors as having meaning only through ideational factors: 'After all material (economic) structures are "ideational" to their core. We may refer to individuals or classes acting in their material interests, but what precisely are such interests if not knowledge constructs? Similarly, we may speak of the distribution of wealth as a brute material fact, but that is just a way of speaking. There is no way that a particular distribution of "wealth" can be instituted—or redistribution pursued as a political project—except through the entrenchment of particular conceptions of value and through the operation of the knowledge practices through which such conceptions are constituted. The material is inseparable from the ideational.' A Lang, 'Rejoinder', (2014) 23(3) *Social & Legal Studies* 453, 454.

[15] Chapter 2.D(4)(c).

[16] A 'structural coupling' between law and society: G Teubner, *Constitutional Fragments: Societal Constitutionalism and Globalization* (Oxford, Oxford University Press 2012) 105–10.

[17] See Rio Declaration on Environment and Development (3–14 June 1992) A/Conf.151/26 (Vol. I) Principle 3 and Principle 21.

[18] Preamble to the GATT 1947, second recital: 'Recognizing that their relations in the field of trade and economic endeavour should be conducted with a view to raising standards of living, ensuring full employment and a large and steadily growing volume of real income and effective demand, developing the full use of the resources of the world and expanding the production and exchange of goods.'

[19] Relating to the protection of human, animal, or plant life or health and the conservation of exhaustible natural resources respectively.

[20] For a vivid account: J Ruggie, 'International Regimes, Transactions and Change: Embedded Liberalism and the Post-war Economic Order', (1982) 36(2) *International Organization* 379.

not that it encapsulated conceptions of fairness but rather that this developed *over time*.[21] It is the openness of such terms that permits the continual contestation over their application.

In an especially interesting account of such contestations over foundational concepts is Andrew Lang's analysis of how the term 'free trade' has altered over time, moving from a preoccupation with customs administration in nineteenth century France, to prioritizing non-discrimination as a central characteristic in the postwar period, and more recently to its relationship with a 'global marketplace'.[22]

By looking at how such a foundational term can change in its content over time, Lang states:

> Transformational change in the institutions and politics of international trade, it seems, goes hand in hand with *cognitive* change. Different epochs in the history of international trade are characterised by differences in the prevailing meaning of free trade—meanings which are embedded and expressed in the concrete institutions and policy choices associated with a given trading order.[23]

The relationship between ideas (in particular values), law, and economic structures is thus complimentary; one does not develop without the other, their relationship is dynamic and constitutive.[24] It is the argument here, and made in more detail in the following two sections, that law is central to *both* the process of embedding meanings in institutions (i.e. what they are, what they are for, and how we understand them) as well as the ways in which institutions stimulate changes to identities.

2. Law's constitutive effect on the State and other institutions

Just as law plays a constitutive role in the identity (and thus interests) of the individual engaged in trade matters, so it does for other autonomous institutions such as the State. It does this by legitimating its existence in the eyes of other members of the community, influencing the way in which the State or institution understands its own interest. This is an understanding of the State as an entirely distinct and 'real' entity that has interests that go beyond that of its component institutions or actors. Not that the 'State' is a useful fiction and that it is really the manifestation of interests of others through the government bodies or agents. Instead, in the

[21] On its relationship to intergenerational fairness, through the principle of sustainable development: Panel Reports, *China—Measures Related to the Exportation of Rare Earths, Tungsten, and Molybdenum*, WT/DS431/R/WT/DS432/R/WT/DS433/R/ and Add.1, adopted 29 August 2014, para. 7.277.

[22] This is a simplification of Lang's nuanced analysis: A Lang, 'Reflecting on "Linkage": Cognitive and Institutional Change in The International Trading System', (2007) 70(4) *Modern Law Review* 523, 528–9.

[23] Ibid., 529.

[24] D Kennedy, 'Three Globalizations of Law and Legal Thought: 1850–2000', in D Trubek and A Santos (eds), *The New Law and Economic Development: A Critical Appraisal* (Cambridge, Cambridge University Press 2006) 19.

constructivist tradition, that the State is understood as a separate entity with its own objectives and values.[25]

The existence of the State as a 'real' entity is not dependent on its international legal personality, though the legitimacy that legal personality grants States is considerable. The efforts of the Palestinian National Authority to have Palestine's 'non-member observer State' status accepted at the UN and other institutions is well documented.[26] Indeed, the recognition of States is a highly contentious area of international law precisely because of the legitimacy that such an act entails, permitting recognized States to engage with the international community as sovereign equals.[27]

The law's strength in legitimating States is so great that it can do so in situations that would not normally give rise to such recognition.[28] The constitutive role of the Fourth Geneva Convention in the 'reconstruction' of Iraq is one notable example.[29] In this instance, it is arguable that the Iraqi State was restructured beyond what would traditionally be considered permissible under the authority claimed by occupying powers.[30] The current use of IMF conditionality and Letters of Intent to conduct fundamental changes to the structures of States in the face of the 2007/8 financial crisis is another.[31] Foreign intervention on such a scale would normally raise serious alarm yet the role of international law in legitimizing this process has served to soften some of the criticism.[32]

It is not only the State that is legitimated by the law but also other autonomous institutions. Just as we can understand the State as an actor in its own right, we can extend these insights to other forms of association such as international organizations and the institutions within.[33] Just as States pursue their own objectivities, influenced by the way in which law has constituted them, so do other forms of

[25] 'States are people too': A Wendt, *Social Theory of International Politics* (Cambridge, Cambridge University Press 1999) 215. See also, PT Jackson, 'Hegel's House, or "People are States Too" ', (2004) 30 *Review of International Studies* 281; and C Wight, 'State Agency: Social Action Without Human Activity?', (2004) 30 *Review of International Studies* 269.

[26] United Nations General Assembly Resolution 67/19 (A/RES/67/19A) 29 November 2012, and the subsequent discussion: D Akande, 'Palestine as a UN Observer State: Does this Make Palestine a State?' 3 December 2012, EJIL: *Talk!* <http://www.ejiltalk.org/palestine-as-a-un-observer-state-does-this-make-palestine-a-state/>.

[27] On the competing approaches to recognition: S Talmon, 'The Constitutive versus the Declaratory Theory of Recognition: Tertium Non Datur?', (2005) 75 *British Year Book of International Law* 101.

[28] A Anghie, *Imperialism, Sovereignty and the Making of International Law* (Cambridge, Cambridge University Press 2005) 310.

[29] M Craven, S Marks, G Simpson, and R Wilde, 'We Are Teachers of International Law', (2004) 17 *Leiden Journal of International Law* 363, 372.

[30] S Wheatley, 'The Security Council, Democratic Legitimacy and Regime Change in Iraq', (2006) 17(3) *European Journal of International Law* 531, 533.

[31] The legal basis for which is commonly attributed to Art. V(3) Articles of Agreement of the International Monetary Fund (concluded and entered into force 27 December 1944) 2 UNTS 39.

[32] Clearly not all as there is considerable opposition within receiving States to IMF intervention, by popular protest (in Greece, for example) and legal action (Judgment of the Constitutional Court of Latvia, 'On the compliance of Article 2, Paragraph One of the Law "On State Pension and State Allowance Disbursement in the Period from 2009 to 2012" with Articles 1 and 109 of the Constitution of the Republic of Latvia and on the compliance of Article 3, Paragraph One of the above Law with Articles 1, 91, 105 and 109 of the Constitution of the Republic of Latvia.' Case No. 2009-43-01).

[33] S Cho, n. 5, 77–81.

association. International organizations have their own identity, separate to that of their membership: indeed, this is considered a defining feature of international organizations as separate legal persons.[34]

The Appellate Body of the WTO serves as an excellent example: an institution that enjoys an independent identity beyond the wishes of the membership or the superficial strictures of its constitutive text (the Dispute Settlement Understanding).[35] Rather, it is the institution's interpretation of its constituent instrument that has had such unexpected results. This development of the Appellate Body into a 'World Trade Court' was by no means inevitable, and has influenced the way that the Appellate Body examines cases as part of its judicial process.[36]

It was not clear at the founding of the WTO, that the Appellate Body would take the form that it has since taken.[37] Indeed, the negotiating history clearly indicates that the GATT Contracting Parties considered dispute settlement under the WTO to be an entirely different creature to that found in other areas of international relations,[38] not concerned with the development of a clear jurisprudence[39] but rather to settle specific disputes between the parties to it.[40] The proposal of appellate review raised concerns not of potential institution building (at that point in time) but rather that it would add delays to the settlement of disputes with all members lodging appeals.[41]

[34] See *Reparation for Injuries Suffered in the Service of the Nations*, Advisory Opinion, [1949] ICJ Rep 174. Otherwise, the organization does not enjoy legal personality as distinct from the States: *Case Concerning Certain Phosphate Lands in Nauru* (*Nauru v Australia*) [1992] ICJ Rep 240 and discussion in D Sarooshi, *International Organizations and their Exercise of Sovereign Powers* (Oxford, Oxford University Press 2005) 34.

[35] Understanding on Rules and Procedures Governing the Settlement of Disputes (15 April 1994) LT/UR/A-2/DS/U/1 <http://docsonline.wto.org> ('DSU').

[36] Former Appellate Body Member C-D Ehlermann: 'Six Years on the Bench of the "World Trade Court": Some Personal Experiences as Member of the Appellate Body of the WTO', (2002) 36 *Journal of World Trade* 605. An alternative name previously suggested is the 'International Court of Economic Justice': JHH Weiler, 'The Rule of Lawyers and the Ethos of Diplomats: Reflections on the Internal and External Legitimacy of WTO Dispute Settlement', (2001) 35(2) *Journal of World Trade* 206; Appellate Body Member P Van Den Bossche, 'The Making of the "World Trade Court": the Origins and Development of the Appellate Body of the World Trade Organization', in R Yerxa and B Wilson, *Key Issues in WTO Dispute Settlement: The First Ten Years* (Cambridge, Cambridge University Press 2005) 63–4. Also, P Van Den Bossche, 'From Afterthought to Centerpiece: The WTO Appellate Body and its Rise to Prominence in the World Trading System', Maastricht Faculty of Law Working Paper 2005/1.

[37] R Steinberg, 'Judicial Lawmaking at the WTO: Discursive, Constitutional, and Political Constraints', (2004) 98(2) *American Journal of International Law* 247, 250.

[38] 'The GATT dispute settlement machinery is original and specific; there is no equivalent in other areas of international relations.' Communication from EEC (24 September 1987) GATT Doc. MTN. GNG/NG13/W/12, para. 1.

[39] Ibid. 'The machinery cannot and must not be used to create, through a process of deductive interpretation, new obligations for contracting parties, or to replace the negotiating process. One of the objectives of the Uruguay Round is to eliminate certain ambiguities and diverging interpretations of the General Agreement and Codes, and this will make a fundamental contribution to dispute settlement.'

[40] 'The dispute settlement procedures should be used essentially as a conciliation mechanism whose final stage, if conciliation fails, should not be of a judicial nature.' Communication from Brazil (7 March 1988) GATT Doc. MTN.GNG/NG13/W/24.

[41] See: Note by the Secretariat (13 November 1989) GATT Doc. MTN.GNG/NG13/16, para. 21; Note by the Secretariat (15 December 1989) GATT Doc. MTN.GNG/NG13/17, para. 9; Note by the Secretariat (28 May 1990) GATT Doc. MTN.GNG/NG13/19, para. 8.

Article 17 DSU sets out the competences of the Appellate Body and is cautious in its terminology.[42] There is no mention of a 'court', 'tribunal', or 'judges' and the number of permanent members is considerably lower than comparable international tribunals.[43] Though permanent, members of the Appellate Body are not contracted on a full-time basis but rather maintained on a monthly retainer with daily fees factored in.[44] They do not sit together but in divisions of three,[45] potentially minimizing their ability to lay down particularly authoritative decisions of the full Appellate Body as is customary in other legal systems.[46] The Appellate Body does not issue judgments but instead 'reports' which are subject to adoption:[47] the Dispute Settlement Body, a political organ of all members of the WTO, must adopt reports of the Appellate Body which though in practice a formality due to the negative consensus rule,[48] in theory it constitutes a limitation on the autonomy of the Appellate Body, as it creates opportunities for the public criticism of reports by the membership.[49]

The role of judicial actors in creating novel institutions is not new; Stein identified the process in the European context in 1981.[50] More cautious than the European Court of Justice, the Appellate Body has acted to consolidate its position and maintain its own legitimacy.[51]

In spite of limited, though central, guidance from the DSU[52] and a weak mandate from its accompanying negotiating history, the Appellate Body created and moulded an identity for the institution through legal decisions (some considered

[42] Though nonetheless using the term 'appellate' which does conjure up legal images. I am grateful to David Zharing for raising this point.

[43] P Van Den Bossche, 'The Making of the "World Trade Court"', n. 36, at 65–6 citing the numbers of other permanent judges on international tribunals: fifteen on the International Court of Justice, eighteen on the International Criminal Court, and twenty-one on the International Tribunal for the Law of the Sea.

[44] Establishment of the Appellate Body: Recommendations by the Preparatory Committee for the WTO approved by the Dispute Settlement Body on 10 February 1995 (19 June 1995) WT/DSB/1, paras 10–12.

[45] Article 17.1 DSU.

[46] Note discussions over the differing weight of judgments of chambers rather than a full court of the International Court of Justice: A Zimmermann, C Tomuschat, K Oellers-Frahm, and C Tams, *The Statute of the International Court of Justice: A Commentary* (2nd edn, Oxford, Oxford University Press 2012) 468.

[47] D McRae, 'What is the Future of WTO Dispute Settlement', (2004) 7(1) *Journal of International Economic Law* 3, 7–8.

[48] Article 17.14 DSU.

[49] For an illustrative example: P Mavroidis, 'Amicus Curiae Briefs Before the WTO: Much Ado About Nothing', Jean Monet Working Paper 2/01, 8.

[50] E Stein, 'Lawyers, Judges, and the Making of a Transnational Constitution', (1981) 75(1) *American Journal of International Law* 1.

[51] P Van Den Bossche, 'The Making of the "World Trade Court"', n. 36, at 69: 'most, if not all, members appointed in November 1995 shared a nearly missionary belief in the importance of the task entrusted to them.' S Picciotto, 'The WTO's Appellate Body: Legal Formalism as a Legitimation of Global Governance', (2005) 18 *Governance* 3.

[52] The limited guidance offered by the DSU to the members of the Appellate Body may well further explain their fixation with what little guidance exists: that is Art. 3.2 DSU and thus the textual methodology on which their legitimacy rests.

of particular 'constitutional' importance)[53] as well as fleshing out a number of procedural obligations under the DSU.[54] The drafting of its own Working Procedures has also served to 'cure' some of the obstacles to the Appellate Body's legitimacy;[55] Van den Bossche identifies Rule 4 of the Working Procedures, which sets out a mechanism for the 'exchange of views' between all members before finalizing a report, as a key way to resolve the dangers of inconsistency and reduced authority that the three member divisions might otherwise have caused.[56] More generally the Working Procedures have served to ensure the judicial character of the procedures at the Appellate Body.[57]

Just as law influences the identities and interests of actors and institutions, it similarly plays a constitutive role in the relationship between public and private authority. This is the subject of the following section.

3. Law's constitution of the public–private relationship

In its second report, the Appellate Body set out what it considered to be the focus of the WTO: 'The GATT 1994 is a commercial agreement, and the WTO is concerned, after all, with markets.'[58] In spite of the WTO's concern with markets, its focus is not traders but rather governments. The distinction between the public and the private is central to the way in which the WTO regulates international trade. The WTO regulates the behaviour of the membership (principally States) directly: though private actors constitute the vast majority of traders, WTO rules do not apply to them but rather the membership.[59]

By regulating one class of actor (public) but focussing on the outcomes for another (private), WTO law is required to engage with the distinction between the public and the private on a continual basis, a situation that becomes more complex in light of changes at both domestic and international levels.[60] At the domestic

[53] JH Jackson, 'The Varied Policies of International Juridical Bodies—Reflections on Theory and Practice', (2004) 25 *Michigan Journal of International Law* 869; D Cass, 'The "Constitutionalization" of International Trade Law: Judicial Norm Generation as the Engine of Constitutional Development in International Trade', (2001) 12 *European Journal of International Law* 39.

[54] See Howse's analysis of Art. 7.2 DSU and other 'procedural' provisions: R Howse, 'Adjudicative Legitimacy and Treaty Interpretation in International Trade Law: The Early Years of WTO Jurisprudence', in JHH Weiler (ed.), *The EU, the WTO, and the NAFTA: Towards a Common Law of International Trade?* (Oxford, Oxford University Press 2001) 44ff.

[55] Currently: *Working Procedures for Appellate Review* (16 August 2010) WT/AB/WP/6.

[56] P Van Den Bossche, 'The Making of the "World Trade Court"', n. 36, at 69–71.

[57] R Hudec, 'The New Dispute Settlement System of the WTO: An Overview of the First Three Years', (1999) 8 *Minnesota Journal of Global Trade* 1.

[58] *Japan—Taxes on Alcoholic Beverages*, Report of the Appellate Body, WT/DS8/AB/R—WT/DS10/AB/R—WT/DS11/AB/R (4 October 1996), p. 25.

[59] On the consequences of this bifurcation: G Shaffer, *Defending Interests: Public–Private Partnerships in WTO Litigation* (Washington DC, Brookings 2003) 3.

[60] See M de Bellis, 'Public Law and Private Regulators in the Global Legal Space', (2011) 9(2) *International Journal of Constitutional Law* 425; A Supiot, 'The Public–Private Relation in the Context of Today's Refeudalization', (2013) 11(1) *International Journal of Constitutional Law* 129.

level, many States are liberalizing the provision of public services, blurring the line between public and private.[61] At the international level, the distinction between public State action, and private commercial action is also becoming blurred.[62] The proliferation of private standards which increasingly effect trade (at times to a greater extent than governmental standards) is one such example: ought the WTO regulate private standard setting bodies, or ought the membership accept that the WTO's competence is limited to public standards, no matter the discriminatory impact that private standards may have for traders?[63]

The underlying logic of the WTO, it is said, is the theory of comparative advantage.[64] Whether world trade law truly embodies such a principle is contested, arguably favouring 'enlightened mercantilism' rather than true free market rationales.[65] Equally, the effectiveness of the underlying theory of free trade is also contested, most notably in the development context.[66] Nonetheless, the crude thrust of the covered agreements is that public action (i.e. government) is to be restrained from distorting conditions of competition within the market (i.e. between private actors). This is the case even where the same action by private actors would have the same effect; under the national treatment provisions of Art. III:4 GATT, the WTO's concern 'is merely the *governmental* intervention that affects the conditions under which like goods, domestic and imported, compete in the market within a Member's territory'.[67]

States are thus conflicted: on the one hand, governmental action has been central to the historical success of many industries, from cotton to computers,[68] while on the other, the general atmosphere in trade relations adheres to the relationship between free trade and honest dealing.[69] And all the while, different interest groups lobby policy makers to either increase or reduce governmental involvement.[70]

[61] Most notably through Public-Private Partnerships and Private Finance Initiatives. See also J Resnik, 'Globalization(s), Privatization(s), Constitutionalization, and Statization: Icons and Experiences of Sovereignty in the 21st Century', (2013) 11(1) *International Journal of Constitutional Law* 162.

[62] Various different frameworks speak to this development, such as transnational legal process, the *lex mercatoria*, International Public Authority, and Global Administrative Law.

[63] See Note by the Secretariat, 'Proposed Working Definition On SPS-Related Private Standards' (6 March 2012) G/SPS/W/265; A Arcuri, 'The TBT Agreement and Private Standards', in M Trebilcock and T Epps (eds), *Research Handbook on the TBT Agreement* (Cheltenham, Edward Elgar 2013).

[64] For example, M Herdegen, *Principles of International Economic Law* (Oxford, Oxford University Press 2013) 13–15; JH Jackson, *The Jurisprudence of GATT & the WTO* (Cambridge, Cambridge University Press 2000) 3–14; P Ven den Bossche and W Zdouc, *The Law and Policy of the World Trade Organization* (3rd edn, Cambridge, Cambridge University Press 2013) 4–30.

[65] K Bagwell and R Staiger, 'An Economic Theory of GATT', (1999) 89(1) *The American Economic Review* 215.

[66] See generally, S Rolland, *Development at the WTO* (Oxford, Oxford University Press 2012).

[67] *Korea—Measures Affecting Imports Of Fresh, Chilled and Frozen Beef*, Report of the Appellate Body, WT/DS161/AB/R—WT/DS169/AB/R (11 December 2000) para. 149.

[68] On the role of the State in developing industrial cotton production: S Beckert, *Empire of Cotton: A New History of Global Capitalism* (London, Allen Lane 2014) xiv–xv. On US policy of R&D subsidies in the semi-conductor industry: D Sarooshi, n. 34, 90–1.

[69] For example, the pursuit of 'free and fair trade' in the external action of the EU: Art. 3.5 Treaty on European Union [2010] OJ C83/13.

[70] Subsidies (and their regulation) are the most obvious example: see Chapter 6.

The way each member responds to these competing difficulties alters the conditions for actors within that jurisdiction. Indeed, the Appellate Body has drawn attention to the difficulties that such a process has on examining whether consumers consider two products to be 'like'—government regulation may well create distinctions between products that would otherwise not exist. For example, is beef sold only in specialized shops viewed differently by consumers to beef that is sold in supermarkets? Though one may be imported and the other domestic, all else being equal, the distinction for the consumer has been determined by the point of sale, not the point of origin.[71] The legal framework in which those products exist thus effects the consumer's understanding of whether two products are alike.[72]

The way in which States structure the relationship between the public and private spheres in trade is multifaceted but law plays a central role. The market depends on law for its existence: the enforcement of contracts, settlement of disputes, all require a legal framework that does not depend solely on the goodwill of those within the community.[73] The structure of the public–private relationship is thus historically conditioned and reflects the biases of those who were involved in its creation.[74] It represents, and provides a space for, the determination of the 'correct' balancing of values in trade, including the scope of public and private authority. It is in light of this that law motivates actors to encourage the development of law that impacts upon them.

4. The constitutive influence of law as motivation for actors

The previous sections have presented a view of law as an arbiter and transmitter of values, influencing and at times even creating the identities and interests of actors. As a consequence of the syllogistic relationship between law and values, international organizations such as the WTO offer globalized actors the opportunity to embed their preferences in the international legal system. By providing a space for members to negotiate, create rules, and resolve disputes at the international level, the WTO offers a forum for actors who want to ensure that their own value preferences are established (as far as possible) as the international standard via contestations that result in the acceptance of certain norms.

Norms, in this context, are defined as a 'prescription for action in situations of choice'.[75] They 'give rise to feelings of obligation and when violated engender

[71] The subject of the *Korea–Beef* dispute, n. 67.

[72] See the discussion in *European Communities—Measures Affecting Asbestos and Asbestos-Containing Products*, Report of the Appellate Body, WT/DS135/AB/R (12 March 2001), at para. 122.

[73] CAE Goodhart, 'Economics and the Law: Too Much One-Way Traffic?', (1997) 60(1) *Modern Law Review* 4–10.

[74] J Goldstein, 'Ideas, Institutions, and American Trade Policy', in GJ Ikenberry, D Lake, and M Mastanduno (eds), *The State and American Foreign Economic Policy* (Ithaca, Cornell University Press 1988) 180.

[75] A Chayes and AH Chayes, *The New Sovereignty: Compliance with New Regulatory Agreements* (Cambridge MA, Harvard University Press 1995) 113.

regret or a feeling that the deviation or violation requires justification'.[76] Norms encourage actors to understand and interpret their obligations in a determined way, taking into account the underlying values within a legal agreement.[77]

The idea that globalized actors might use the institutions of the State to pursue their objectives at the international level is well documented: this is the State as 'a representative institution constantly subject to capture and recapture, construction and reconstruction by coalitions of social actors'.[78]

In this account, the State is the prize, allowing the use of its personality at the international level by actors to pursue their objectives. The State is a forum for the development of values but also the prize for those competing to get their approach considered as the dominant or nationally accepted one.[79]

For these actors to maintain the dominance of their values, it becomes necessary not only to maintain control but also embed such values where possible.[80] Having captured certain institutions, there is an interest in ensuring that the values of the actors are entrenched as much as possible. By prescribing certain forms of behaviour within these institutions, actors protect their own value preferences.[81] This applies within the State but also, importantly, within institutions that claim authority over the State such as the WTO.[82]

Actors can protect their preferences from threats both within the State and without by creating new obligations (e.g. through negotiations of new agreements) or during judicial processes of interpretation, during administrative processes at the committees of the WTO and elsewhere. In each instance, actors contest existing conceptions of the correct balance between, for example, the market and government with the expectation that the 'correct' interpretation filters down through the WTO membership via their obligations under the covered agreements.[83]

Thus, instead of coercing or co-opting other States, a State might instead attempt to influence the structure and activity of the WTO. The logic is clear:

> If a country can shape international rules that are consistent with its interests and values, its actions will more likely appear legitimate in the eyes of others. If it uses institutions and

[76] A Cortell and J Davis, 'When Norms Clash: International Norms, Domestic Practices and Japan's Internalisation of the GATT/WTO', (2005) 31 *Review of International Studies* 3, 4.

[77] See n. 17 and accompanying text.

[78] A Moravcsik, 'Taking Preferences Seriously: A Liberal Theory of International Politics', (1997) 51(4) *International Organization* 513, 518.

[79] Similar insights can be drawn from public choice theory where policymakers compete in a policy marketplace, attempting to 'sell' their policies for political capital. See, for example: GS Becker, 'A Theory of Competition Among Pressure Groups for Political Influence', (1983) 98(3) *The Quarterly Journal of Economics* 371.

[80] Embedding values can be understood as encouraging a form of structural bias, the influence of which is well documented: J Goldstein, n. 74; M Koskenniemi, 'The Politics of International Law—20 Years Later', (2009) 20(1) *European Journal of International Law* 7.

[81] J Nye, *Soft Power: The Means to Success in World Politics* (New York, PublicAffairs 2004) 10.

[82] The EU is in a peculiar position, straddling both conceptions. See I Manners, 'Normative Power Europe: A Contradiction in Terms?', (2002) 40 *Journal of Common Market Studies* 23.

[83] See D Sarooshi, 'Sovereignty, Economic Autonomy, the United States and the International Trading System', (2004) 15 *European Journal of International Law* 4, for an account of the US–UK steel dispute in light of a debate over competing values.

follows rules that encourage countries to channel or limit their activities in ways it prefers, it will not need as many costly carrots and sticks.[84]

At the WTO there are numerous cases of such behaviour, indeed, policy-makers openly use the potential success of norm export through international legal structures to justify their positions. For example, President Clinton did so writing on China's accession to the WTO. While he made the traditional arguments about the benefits to US traders and farmers from the reduction of tariffs and inclusion of China into the WTO's dispute settlement system, the President also placed considerable focus on the importance of projecting US values through the trading system, stating:

This deal [China's accession to the WTO] not only expands trade, it also projects our values and enhances our security. To understand why, we need to see China clearly—its progress and problems, its policies and perceptions of us, of itself, and the world . . .

The agreement obligates China to deepen its market reforms, empowering leaders who want their country to move further and faster toward economic freedom . . .

In the past, the Chinese state was employer, landlord, shopkeeper, and news provider all rolled into one. This agreement will accelerate a process that is removing the government from vast areas of China's economic life. China's people will have greater scope to live their lives as they see fit. And as they become more mobile, more prosperous, more aware of alternative ways of life, they will seek greater say in the decisions that affect their lives.[85]

The expectations were that China would bring its national law into conformity with its WTO obligations but also that the WTO would provide a framework in which compliance procedures (both formal and informal) would be available.[86]

The preceding sections have highlighted the constitutive effect of law on individual actors, on autonomous institutions, and on the structures that determine the relationship between market and government. The influence here has been on the identities and interests of those involved, encouraging actors to develop WTO law in a way that protects their value preferences. What follows is an examination of how actors pursue these objectives: the way in which the instrumental use of law at the WTO influences its development.

C. The Instrumental Effect of Law at the WTO

Globalized actors use law to pursue their objectives. This is the fundamental premise behind a number of accounts of how law functions and how it develops.[87] Indeed, common political conceptions of the role of law are based on

[84] J Nye, n. 81, 10–11.

[85] WJ Clinton, 'Expanding Trade, Projecting Values', *The New Democrat* (1 January 2000).

[86] Of particular interest are Art. 2.A on uniform administration, Art. 2.C on transparency obligations, and most notably, Art. 5 on ensuring a right to trade for enterprises in China. 'Accession of the People's Republic of China' Decision of 10 November 2001, WT/L/432 (23 November 2001). See further, Chapter 6.C(3).

[87] Chapter 2.D(4).

the idea that we use law to get what we want. Of course, the picture is not so simple as outcomes can frustrate expectations (a recurring theme in the following chapters). Nonetheless, the use of law affects its development: legislative activity (that is rule-making) or stimulating an exercise in rule-making or rule-changing (through judicial or legislative means) alters the law and encourages its development.

In general terms, the instrumental use of law allows actors to use law in two ways: using law to embed norms within a legal system and using law to stimulate an interaction between competing conceptions of a norm. These are different ways to stimulate contestations over the meaning and scope of the law so as to encourage its development. The process of claim and counter-claim, the act of interpretation, the pursuit of an interest not shared by others: in each instance, a contestation takes place.

This section examines the ways in which globalized actors use law to pursue their goals at the WTO: the creation of new legal obligations such as treaty obligations (1); via the membership's representative institutions, the Ministerial Council, and the General Council and its sub-Committees (2); and by stimulating an interaction between competing conceptions of a norm by raising and intervening in disputes at the WTO (3) and challenging coterminous WTO obligations at the domestic level (4).

1. Embedding norms as treaty obligations: The covered agreements

As actors seek to prioritize their normative preferences, one obvious target is the creation of new international obligations in treaties such as the covered agreements. Determining what is to be regulated by international agreement at the WTO, and how the related rights and obligations under the covered agreements are defined and developed is key to ensuring that actors' objectives are met, both setting the agenda and the rules of the game from that point onward.[88] As the members of the WTO are bound by their obligations under the covered agreements as a matter of international law (and, depending on their own legal systems, as a matter of domestic law), one might expect that inserting a treaty provision that incorporates an actor's preferences would be a logical objective.

While crystallizing norms as treaty obligations is an obvious choice for actors, it is limited in effect due to numerous factors. These include material factors (the need for power asymmetries), temporal factors (the timing must be right to gain agreement for a new treaty or amendment), and the unintended consequences as embedded norms may interact with other norms producing unexpected results.

[88] On this process: G Messenger, 'National Law As An Unpredictable Generator Of International Law: the Case of Norm Export at the World Trade Organization', *ESIL Conference Paper Series* 10/2014, <http://ssrn.com/abstract=2546185>.

The material limitation results from the influence of the principle of sovereign equality and the *pacta tertiis* rule.[89] As the consent of all relevant parties is traditionally required to incorporate a desired treaty obligation wholesale, considerable power asymmetries are needed to be able to achieve this aim. This has occurred previously: of the twenty-six articles in the GATT 1947, twenty-three were almost entirely based on the US's proposals.[90] While examples of US and EU influence in the remaining covered agreements exist, the wholesale dictation of a treaty by one party has not repeated itself in the multilateral trading system.[91] This is a consequence, in part, of the relative decline of US dominance in the international trading system. While 'declinism' is a recurring theme in US perceptions of its place in the world,[92] in the context of trade its *relative* position to other WTO members has narrowed. Coupled with the representation of the EU as a (largely) single voice in the WTO, the rise of China and the increasing economic strength of other emerging economies, the allocation of power within the international trading system is less concentrated than it was in the 1940s.

With a larger group of powerful trading States and regional bodies involved in the negotiations on new treaties or agreements at the WTO the scope for forcing one provision on the WTO's membership has been diminished.[93] This is particularly the case with new multilateral agreements, which would constitute treaties, require unanimity.[94] More likely, members could act through the Ministerial Conference or General Council and attempt to adopt an authoritative interpretation under Art. IX(2) WTO Agreement, a waiver under Art. IX(3) WTO Agreement, Decision under Art. IX(1) WTO Agreement or amendment by the Ministerial Conference under Art. X WTO Agreement. However, these bodies require (*inter alia*) consensus or majority in the case of Decisions, three-fourths majority for an authoritative interpretation or waiver, and a two-thirds majority for amendments (though the consequences of amendments vary depending on the circumstances).[95] These are not easy hurdles to overcome: with the exception of waivers which have

89 Article 2(1) United Nations Charter (concluded 26 June 1945, entered into force 24 October 1945) 59 Stat 1031 and Art. 34 Vienna Convention on the Law of Treaties (concluded 23 May 1969, entered into force 27 January 1980) 1155 UNTS 331 respectively. The latter is considered fundamental and 'its existence has never been questioned'. M Fitzmaurice, 'Third Parties and the Law of Treaties', (2002) 6 *Max Planck UN Yearbook* 37, 38.

90 D Sarooshi, 'Sovereignty', n. 83 at fn 74.

91 Bilateral trade agreements are a separate matter.

92 Noting in 1989 that declinism had been a feature of US politics since 1950: S Huntington, 'The US—Decline or Renewal?', *Foreign Affairs* (Winter 1988/1989).

93 NB the difficulty concluding the Doha Round.

94 Alternatively, for a new plurilateral agreement to be added to Annex 4, consensus is required: Art. X(9) WTO Agreement.

95 In practice, members do not vote in the majority of these instances and consensus is maintained as the underlying rule: M Footer, 'The WTO as a "Living Instrument"', in T Cottier and M Elsig (eds), *Governing the World Trade Organization: Past, Present and Beyond Doha* (Cambridge, Cambridge University Press 2011) 223.

proved less 'exceptional' than the terms of Art. IX(3) WTO Agreement would indicate,[96] there has only been one amendment[97] and no authoritative interpretations.[98]

The second limitation is the temporal limitation: the need for the timing to be right to arrive at an agreement. Timing plays a role in whether or not consensus can be reached over new agreements or amendments to the existing ones.[99] Not only do the negotiations at the multilateral level need to be favourable but all the parties involved have to be capable of agreeing to a new agreement: this is a frequent issue for the US where the executive requires a congressional delegation of authority in order to conclude trade agreements.[100] With the completion of the Uruguay Round, in stark contrast to the proliferation of preferential trade agreements, there have been few agreements at the multilateral level.[101] Most notably, these are the four protocols to the GATS on financial services,[102] movement of natural persons,[103] and basic telecommunications.[104] Where there has been activity, which will be examined in the following section, it has been in the form of Ministerial Declarations such as the Information Technology Agreement[105] or documents passed by a specific working group such as the Telecommunications Services Reference Paper.[106]

2. Embedding norms through WTO Councils and Committees

Creating new treaty obligations is not the only method of embedding norms in the WTO system. Members can also use a variety of sites with varying possible outcomes affecting the membership: Ministerial Declarations, decisions and standards at either the principal Councils (the Council for Trade in Goods, Council for Trade in Services, and the Council for Trade-Related Aspects of Intellectual Property

[96] Though most waivers have been granted to individual members thus not having the broader systemic impact that an amendment has. Council for Trade-Related Aspects of Intellectual Property Rights—Paragraph 6 of the Doha Declaration on the TRIPS Agreement and Public Health: Note by the Secretariat (24 October 2002) IP/C/W/387 Annex 1.

[97] Decision of the General Council, Amendment of the TRIPs Agreement (6 December 2005) WT/L/641.

[98] There have only been two requests: Communication from the European Communities, 'Request for an Authoritative Interpretation Pursuant to Article IX:2 of the Marrakesh Agreement Establishing the World Trade Organization' (25 January 1999) WT/GC/W/133; and Communication from the European Communities, 'Request for an Authoritative Interpretation Pursuant to Article IX:2 of the Marrakesh Agreement Establishing the World Trade Organization' (5 February 1999) WT/GC/W/143.

[99] Article X WTO Agreement.

[100] See n. 174ff and accompanying text.

[101] The 'Bali package' is the culmination of negotiations thus far. See *Bali Ministerial Declaration* (11 December 2013) WT/MIN(13)/DEC.

[102] Second Protocol to the General Agreement on Trade in Services (24 July 1995) S/L/11 and Fifth Protocol to the General Agreement on Trade in Services (3 December 1997) S/L/45.

[103] Third Protocol to the General Agreement on Trade in Services (24 July 1995) S/L/12.

[104] Fourth Protocol to the General Agreement on Trade in Services (30 April 1996) S/L/20.

[105] Ministerial Declaration on Trade in Information Technology Products (13 December 1996) WT/MIN(96)/16.

[106] Negotiating Group on Basic Telecommunications, 'Telecommunications Services: Reference Paper' (24 April 1996) <http://www.wto.org/english/tratop_e/serv_e/telecom_e/tel23_e.htm>.

Rights),[107] or their sub-Committees, Working Parties, and Working Groups.[108] Actors can use these bodies to disseminate a range of instruments to influence the development of WTO law. While less dramatic than a new agreement, the mechanisms provided for by these bodies (in which all members can be represented) offer ample opportunity for the pursuit of actors' objectives in embedding norms within the world trading system.

In their article, 'The Hidden World of WTO Governance', Lang and Scott seek to open a broader discussion on the role of 'non-judicial governance' at the WTO.[109] While they acknowledge a range of sites of non-judicial governance, they concentrate on the GATS committees and the Committee on Sanitary and Phytosanitary Measures[110] ('SPS Committee').[111] They distinguish between three functions which take place at these non-judicial governance sites: the dissemination and exchange of information between representatives; technical assistance and regulatory co-ordination; and the elaboration and development of norms. They argue that each of these functions influences how the trade regime develops by offering a space for individuals to interact with each other and influence their home-State regulation. As sites of norm elaboration and development they are of particular interest to actors attempting to embed their normative preferences within the WTO framework.

Some committees at the WTO provide a clear opportunity to embed norms within the international system. Some of the most notable of these are the SPS Committee, the Working Party on Domestic Regulation,[112] and the Committee on Technical Barriers to Trade ('TBT Committee').[113] These committees offer actors the prospect of influencing the ways in which the committee and the membership conduct themselves in a range of fields. The comprehensive guidance given by the TBT Committee in its decisions and recommendations, for example, gives guidance on a wide range of matters for members from notification requirements to the proper running of enquiry points.[114] These decisions can have far-reaching consequences. While the broader process of institutional learning is important, there is increasing scope for such documents to become relevant in judicial decision-making. For example, the panel in *US–Poultry*[115]referred to a decision of the SPS Committee on

[107] Article IV(5) WTO Agreement. [108] Article IV(6) WTO Agreement.

[109] A Lang and J Scott, 'The Hidden World of WTO Governance', (2009) 20 *European Journal of International Law* 3, 575.

[110] Ibid., 577–90 and 590–601 respectively.

[111] Article 12, Agreement on the Application of Sanitary and Phytosanitary Measures (15 April 1994) LT/UR/A-1A/12 <http://docsonline.wto.org> ('SPS Agreement').

[112] Replacing the Working Party on Professional Services: Decision on Domestic Regulation adopted by the Council for Trade in Services (26 April 1999) S/L/70.

[113] Article 13, Agreement on Technical Barriers to Trade (15 April 1994) LT/UR/A-1A/10 <http://docsonline.wto.org> ('TBT Agreement').

[114] The Secretariat provides these as a single document: Decisions and Recommendations adopted by the WTO Committee on Technical Barriers to Trade since 1 January 1995 (9 June 2011) G/TBT/1/Rev.10. at 18–29 and 33–6 respectively.

[115] *United States—Certain Measures Affecting Imports of Poultry from China*, Panel Report (29 September 2010) WT/DS392/R.

equivalence[116] in determining the appropriate interpretation of Art. 4 of the SPS Agreement. Acknowledging that the decision was not binding, the panel nonetheless drew on it in this instance:

> The Panel notes, that while this decision is not binding and does not determine the scope of Article 4, we do consider that this Decision expands on the Members' own understanding of how Article 4 relates to the rest of the SPS Agreement and how it is to be implemented.[117]

Indeed, even its observation that the decision is not binding is qualified: it goes on to point out that whereas most decisions contain a note stressing their respect not to alter the rights or duties of the membership under the covered agreements, in this case such a provision was missing.[118] It is unclear exactly what the panel meant here. This could be an acknowledgement that without such a provision decisions may have greater weight. Irrespective, the role of such decisions is likely to increase in importance as they increase in number and scope.[119]

3. Reviewing 'measures' at the WTO: Dispute settlement and other mechanisms

Actors can use law to further their objectives not only by embedding norms within structures such as treaty instruments or other legal instruments but also by stimulating interactions between competing conceptions of a norm's content. This section examines the review of members' measures at the WTO as a method for contesting norms and, in turn, encouraging compliance with the accepted result. The following section (4) evaluates a similar practice at the domestic level.

In his work on transnational legal process, Harold Koh argues that one reason for compliance with international law is the internalization of norms from the international sphere.[120] This takes place in three stages: 'Those seeking to embed certain norms into national conduct seek to trigger *interactions* that yield *interpretations* that are then *internalized* into the domestic law of even resistant nation states.'[121] Koh goes on to give a concrete example to illustrate his point:

> First, suppose you were a human rights lawyer in Great Britain, and you were protesting the treatment of immigrants who were being detained by the British government. What would

[116] Decision of the Committee on Sanitary and Phytosanitary Measures, 'Implementation of Article 4 of the Agreement on the Application of Sanitary and Phytosanitary Measures' (23 July 2004) G/SPS/19/rev. 2.

[117] *US–Poultry* n. 115, para. 7.136. Subsequently followed: *India—Measures Concerning the Importation of Certain Agricultural Products*, Panel Report (14 October 2014) WT/DS430/R, fn 1197.

[118] *US–Poultry* n. 115, fn 345.

[119] Not only from committees within the WTO: Codex standards adopted by majority vote may still apply to members that did not vote in favour of the standard via Art. 2.4 TBT (*European Communities—Trade Description of Sardines*, Report of the Appellate Body (26 September 2002) WT/DS231/AB/R, para. 227).

[120] The others being self-interest and arguments aimed at establishing a shared identity: H Koh, '1994 Roscoe Pound Lecture: Transnational Legal Process', (1996) 75 *Nebraska Law Review* 181, 194ff.

[121] H Koh, 'Jefferson Memorial Lecture: Transnational Legal Process After September 11th', (2004) 22 *Berkeley Journal of International Law* 337, 339.

you do? You would start by challenging the legality of the detention before the British courts. Suppose you lost. Is that the end of the story? Not any more. Today, any British lawyer worth his or her salt would appeal the British court's ruling to the European Court of Human Rights in Strasbourg, an international body, and try to win a judgment invalidating the British government's conduct under European human rights law. To use my terms, you would trigger an interaction in a European court that would promote an interpretation of European law that would lead, you hope, to the internalization of that international rule into British domestic law.[122]

For actors to pursue their interests, dispute settlement systems and compliance mechanisms at the international level serve a dual purpose. The first is, as Koh indicates, that they encourage members to internalize norms that the actor prefers. This is routed in the compliance function of the dispute settlement system and other bodies. It is a key advantage of the WTO that has, by international standards, a very high success rate in compliance and monitoring.[123] While the dispute settlement system exercises a constraint upon actors, it also serves as a forum for actors to stimulate contestations. Other oversight structures such as the Trade Policy Review Mechanism ('TPRM')[124] and the Committees serve a similar purpose.[125] The involvement of the EU as a 'strategic litigant' at the WTO has been documented, encouraging a clarification (or shift depending on one's perspective) on zeroing, for example.[126]

The scope of the WTO bodies' powers of scrutiny is at the heart of how actors stimulate these challenges. They can only stimulate an interaction by challenging (in the dispute settlement system) or questioning (in the case of the Committees) measures that are within the purview of the WTO system.

Within the dispute settlement system, actors are in the first instance limited by the membership and standing requirements of the WTO: only members (States or customs unions) may raise claims under the DSU. While they may only act under the aegis of a State or custom union, the dispute settlement system at the WTO still offers many opportunities for globalized actors to engage in challenging the interpretation and the application of norms in the international trade system. So long as they can utilize the legal personality of a member, the dispute settlement procedures at the WTO provide plenty of opportunities to contest the understanding of a given rule (particularly when compared to other areas of

[122] Ibid., 339–40.

[123] M Footer, 'Some Theoretical and Legal Perspectives on WTO Compliance', (2007) 38 *Netherlands Yearbook of International Law* 61, 100; J Crawford, 'Continuity and Discontinuity in International Dispute Settlement: An Inaugural Lecture', (2010) 1(1) *Journal of International Dispute Settlement* 4, 4.

[124] Trade Policy Review Mechanism (15 April 1994) LT/UR/A-3/TPR/1 <http://docsonline.wto.org> ('TPRM').

[125] Though the manner differs, note Sungjoon Cho's analysis of methods of discourse at the WTO: adjudication, peer-review, and negotiation-consultation. S Cho, *The Social Foundations of World Trade* (Cambridge, Cambridge University Press 2014) 130–50.

[126] T Krüger, 'Shaping the WTO's Institutional Evolution: The EU as a Strategic Litigant in the WTO', in D Kochenov and F Amtenbrink (eds), *The European Union's Shaping of the International Legal Order* (Cambridge, Cambridge University Press 2013).

international law).[127] First, members are given considerable discretion to decide on whether they have an interest in the dispute,[128] either when requesting consultations[129] or as third parties,[130] and are under no requirement to show any legal interest.[131] Beyond the ease with which claims may be raised (as a matter of law rather than of resources), dispute settlement at the WTO also permits the examination of a wide range of what it considers 'measures' that may be subject to a complaint.

Panels and the Appellate Body have encouraged a broad interpretation of what constitute the 'specific measures at issue' that must be raised to establish a panel.[132] Starting with an expansive interpretation, the Appellate Body has stated: 'In principle, any act or omission attributable to a WTO Member can be a measure of that Member for purposes of dispute settlement proceedings.'[133] Usually, such acts or omissions would be those of an organ of that State (though not necessarily).[134] Furthermore, the measure in question need not be only a legislative instrument: the Appellate Body has acknowledged that where the agreement in question provides a list it is not necessarily exhaustive. This is the case with the SPS Agreement that includes 'laws, decrees or ordinances which are applicable generally'[135] as examples of SPS regulations that are subject to the disciplines on transparency within Annex B. In *Japan–Agricultural Products II*,[136] the Appellate Body made it clear that this was not an exhaustive list and would consider other measures of similar character as included.[137] Notably, it is for the panel or Appellate Body to determine the nature of the instrument in question and whether or not it constitutes a measure by reference to its content and substance, irrespective of its name or form.[138]

The challenge of measures under the dispute settlement system is not only broad in terms of targets (i.e. what constitutes a measure) but also in the effect of that

[127] cf. third party interventions at the International Court of Justice under Art. 62 Statute of the ICJ and Art. 81(2) Rules of the Court, and their strict interpretation as in, for example, *Continental Shelf (Tunisia/Libyan Arab Jamahiriya) Application to Intervene* (Judgment) [1981] ICJ Rep 3.

[128] *European Communities—Regime for the Importation, Sale and Distribution of Bananas*, Report of the Appellate Body (9 September 1997) WT/DS27/AB/R, para. 135: '[W]e believe that a Member has broad discretion in deciding whether to bring a case against another Member under the DSU. The language of Article XXIII:1 of the GATT 1994 and of Article 3.7 of the DSU suggests, furthermore, that a Member is expected to be largely self-regulating in deciding whether any such action would be "fruitful".'

[129] Article 4.11 DSU.

[130] Article 10.2 DSU.

[131] *European Communities—Regime for the Importation, Sale and Distribution of Bananas*, n. 128, para. 132.

[132] Article 6.2 DSU.

[133] *United States—Sunset Review of Anti-Dumping Duties On Corrosion-Resistant Carbon Steel Flat Products From Japan*, Report of the Appellate Body (15 December 2003) WT/DS244/AB/R, para. 81.

[134] Ibid.

[135] SPS Agreement, Annex B Art. 1, fn 5.

[136] *Japan—Measures Affecting Agricultural Products*, Report of the Appellate Body (22 February 1999) WT/DS76/AB/R.

[137] Ibid., para. 105.

[138] *United States—Sunset Review of Anti-Dumping Duties On Corrosion-Resistant Carbon Steel Flat Products From Japan*, n. 133, fn 87.

measure. Under the dispute settlement system there is scope for raising a complaint in light of both how a measure is applied as well as (and more far-reaching) the measure 'as such'.[139] These claims are interpreted strictly and the expectation is that members will be selective in raising 'as such' claims as they constitute preventative litigation, initiating dispute settlement before a member has engaged in certain conduct.[140]

Limited restrictions on raising claims and a broad interpretation of what constitutes a 'measure' offer globalized actors a range of options to stimulate challenges at the WTO level. Engaging in the dispute settlement procedures under the DSU is costly and time-consuming, however.[141] The final result also rests with the members of the panel or Appellate Body. Such an approach is potentially a risky one, even with the theoretical 'handbrake' of the Dispute Settlement Body.[142] Instead of viewing dispute settlement as the main weapon in the armoury of the globalized actor, it is more helpful to view it as another arrow in its quiver with other methods of stimulating a contestation at the WTO level available: the Committees, Councils, and Trade Policy Review Body all offer alternatives to challenge the meaning and application of key obligations.[143]

These bodies provide a forum for members to discuss the compliance of other members' domestic procedures and thus encourage a discussion over the 'appropriate' interpretation or application of a measure. This usually arises as a result of the notification requirements under various agreements at the WTO.[144] Following notification of the relevant measure, representatives at the Committee then question the members on the potential compliance consequences of their domestic instruments.

The role of these committees is, in part, a process that encourages certain types of behaviour by creating an environment where WTO consistent behaviour is expected.[145] One example is the Trade Policy Review Mechanism under the WTO where the behaviour of members is scrutinized and serves as 'a venue for

[139] Article XXIII.1(a) GATT, confirmed in *United States—Anti-Dumping Act of 1916*, Report of the Appellate Body (28 August 2000) WT/DS/136/AB/R, paras 60–1.

[140] *United States—Sunset Reviews of Anti-Dumping Measures on Oil Country Tubular Goods From Argentina*, Report of the Appellate Body (29 November 2004) WT/DS268/AB/R, paras 172–3.

[141] Conservative estimates suggesting anything from $128,500 to $706,000 depending on the complexity of the case. Certain cases have been particularly expensive: fees for the Kodak and Fuji dispute (*Japan—Measures Affecting Consumer Photographic Film and Paper*, Panel Report (31 March 1998) WT/DS44/R) is reputed to have exceeded 10 million dollars: H Nordstrom, 'The Cost of WTO Litigation, Legal Aid and Small Claim Procedures', Paper presented at conference on WTO Dispute Settlement and Developing Countries: Implications, Strategies, Reforms. Center for World Affairs and the Global Economy, University of Wisconsin (20–1 May 2005).

[142] On the political oversight of the dispute settlement system see below, D(4).

[143] M Footer, 'Some Theoretical and Legal Perspectives on WTO Compliance', (2007) 38 *Netherlands Yearbook of International Law* 61–112.

[144] Generally, Ministerial Decision on Notification Procedures of the Trade Negotiations Committee (15 April 1994) LT/UR/D-1/5 <http://docsonline.wto.org> and Art. X GATT.

[145] A Lang, 'Some Sociological Perspectives on International Institutions and the Trading System', in C Picker, I Bunn, and D Arner (eds), *International Economic Law: The State and Future of the Discipline* (Oxford, Hart Publishing 2008) 73–88, 78.

persuasion and ideological diffusion, for "teaching" members norms of appropriate behaviour'.[146] These bodies provide a forum for members to challenge the interpretation or application of measures and, in this way, other members' understanding of the core value judgments underpinning such measures. This can be viewed as a softer alternative to dispute settlement: less confrontational, more cost-effective and, to a degree, less risky as there is no final authoritative statement of a third party (a panel or the Appellate Body).[147]

Just as the WTO offers opportunities for globalized actors to stimulate contestations, so do other regional and domestic legal systems which incorporate coterminous WTO obligations. This is the subject of the following section.

4. Challenging coterminous WTO obligations under other legal systems

Actors stimulate challenges not only at the WTO but also under other legal systems. Article XVI:4 WTO Agreement requires 'conformity of [members'] laws, regulations and administrative procedures with [their WTO] obligations'.[148] More specifically many of these obligations require members to introduce and maintain procedures relating to, for example, the conduct of trade remedy investigations or the possibility of judicial review in a number of trade areas.[149] As a result, there exist a number of coterminous WTO obligations in domestic legal systems.[150]

Note, these differ from the coterminous obligations under other international legal orders such as preferential trade agreements ('PTAs'). Until now, cases which have involved overlapping PTA and WTO obligations have been resolved on the system in question's own terms: for example, a MERCOSUR tribunal using more detailed WTO provisions to interpret a MERCOSUR Decision[151] or the Appellate

[146] Ibid.

[147] S Laird and R Valdés, 'The Trade Policy Review Mechanism', in A Narlikar, M Daunton, and R Stern, *The Oxford Handbook on the World Trade Organization* (Oxford, Oxford University Press 2012) 468.

[148] Over and above the general obligation to comply in good faith with obligations under international law: Art. 26 Vienna Convention on the Law of Treaties (VCLT) (23 May 1969) 1155 UNTS 331.

[149] Article 13 AD; Art. 23 SCM; Art. 3 Agreement on Trade Facilitation.

[150] 'Coterminous' is used to describe those rights and duties that members have incorporated into their own legal systems to comply with the covered agreements. These may be incorporations by reference to the covered agreements themselves, verbatim repetition of the relevant provisions of the covered agreements in a domestic legal instrument, or alternatively may be worded differently but held to be compliant (by the member) with their obligations under the covered agreements. While they constitute separate legal obligations (domestic and not international), their substance is such that they *necessarily* imply consequences for the member at the WTO level where they are not WTO compliant. Parallels can be drawn with the concept of 'Multi-Sourced Equivalent Norms' developed in T Broude and Y Shany (eds), *Multi-Sourced Equivalent Norms in International Law* (Oxford, Hart Publishing 2011).

[151] Laudo II, Laudo del Tribunal Ad Hoc del Mercosur, Constituido para Entender en la Reclamación de la República Argentina al Brasil, sobre Subsidios a la Producción y Exportación de Carne de Cerdo (09/1999), para. 57.

Body acknowledging NAFTA obligations but not seeing any basis for adjudicating upon them directly.[152]

While some PTAs such as NAFTA contain fork-in-the-road provisions or primacy clauses, many do not and the practice of those that do has been mixed.[153] Note, the discussions over the *US–Tuna II (Mexico)* dispute which saw Mexico and the US attempting to resolve their dispute under different dispute settlement systems.[154]

A new set of free trade agreements seem to be taking a different approach. The EU–US Transatlantic Trade and Investment Partnership ('TTIP') currently under negotiation, the EU–Singapore Free Trade Agreement, and EU–Canada Comprehensive Trade and Economic Agreement ('CETA') all offer a 'softer' and more transparent way of trying to accommodate obligations under both the WTO and free trade agreements by requiring dispute settlement panels constituted under these treaties to take into account the reports of the WTO Dispute Settlement Body when interpreting relevant provisions of the PTA in question.[155]

As is often the case with the interpretative process in judicial decision-making, it may not be clear how the obligation to 'take into account' extends. As such, it is possible that contestations may be stimulated in competing (or perhaps, complementary) legal orders, yet the scope and application of such a relationship is not yet clear.

Domestic legal orders, on the other hand, offer a qualitatively different dynamic for globalized actors interested in stimulating the development of WTO law. Rather than enjoying a conflictual relationship with WTO law, domestic trade remedies legislation (for example) customarily mirror WTO obligations. Their judicial review processes are supplementary to, rather than in competition with, WTO law.[156]

The overlap between the content of legal obligations at the WTO and other legal systems allows globalized actors to stimulate contestations over WTO obligations within domestic (or regional) legal systems. Take the example of a producer who feels that they are being undermined by a foreign producer who is exporting goods at below value. The domestic producer petitions for an investigation into whether dumping is taking place, and whether anti-dumping duties

[152] *Mexico—Tax Measures on Soft Drinks and Other Beverages*, Appellate Body Report, WT/DS308/AB/R (6 March 2006) paras 54–6.

[153] NAFTA Art. 2005:6 and Art. 103:2 respectively.

[154] *United States—Measures Concerning the Importation, Marketing and Sale of Tuna and Tuna Products*, Request for Consultations by Mexico, WT/DS381/1 (28 October 2008), Dispute Settlement Body Minutes of Meeting 20 April 2009, WT/DSB/M/267 (26 June 2009) para. 77. See also Simon Lester's discussion at the International Economic Law and Policy Blog: <http://worldtradelaw.typepad.com/ielpblog/2010/09/the-tunadolphin-nafta-panel.html>.

[155] See G Messenger, 'Anti-Fragmentation Strategies: the Curious Case of the EU and World Trade Law', 20 February 2015, EJIL: *Talk!* <http://www.ejiltalk.org/anti-fragmentation-strategies-the-curious-case-of-the-eu-and-world-trade-law/>.

[156] M Yilmaz (ed.), *Domestic Judicial Review of Trade Remedies* (Cambridge, Cambridge University Press 2013) 5.

should be imposed upon the foreign imports.[157] This investigation, the process whereby an actor requests the governing structures of a member to investigate a perceived breach of WTO or coterminous domestic rights or duties through internal administrative bodies, *necessarily* requires an interpretation of the correct application of the rule in question. By initiating an administrative investigation, actors encourage an evaluation of how a member should apply WTO rules in its territory.[158]

WTO law not only prescribes certain requirements for members as they conduct investigations but it also requires judicial review for those affected.[159] Many systems allow not only the review of a determination but also the review of a decision *not* to act, thus granting actors a legal mechanism to require members to act in ways which may open them to scrutiny at the WTO.[160] The liberal approach that domestic systems tend to take vis-à-vis standing in raising matters, especially in comparison to the WTO itself further highlights this mechanism.[161]

Through the process of judicial review of administrative decisions relating to WTO obligations, a globalized actor may attempt to appeal to the rights and duties under the covered agreements in raising a claim at the domestic level. While the success of such an appeal may be limited in terms of formal responses,[162] judicial bodies nonetheless frequently follow the WTO *acquis* through a process of 'muted dialogue'.[163] Even where systems openly reject the prioritization of 'external' law in instances of apparent conflict, the interpretation of domestic rules in line with international obligations is a common feature of many domestic legal systems.[164]

D. The Systemic Effect of Law on Globalized Actors at the WTO

When framing the types of cause that influence the development of international law, we identified the key role of law as a system; that is, constraining or enabling

[157] Article 9 Agreement on Implementation of Art. VI of the General Agreement on Tariffs and Trade 1994 (15 April 1994) LT/UR/A-1A/3 <http://docsonline.wto.org> ('AD Agreement').

[158] For this reason, many legal systems attempt to limit 'external' actors (that is, competitors) from using domestic systems against the host member: *Opinion 1/94* (*WTO*) [1994] ECR I-05267.

[159] Judicial in the broadest sense: this may be undertaken by 'judicial, arbitral or administrative tribunals or procedures'. Art. 13 AD Agreement; Art. 23 SCM Agreement.

[160] See Case C-76/01, *Eurocoton and Others v Council* [2003] ECR I-1091.

[161] For an analysis of a number of jurisdictions reaching this conclusion: M Yilmaz (ed.), *Domestic Judicial Review of Trade Remedies* (Cambridge, Cambridge University Press 2013) 424.

[162] Note the reticence of US domestic courts to implement WTO obligations vis-à-vis the practice of zeroing in calculating anti-dumping margins: for example, *Corus Staal BV v United States*, 259 F. Supp. 2d 1253, 1264 (CIT 2003).

[163] In the EU context: M Bronckers, 'From "Direct Effect" to "Muted Dialogue": Recent Developments in the European Courts' Case Law on the WTO and Beyond', (2008) 11(4) *Journal of International Economic Law* 885.

[164] For example, the 'Charming Betsy' doctrine: *Murray v The Charming Betsy*, 6 US 2 Cranch 64 (1804).

causes that restrict or empower certain types of behaviour. Unlike constitutive causes which impact upon identities, or instrumental causes which influence the law as it is used by interested actors, the systemic effect of law is on those within the legal system in question. It varies in intensity within the system, as well as across the different jurisdictions in which globalized actors engage.

Globalized actors do not behave in a normative vacuum: as they attempt to embed their own value-preferences at the WTO or challenge others, they are constrained and enabled by law. There are a number of constraining and enabling causes on actors besides law: the distribution within international society of resources or power, for example. Yet, while much literature has been dedicated to the importance of resource asymmetries and their consequence on relations between States,[165] their relevance is to the *strength* of the law's causal influence.

For example, let us take sovereign equality as a founding principle of the international legal system, tentative though it may be.[166] Where properly constituted States are equal as a matter of international law, the relative power of one compared to another is not important in the way that it might be from a political perspective. Insofar as power asymmetries effect the examination of legal influences, they serve as a background for all causes rather than constituting a discrete category: the ability to use law instrumentally, the ability to resist the constraints of law, and the relative influence on constituting interests and identities are all related to power, not as a separate cause but contributing to the strength of the causal influence. In the case of systemic causes, the strength of the influence is particularly important.

In the following sections the four principal constraining and enabling influences on globalized actors at the WTO are examined: (1) the domestic rules that grant actors access to the WTO; (2) the rules that allow actors to raise claims based on WTO law under non-WTO systems; and finally (3) the systemic influence of law at the WTO under the covered agreements; and (4) through its institutions.

1. The rules applicable to granting globalized actors access to the WTO

The domestic legal systems of WTO members constrain and enable actors as they attempt to influence the international trade policy of the State, engage on the international plane, and respond to influences from the WTO. In doing so, law restricts some actors from accessing the WTO while giving others a privileged position. Such divergences both reflect the social choices made within the community but also influence the ways in which actors pursue their objectives. Importantly, here the law advantages some over others, unlike the case of constitutive causes where the law plays a deeper ideational role. There may well be an overlap between

165 For example, K Knorr, *Power and Wealth—The Political Economy of International Power* (New York, Basic Books 1973); S Krasner, 'State Power and the Structure of International Trade', (1976) 28(3) *World Politics* 317; R Keohane and J Nye, *Power and Interdependence* (New York, Longman 2000).

166 Article 2(1) UN Charter. For a contemporaneous analysis: H Kelsen, 'The Principle of Sovereign Equality of States as a Basis for International Organization', (1944) 53(2) *Yale Law Journal* 207.

the legal instruments in question, but it is their distinct influences which are of interest here.[167]

If we look to the US as an example, systemic influences that result from internal priorities influence the way that globalized actors within that jurisdiction pursue their objectives at the WTO.

Under the US Constitution, the Executive is granted the authority to 'make' treaties with the 'Advice and Consent of the Senate',[168] leading to a centralization of foreign affairs competences to it.[169] In trade relations, however, Congress enjoys explicit competences to 'regulate Commerce with foreign Nations'.[170] Congress is granted the 'Power To lay and collect Taxes, Duties, Imposts and Excises',[171] thus limiting the authority of the Executive in international trade relations.[172] One outcome of this shared relationship is the difficulty associated with the Executive negotiating a complex agreement internationally and then having Congress demand changes domestically. Not only does this lead to a longer and more complex process, but it also limits the capacity of the US to engage with its trading partners that may not take commitments made at the negotiating table seriously.[173] In order to resolve this problem Congress utilises controlled delegations to the Executive to negotiate trade agreements.[174]

The fast-track system, 'a *quid pro quo* between Congress and the President',[175] provides for consultation with both Congress and the private sector during the negotiation process. The delegation period is limited, with each renewal requiring presidential petitions to Congress. Importantly, the private sector is represented by proxy through congressional consultation[176] and directly through the Advisory Committee for Trade Policy and Negotiations ('ACTPN').[177] There are also further advisory committees dedicated to specific sectors or policies.[178] These representatives maintain close contact with the United States Trade Representative

[167] Chapters 2(D), 4(E).

[168] US Constitution Art. II s. 2 cl. 2.

[169] The President 'alone has the power to speak or listen as a representative of the nation. He makes treaties with the advice and consent of the Senate; but he alone negotiates.' *United States v Curtiss-Wright Export Corp.*, 299 US 304 (1936) 220.

[170] US Constitution Art. I s. 8 cl. 3.

[171] US Constitution Art. I s. 8 cl. 1.

[172] 'Congress reigns supreme on trade, unless and until it decides otherwise.' IM Destler, *American Trade Politics* (4th edn, Institute for International Economics 2005) 14.

[173] For example, the negotiation of the Kennedy Round Agreements and the US's subsequent failure to implement them, though note the possibility that requiring domestic ratification may strengthen a State's bargaining position: the 'Schelling Conjecture', in R Putnam, 'Diplomacy and Domestic Politics: The Logic of Two-Level Games', (1998) 42(3) *International Organization* 427.

[174] Starting as early as 1897, though now found in the *US Trade Promotion Authority Act* of 2002 [Pub L 107-210, 116 Stat 993]. The fast-track system was introduced in the *Trade Act of 1974* [Pub L 93-618, 88 Stat 1978] and amended by the *Omnibus Foreign Trade and Competitiveness Act of 1988* [Pub L 100-418, 102 Stat 1107] for the purposes of negotiating the Uruguay Round Agreements.

[175] D Leebron, 'Implementation of the Uruguay Round Results in the United States', in JH Jackson and A Sykes (eds), *Implementing the Uruguay Round* (Oxford, Clarendon Press 1997) 191.

[176] On the relationship between Congress and private interests: IM Destler, n. 172, Chapter 2.

[177] 19 USC s. 2155(b)(1).

[178] Approximately 1,000 individuals were involved in the committee system during the Uruguay Round negotiations; D Leebron, 'Implementation of the Uruguay Round Results in the United States', n. 175, 197.

('USTR'), giving recommendations and reports to Congress, the President, and the USTR.[179] The subsequent implementing bill is voted on within a short time frame and may not be amended. As a congressional–executive agreement and not a treaty, the vote requires a simple majority in both Houses rather than the more onerous two-thirds majority in the Senate.[180]

The systemic influence of US law on the conclusion of trade agreements channels and prioritizes some actors over others. The Executive (traditionally in favour of liberal trade policies)[181] is constrained first, by needing authorization from Congress to initiate negotiations[182] and second, by the involvement of Congress and the ACTPN. By enabling industry interests to engage with the negotiating process directly, the US system offers more avenues for private involvement than might otherwise be the case. Indeed, it is notable that the EU has only recently begun to engage more openly with non-governmental interests in trade negotiations through consultations and the formation of groups of experts.[183]

2. The role of domestic procedural requirements in challenging incorporated WTO obligations

The rules that permit certain actors to engage with WTO matters limits access for others. Globalized actors do not behave at only one level, however, for many, it is within a separate legal system that WTO-relevant provisions can be raised.[184] We have seen how actors stimulate contestations over the appropriate interpretation or use of legal provisions in pursuit of their interests. One way to do this is through initiating administrative investigations or judicial determinations under domestic law to challenge coterminous WTO obligations.

As they attempt to stimulate such challenges within the domestic legal systems of members, they are subject to the systemic influence of the rules applicable to

[179] D Leebron, 'Implementation of the Uruguay Round Results in the United States', n. 175, 198.

[180] Notably, the North American Free Trade Agreement ('NAFTA') implementing legislation, having passed through the House successfully, was passed by a vote of sixty-one to thirty-eight in the Senate, short of the two-thirds required had it been a 'treaty'. Had this been the case, of course, it would not have had to pass through the House of Representatives; B Ackerman and D Golove, 'Is NAFTA Constitutional?', (1995) 108 *Harvard Law Review* 799. Most trade agreements are negotiated as congressional–executive agreements. Their constitutionality was challenged in *Made in the USA Foundation v US* 242 F 3d 1300 (11th Cir 2001) where it was held that 'the question of just what constitutes a "treaty" requiring Senate ratification presents a nonjusticiable political question' (Judge Fletcher at 1302).

[181] SD Nollen and DP Quinn, 'Free Trade, Fair Trade, Strategic Trade, and Protectionism in the U.S. Congress, 1987–1988', (1994) 48(3) *International Organization* 491, 493.

[182] While technically not necessary, the US's trading partners view such authority as necessary in most instances (above, n. 173), in spite of the positive words of some Senators ('I want to reassure all of our trading partners that, with fast track or without fast track, a good trade agreement will win congressional support.' Senator Max Baucus, Opening Statement, Hearings Before The Committee on Finance, United States Senate, 20 and 21 June 2001 S. HRG. 107–71).

[183] Largely seen as a response to the European Parliament's rejection of the Anti-Counterfeiting Trade Agreement. See 'Decision of the European Ombudsman closing her own-initiative inquiry OI/10/2014/RA concerning the European Commission' (6 January 2015).

[184] M Yilmaz (ed.), *Domestic Judicial Review of Trade Remedies* (Cambridge, Cambridge University Press 2013) 3.

such challenges: the rules on how, when, and why such claims may be raised within the legal system of a member. The structure of the domestic rules on international trade regulation constrains and enables actors as they seek to stimulate these interactions. Consequently, the rules influence the types of actors that can engage in these processes by determining standing and other procedural requirements that channel behaviour in one direction or another.

The requirements for globalized actors to petition authorities to investigate a potential breach of WTO obligations or to challenge a measure under domestic courts influence their ability to pursue their objectives. While South Africa requires a person to have their rights affected by the measure under challenge, Colombia places no restrictions on standing for such cases, 'which literally may be initiated by anyone. There is no need even to be an interested party in the underlying proceeding'.[185]

By setting out the procedures and requirements for actors to engage within their own legal systems with WTO-based obligations, domestic legal systems constrain and enable globalized actors to pursue their objectives in certain ways. These procedural requirements can have a considerable influence on the way in which these actors then pursue their objectives, not only within their own legal systems but also at the international level, encouraging greater focus on potentially more productive avenues of engagement.

It is not only the domestic rules applicable to globalized actors that have a constraining or enabling influence on them; the rules at the international level also constrain and enable. The following two sections examine the systemic influence of international law as actors pursue their objectives at the WTO.

3. International law obligations under the covered agreements: Constraining and enabling on the international plane

The obligations under the covered agreements bind WTO members (and by extension restrain the actors that act through them) in two ways: first, by virtue of the substantive obligations contained in the covered agreements themselves and second, members are obliged to comply with the recommendations or rulings of the Dispute Settlement Body (DSB).[186] While the obligation to comply with these

[185] Ibid., 425, fn 1. For more detail: M Clara Lozano, 'Colombia: A Complex Court System With the Possibility of Three Instances' and G Brink, 'South Africa: A Complicated, Unpredictable, Long and Costly Judicial Review System' both in M Yilmaz (ed.), *Domestic Judicial Review of Trade Remedies* (Cambridge, Cambridge University Press 2013).

[186] The possibility of customary rules of international law arising from the GATT and WTO obligations is contentious and not widely accepted. 'The emphasis in International Economic Law is on treaties.' G Schwarzenberger, 'The Principles and Standards of International Economic Law', (1966) I *Recueil des Cours* 12. Rules of customary international law do, however, play a role in the interpretation of the covered agreements (*United States—Standards for Reformulated and Conventional Gasoline*, Report of the Appellate Body (29 April 1996) WT/DS2/AB/R, 17) and may even have further application (though this is highly contested). See generally, J Pauwelyn, 'The Role of Public International Law in the WTO: How Far Can We Go?', (2001) 95 *American Journal of International Law* 595; and L Bartels, 'Applicable Law in WTO Dispute Settlement Proceedings', (2001) 35 *Journal of World Trade* 499.

reports is based on the Agreements (particularly the DSU),[187] the report creates a distinct obligation for the parties in a case. As the report determines the existence of a breach of the covered agreements, this determination binds the parties to the dispute.[188]

Key to the foundations of the international legal system is that obligations under a treaty are binding on the parties to it.[189] Under the covered agreements, members are subject to a host of obligations and granted rights in trade-related areas. Whilst many of these obligations relate to the external acts of the members, there are certain requirements that permeate into the legal system of the member. Article XVI:4 of the WTO Agreement, requires that 'Each Member shall ensure the conformity of its laws, regulations and administrative procedures with its obligations as provided in the annexed Agreements.' Whereas Art. 27 VCLT precludes the use of domestic law as an excuse for failure to comply with a treaty obligation, the WTO obligation extends further: Art. XVI.4 of the WTO Agreement 'not only precludes pleading conflicting internal law as a justification for WTO inconsistencies, but requires WTO Members actually to ensure the conformity of internal law with its WTO obligations'.[190]

While there is no obligation to incorporate WTO obligations into domestic law directly,[191] members are still bound at all times to maintain WTO consistent positions. However, while members are expected to comply with their obligations at the WTO this is not to say that they always do.

A member may be bound by an obligation and breach it: the issue when understanding this obligation as a 'constraining' cause is that if the member breaches its obligation it incurs a cost (political, reputational, etc.). Rather than a binary choice, the obligation is examined for its casual strength. The strength of this cause is dependent on other factors: whether the normativity of the obligation is accepted (i.e. the member views it as law) or where the member views the rule as a legitimate one.

The international law obligations under the covered agreements do not only constrain or enable on the basis of substantive rules of international trade law. They also influence members by determining who may *be* a member. Under Art. XII(1) WTO Agreement, States and customs territories can become members of

[187] John Jackson cites Arts 3(4), 3(5), 3(7), 11, 19(1), 21(1), 21(6), 22(1), 22(2), 22(8), and 26(1)(b) DSU as relevant for the determination of the obligation to comply with an adopted report; J Jackson, 'The WTO Dispute Settlement Understanding—Misunderstandings On the Nature of Legal Obligation', (1997) 91 *American Journal of International Law* 63. Most relevant is Art. 21(1) DSU: 'Prompt compliance with recommendations or rulings of the DSB is essential in order to ensure effective resolution of disputes to the benefit of all Members.'

[188] J Pauwelyn, *Conflict of Norms in Public International Law* (Cambridge, Cambridge University Press 2003) 27–8.

[189] This is embodied in the rule *pacta sunt servanda*, 'one of the most fundamental in international law', V Lowe, *International Law* (Oxford, Oxford University Press 2007) 74.

[190] *United States—Sections 301–310 of the Trade Act 1974*, Panel Report (22 December 1999) WT/DS152/R, 314, fn 652. It appears that the aim of the negotiators to maintain a standard higher than that found in public international law more generally; see S Bhuyian, *National Law in the WTO* (Cambridge, Cambridge University Press 2007) 59–61.

[191] *US–Sections 301–10*, n. 190, para. 7.20.

the WTO.[192] By restricting membership to States and separate customs territories such as the EU or China Hong Kong, globalized actors are encouraged to act through such institutions and bodies in order to pursue their objectives. Use of the WTO dispute settlement system is principally restricted to members of the organization,[193] which also encourages engagement with the State as a representative institution or other independent customs territories in order to pursue claims or stimulate contestations between differing interpretations of rules at the WTO.

The use by globalized actors of the legal personality of members to raise claims at the WTO is not uncommon.[194] While the most obvious is the dispute between Japan and the US over photographic film[195] (commonly referred to as Kodak/Fuji after the companies concerned), the Boeing/Airbus dispute is another notable example.[196] There are less obvious instances of such disputes also: the recent involvement of large tobacco companies with the Ukrainian government in raising tobacco claims (now abandoned),[197] as well as smaller companies which do not fit the customary image of powerful multinational corporations.[198]

The use of members' legal personality by globalized actors to raise claims at the WTO is enabled by the international law rules within the WTO system. The existence of the treaty obligations setting out the requirements for membership is one part of this, while there is also the possible influence of key decisions that have come out of the dispute settlement system, notably the decision of the Appellate Body in *EC–Bananas III*[199] to allow the use of private legal representation in disputes between members.

There are many more rules, specifically related to the use of the dispute settlement system, that constrain and enable actors at the international level. Indeed, many of the arguments concerning the systemic influence of the rules of the WTO are shared with the constraining and enabling influence of its dispute settlement system and other compliance mechanisms. This is the focus of the following section.

[192] 'Any State or separate customs territory possessing full autonomy in the conduct of its external commercial relations and of the other matters provided for in this Agreement and the Multilateral Trade Agreements may accede to this Agreement, on terms to be agreed between it and the WTO. Such accession shall apply to this Agreement and the Multilateral Trade Agreements annexed thereto.'

[193] Inter alia: Arts 3.2, 3.3, 3.7, and 10.2 DSU making reference to members in raising claims under the DSU.

[194] For an account of the influence of private parties on governmental decisions to litigate and the networks between them: G Shaffer, *Defending Interests: Public-Private Partnerships in WTO Litigation* (Washington DC, The Brookings Institution Press 2003).

[195] *Japan—Measures Affecting Consumer Photographic Film and Paper*, Panel Report (31 March 1998) WT/DS44/R.

[196] *European Communities and Certain Member States—Measures Affecting Trade In Large Civil Aircraft*, Report of the Appellate Body (18 May 2011) WT/DS316/AB/R; and *United States—Measures Affecting Trade In Large Civil Aircraft (Second Complaint)*, Report of the Appellate Body (12 March 2012) WT/DS353/AB/R.

[197] 'Hidden hand of big tobacco leads to WTO challenge', The Sydney Morning Herald, 20 August 2012. See also the discussion below relating to the role of private parties in the *US–Gambling* dispute: n. 217 and corresponding text.

[198] See G Shaffer, *Defending Interests*, n. 194, 96–7.

[199] *European Communities—Regime for the Importation, Sale and Distribution of Bananas*, Report of the Appellate Body (9 September 1997) WT/DS27/AB/R, para. 10.

4. The systemic influence of the dispute settlement system: Examining causal strength

Just as the normative framework of the WTO influences actors involved, so do the institutions through which the norms are given force. As identified earlier, a range of committees and compliance structures exist at the WTO, though the most visible is the dispute settlement system. This system enables members of the WTO to litigate against other members and gives greater weight to the constraining force of the covered agreements by opening the way to public determinations at the WTO that a member is in breach of its obligations and potentially permitting the use of counter-measures.[200]

There has been some discussion as to the exact nature of the obligation to obey the recommendations of an adopted panel or Appellate Body report, most notably in an exchange in the American Journal of International Law between John H Jackson and Judith H Bello.[201] Whilst ostensibly looking at WTO obligations in the round, the primary focus was on the relationship between the existence of an obligation and the existence of an effective enforcement mechanism. Bello's argument was as follows:

> WTO rules are simply not 'binding' in the traditional sense ... there is no prospect of incarceration, injunctive relief, damages for harm inflicted or police enforcement. The WTO has no jailhouse, no bail bondsmen, no blue helmets, no truncheons or tear gas.[202]

Jackson's response is largely centred on the statement that WTO rules 'are binding in the traditional *international law* sense', that is, the obligations exist, though they may have weak enforcement mechanisms.[203] In a similar vein, JHH Weiler has argued that the withdrawal of concessions in the WTO dispute settlement system ought properly to be conceived of as sanctions and 'not an indulgence you buy to expiate your wrong doing'.[204]

In this light, the debate becomes more concerned with the potential effectiveness of WTO enforcement and not the existence of an obligation in and of itself.[205] These are two separate issues. The first question is whether WTO obligations bind

200 Article 22 DSU.

201 J Bello, 'The WTO Dispute Settlement Understanding: Less is More', (1996) 90 *American Journal of International Law* 416; J Bello, 'Review: The Jurisprudence of the GATT and the WTO: Insights on Treaty Law and Economic Relations by John H. Jackson', (2001) 95(4) *American Journal of International Law* 984; J Jackson, 'International Law Status of WTO Dispute Settlement Reports: Obligation to Comply or Option to "Buy Out"', (2004) 98 *American Journal of International Law* 109; and J Jackson, 'The WTO Dispute Settlement Understanding—Misunderstandings', n. 187, 60.

202 J Bello, 'The WTO Dispute Settlement Understanding: Less is More', n. 201, 416–17.

203 J Jackson, 'The WTO Dispute Settlement Understanding—Misunderstandings', n. 187, 63.

204 JHH Weiler, 'Written Statement', Testimony to US House of Representatives Committee on the Judiciary, Hearing on Establishing Consistent Enforcement Policies in the Context of Online Wagers, 15 November 2007, 10.

205 J Bello, 'Review: The Jurisprudence of the GATT and the WTO: Insights on Treaty Law and Economic Relations by John H. Jackson', n. 201, 987.

the members. The second question is whether the obligation to obey WTO obligations is undermined if there is no effective enforcement. The proposition that reports of the DSB are not binding is grounded in questions of compliance under WTO obligations. Non-compliance does not strip WTO rules of their normative force.[206] Widespread non-compliance, however, would limit the strength of the systemic influence of the dispute settlement system on actors at the international level. It is argued here, however, that (with a few notable exceptions), the WTO obligations have a commendable compliance record, indicating a strong constraining causal influence.[207]

There are a number of notable instances of non-compliance, the behaviour of the US with regard to the practice known as 'zeroing', for example. Until recently, the US maintained a method of calculating the value of dumped goods that created a higher figure than the method used by other WTO members (i.e. allowing it to impose higher duties on imports to the US than would otherwise be allowed). Panels and the Appellate Body repeatedly held that zeroing (as then applied by the US) was contrary to the WTO provisions on anti-dumping measures[208] (specifically, Art. 2.4.2 Anti-Dumping Agreement).[209] For a long period of time, the US did not change its practice. Indeed, in a dispute with Thailand (*US–Carrier Bags*)[210] it did not contest Thailand's complaint over the use of zeroing and went so far as to recognize that the Appellate Body had found the practice of zeroing incompatible with the Anti-Dumping Agreement in *US–Softwood Lumber V* and that the current case was on all fours with it.[211] While it has since come into conformity with its WTO obligations in this regard (at least in part), the long period of non-compliance demonstrated the ability of States to resist their obligations, even where clear.[212]

Nonetheless, the majority of reports do engender compliance, with delays in bringing measures into conformity principally where legislative amendment is required as opposed to administrative action.[213]

[206] See Chapter 2.D(4)(a).

[207] A more specific application of Henkin's wider observation regarding compliance in international law: L Henkin, *How Nations Behave* (2nd edn, New York, Columbia University Press 1979) 47; similarly, Franck commenting that 'most states observe systemic rules much of the time in their relations with other states', T Franck, 'Legitimacy in the International System', (1988) 82 *American Journal of International Law* 705.

[208] Most importantly, *European Communities—Anti-Dumping Duties on Imports of Cotton-Type Bed Linen From India*, Report of the Appellate Body (12 March 2001) WT/DS141/AB/R and *United States—Final Dumping Determination on Softwood Lumber from Canada*, Report of the Appellate Body (31 August 2004) WT/DS264/AB/R.

[209] Agreement on Implementation of Art. VI (Anti-dumping) (15 April 1994) LT/UR/A-1A/3 <http://docsonline.wto.org>.

[210] *United States—Anti-Dumping Measures on Polyethylene Retail Carrier Bags From Thailand*, Panel Report (22 January 2010) WT/DS383/R.

[211] Ibid., para. 3.3.

[212] The altered practice was published in the Federal Register, 'Calculation of the Weighted-Average Dumping Margin and Assessment Rate in Certain Antidumping Duty Proceedings; Final Modification' 77 Fed Reg 8101 (14 February 2012).

[213] B Wilson, 'Compliance by WTO Members With Adverse WTO Dispute Settlement Rulings: The Record to Date', (2007) 2(1) *Journal of International Economic Law* 398.

The focus here, however, is not on whether WTO dispute settlement works as well as it should do, or as well as it might be wished: indeed, its praise in many ways points to the weakness of other international dispute settlement systems rather than its own strength per se. The key point is that the obligatory nature of adopted panel and Appellate Body reports is not illusory, undermined by a weak or non-existent enforcement mechanism either as a matter of principle or practice. By stressing the influence of the disputes settlement system in constraining or enabling actors, the existence of a cost (whether it be reputational, political, or financial) for non-compliance with a panel or Appellate Body report is sufficient to exert a causal influence. Add to this the normative nature of the obligations under the DSU, we can expect it to exert a greater constraining influence.

The importance that panels and the Appellate Body have placed on augmenting their own perceived legitimacy has further added to the strength of the systemic influence of the WTO dispute settlement system.[214] As we will see later, most notably in the field of SPS measures but also safeguard measures, the practice of panels and the Appellate Body under the DSU has been motivated by an attempt to legitimize their role and, in this way, minimize potential non-compliance by members.[215] It is an attempt to maintain their legitimacy in the face of criticism that would undermine their ability to constrain or enable actors within the WTO system and thus limit the strength of the constraint that WTO institutions provide. This is an example of how causes cause things in different ways: the instrumental use of law by panels and the Appellate Body to further their own objectives by augmenting their legitimacy, is interrelated to and dependent on, the systemic influence of the WTO on other globalized actors.

E. Concluding Remarks

Examining the constitutive role of law on the identities and interests of actors helps explain the development of WTO law as it helps answer deeper questions of the behaviour of those catalysing legal change. If we look at all three causes of change in WTO law we can see how they each answer a different question about why the law has changed, who changed it and in what way.

In accepting the three different types of cause that cause things *in different ways* many of the ideological divisions that separate the literature are no longer

[214] Concerning legitimacy: R Howse, 'Adjudicative Legitimacy and Treaty Interpretation in International Trade Law: The Early Years of WTO Jurisprudence', in JHH Weiler (ed.), *The EU, the WTO and the NAFTA: Towards a Common Law of International Trade* (Oxford, Oxford University Press 2000); JHH Weiler, 'The Rule of Lawyers and the Ethos of Diplomats: Reflections on the Internal and External Legitimacy of WTO Dispute Settlement', (2001) 35 *Journal of World Trade* 206.

[215] Suggesting that the Appellate Body balances its role as a legal decision-maker with a desire to encourage compliance with its reports: J McCall Smith, 'WTO Dispute Settlement: The Politics of Appellate Body Rulings', (2003) 2 *World Trade Review* 65.

relevant.[216] It is not that a realist account of the instrumental use of law is inaccurate or that a constructivist account of the role of ideas is sufficient. Rather, that each cause is part of the analysis and that each type of influence corresponds to a different way in which law develops.

In examining the different ways in which law develops, some key issues have been identified. The ability of actors to crystallize norms in treaty form is likely limited and is subject to the interaction of other norms. This is expected to create uncertainty in tracing the objectives of some actors and the outcomes as the law develops. The possibility of actors pursuing their objectives across jurisdictional lines is also to be expected, especially in light of the different rules that apply within members' legal systems. The picture we are left with is a complex one with globalized actors spanning jurisdictions and pursuing their objectives at numerous levels of governance.

A picture of globalized actors engaging across numerous jurisdictions and attempting to manipulate the way in which law develops may seem a complex one though it is far closer to the reality of litigation at the WTO, for example, than a State-centred view. If we take the *US–Gambling*[217] dispute as an example: nominally this is a dispute between the US and Antigua & Barbuda, however, private individuals are key to understanding the dispute. Jay Cohen, a US citizen constituted an online gambling company (World Sports Exchange) in Antigua and was subsequently prosecuted by the US[218] for violations of the Wire Wager Act that prohibits the use of wire communication facilities in betting.[219] Cohen's own involvement, the US government's zealous pursuit of online gambling companies, and Antigua's diminishing appeal as a host for such businesses all contributed to the initiation of the WTO dispute, as did the involvement of other private individuals and firms.[220] To view it only in terms of States (or customs unions) or single jurisdictions misses the wider influences on the way in which the dispute (and, therefore, the law) evolves.[221]

[216] The divisions in International Relations scholarship, commonly known as the 'Great Debates'. For an overview: R Baumann, P Mayer, and B Zangl (eds), *International Relations: The Great Debates* (Cheltenham, Edward Elgar 2011).

[217] Principally (and still on-going): *United States—Measures Affecting the Cross-Border Supply of Gambling and Betting Services*, Panel Report (10 November 2004) WT/DS285/R; *United States—Measures Affecting the Cross-Border Supply of Gambling and Betting Services*, Report of the Appellate Body (7 April 2005) WT/DS285/AB/R; *United States—Measures Affecting the Cross-Border Supply of Gambling and Betting Services: Recourse to Article 21.5 of the DSU by Antigua and Barbuda*, Panel Report (30 March 2007) WT/DS285/RW.

[218] *United States v Jay Cohen* 260 F 3d 68 (2nd Cir 2001).

[219] 18 U.S.C § 1084: 'Whoever being engaged in the business of betting or wagering knowingly uses a wire communication facility for the transmission in interstate or foreign commerce of bets or wagers or information assisting in the placing of bets or wagers on any sporting event or contest, or for the transmission of a wire communication which entitles the recipient to receive money or credit as a result of bets or wagers, or for information assisting in the placing of bets or wagers, shall be fined under this title or imprisoned not more than two years, or both.'

[220] For an overview of the key actors: A Cooper, *Internet Gambling Offshore: Caribbean Struggles Over Casino Capitalism* (Basingstoke, Palgrave Macmillan 2011) 80–94.

[221] A partial analogy can be drawn with *Tokios Tokelés v Ukraine* (Jurisdiction) ICSID Arbitration Case No ARB/02/18 (2004) where a business owned by Ukrainian nationals and conducting business almost exclusively in Ukraine, was incorporated in Lithuania so that it might sue the Ukrainian government under a Ukraine–Lithuania Bilateral Investment Treaty.

4
Safeguard Measures

A. Introduction

This chapter examines how the WTO law on safeguard measures has developed over time. It does this by identifying key issues in safeguards law, examining how globalized actors have embedded their normative preferences within the legal regime. Using the causal approach developed in the previous chapters, this chapter furnishes an account drawing attention to the way in which specific ways of thinking about the law (based on prioritizing one causal influence over another) in turn explains the responses to unexpected developments in the law. As is the case with the other areas of world trade law examined in this book, while WTO law is the principal focus, as part of a globalized legal process, domestic legal influences play a key role in its development.

In the following section (Section B), safeguards are introduced, identifying the underlying value contestation in their use. This sets the ground for the contestations identified in the earlier chapters that stimulate the development of WTO law. Section C then examines how internal US debates encouraged it to embed its own understanding of safeguard measures onto the international system, first in Art. XIX GATT 1947 and then, the Agreement on Safeguards ('AoS'). Section D traces the interpretation of a specific and contentious term in safeguards law (the 'unforeseen developments' clause) as a way of examining how the law has developed over the GATT and later WTO years. Unlike the traditional approaches that focus on the Appellate Body's interpretation of this requirement, this section suggests that the application of the 'unforeseen developments' clause is the result of a complex interplay of causal influences across domestic and international law. Section E examines the way in which the law on safeguard measures may be developing in light of changing practice in this area. It draws attention to the number of alternative spheres in which globalized actors continue to pursue their objectives, outwith the formal dispute settlement system at the WTO, which nonetheless may play a key role in stimulating further change in how safeguard measures are regulated under trade law.

B. The Use of Safeguard Measures and their Underlying Values

This section sets out the key values underpinning the development and use of safeguard measures. This is the key battleground where competing conceptions of the use and interpretation of safeguard measures takes place. It is argued that neither economic nor political economy arguments offer entirely convincing justifications for the use of safeguards and that, instead, they are based on value judgments, competing conceptions of fairness: specifically, outcome-based fairness concerned with the consequences of liberalized trade on specific sections of society and rules-of-the-game fairness which is concerned with 'fair play' and avoiding 'cheating' in international trade.[1]

A safeguard measure is the temporary restriction on the import of a product to protect a domestic industry from serious injury (or threat thereof). The increase in imports must have been the result of unforeseen circumstances arising from a commitment made to reduce tariffs under a trade agreement.[2] Such a clause ensures that where concessions are granted under a trade agreement, and there is an unexpected increase in imports, the importing party has an 'escape clause' permitting the suspension of the previously granted concessions. One of the most important such clauses is Art. XIX GATT, subsequently supplemented by the Agreement on Safeguards 1994.[3]

While it is common to compare safeguards to other trade defence instruments ('TDIs') found in the covered agreements, safeguard measures are different for two reasons. First, their application is subject to high legal standards which are often difficult to satisfy and can be undesirable in their result. The determination process requires a finding of 'serious injury' to the domestic industry, unlike the lesser threshold of 'material injury' in respect of dumping and subsidies.[4] The requirements of 'non-attribution' analyses, whereby investigating authorities must demonstrate that the increase in imports is a cause of the serious injury, and that where other factors may have contributed to the injury, they have not been included further complicate these investigations.[5] The introduction of a safeguard measure requires the negotiation of compensation to the exporting members affected, unlike the case of Anti-Dumping and Countervailing Duties ('AD/CVDs').[6] Again, unlike AD/CVDs, safeguards must be applied 'to a product being imported irrespective of its source'.[7] Safeguards have the potential of costing more to the enacting member than AD/CVDs, in both the costs of conducting complex investigations and in compensation to adversely affected members.[8]

[1] On the questionable distinction between fair and unfair trade: A Lowenfeld, 'Fair or Unfair Trade: Does it Matter?', (1980) 13 *Cornell International Law Journal* 205.

[2] The specific requirements are examined in more detail below, Section C(2)–(3).

[3] There are a number of other 'escape clauses' under the GATT covering a range of issues: *inter alia*, Art. XVIII (balance of payments), Art. XXI (national security), Art. VI (anti-dumping duties), and Art. XXIV (regional trade agreements).

[4] Article XIX:1 GATT, as compared to Art. VI.6(a) GATT. The safeguards requirement is an 'exacting standard': *United States—Definitive Safeguard Measures on Imports of Wheat Gluten from the EC*, Report of the Appellate Body (22 December 2000) WT/DS166/AB/R, ('*US–Wheat Gluten*') para. 149.

[5] Article 4.2(b) AoS.

[6] Article 8 AoS.

[7] Article 2.2 AoS. There is a limited form of selectivity in the Agreement on Safeguards though it is restricted, see Art. 5.2 AoS.

[8] Eighty-two safeguard measures were imposed during the period 1 January 1995 to 31 October 2007 compared to 1997 anti-dumping measures imposed in the period 1 January 1995 to 30 June

The second key difference is in their justification, unlike AD/CVDs that respond to 'unfair' trade practices such as dumping or subsidies.[9] Safeguard measures do not deal with 'cheating' in international trade but instead concern themselves with the inability of a State's industry to adapt to changing times and progressive market liberalization. The protection involved in AD/CVDs is meant to negate the effect of the unfair practice (e.g. negating the benefits of subsidies by increasing tariffs).[10] The motivation behind safeguard measures, however, is not to protect in order to level the playing field but, instead, is intended to be a form of 'time out' from the competitive pressures of certain imports. It is a statement that the domestic industry in the normal course of competition would suffer serious injury and, as such, requires a period of lessened competition to adapt. Clearly, this creates an awkward situation for the State enacting such measures as it signals an inability to adapt to the global market.

Safeguard measures are also often contrasted with 'grey area' measures.[11] This is the generic term for Voluntary Export Restraints ('VERs'), Orderly Marketing Arrangements ('OMAs'), and other similar instruments. 'Grey area' measures are restraint arrangements between two members, where the exporting member agrees to limit exports so as not to harm the domestic producers of the importing member. These agreements are, in essence, de facto quotas and function to limit 'damaging' levels of imports to the member.[12] Clearly this is the role of a safeguard measure, however, 'grey area' measures provide several advantages.

A key advantage is their lack of regulation. 'Grey area' measures are difficult to identify or quantify: they are often concluded between industries though, in fact, governments play a key role.[13] This is often necessary due to the rigours of domestic competition or anti-trust law that would otherwise penalize such market co-ordination. Another advantage is that 'grey area' measures provide an acceptable solution to both parties to the agreement: the importing member cushions its domestic producers from import fluctuations, while the exporting member can benefit from quota rents if the agreement is properly arranged. The exporting member may also view the imposition of a 'grey area' measure as a second-best solution in the face of stricter restrictions on its exports. Equally, the importing member is not required to pay its own compensation and can target individual exporters rather than all exports of a given product (as required for safeguard

2007 alone; 'WTO Secretariat reports decline in safeguard investigations', WTO News Items, 17 November 2008 <http://www.wto.org/english/news_e/news08_e/safeg_nov08_e.htm>.

[9] The fear of being termed a 'wimp': E Vermulst, M Pernaute, and K Lucenti, 'Recent EC Safeguards' Policy: "Kill Them All and Let God Sort Them Out"?', (2004) 38(6) *Journal of World Trade* 955.

[10] See Art. VI.3 GATT and Art. 19.4 Agreement on Subsidies and Countervailing Measures ('SCM Agreement').

[11] On their relationship: EM Hizon, 'The Safeguard Measure/VER Dilemma: The Jekyll and Hyde of Trade Protection', (1994–95) 15 *Northwestern Journal of International Law & Business* 105.

[12] *Consumers Union of US v Kissinger* 506 F 2d 136 (DC Cir 1974), dissenting opinion Judge Leventhal.

[13] Background Note by the Secretariat, 'Grey-Area Measures' (16 September 1987) GATT Doc MTN.GNG/NG9/W/6, para. 8.

measures in the majority of cases).[14] The increasing use (and abuse) of such measures become a problem towards the later GATT years, encouraging legal reform in this area (which would eventually lead to the Agreement on Safeguards).[15]

As an exception to a previously agreed commitment, and potentially in tension with policies of trade liberalization, safeguards must be justified not only in their individual use but also at the systemic level, justifying their inclusion in the GATT (and later, WTO) system. In the following section, the customary accounts for the existence of safeguards are given. While they are not rejected per se, in order to understand why safeguard measures are used, we need to understand their underlying values. Such an exercise places safeguard measures in their wider context, effecting both domestic and international expectations.

1. The justification for safeguard measures

Justifications for safeguard measures can be divided into two general groups. In the first, are arguments based on the economic benefits that may accrue to the member introducing the safeguard. In the second, are arguments that focus on the need to grant domestic industries temporary protection in the face of unexpected import surges as part of a broader international trade liberalizing project.[16]

a. *Economic arguments for the use of safeguard measures and their limitations*

There are a series of arguments that focus on the economic advantages of safeguard measures. It is argued that safeguards can serve as necessary protection for domestic industry whilst it makes 'a positive adjustment to import competition'.[17] This involves either enhancing competitiveness or providing support for the exit of firms or workers from the domestic industry in question. The evidence supporting this proposition, however, is not convincing.[18] Bown and McCulloch identify the weaknesses with the argument that safeguards could provide 'breathing space' for industries as they adapt. They state:

> [A] basic problem with the 'breathing space' approach is that there is no 'pro-adjustment' effect inherent in an import-restricting policy; by itself, temporary protection from imports does nothing to cause an industry to become more internationally competitive. Rather, by

[14] A Sykes, 'Trade Remedy Laws', John M. Olin Program in Law and Economics Working Paper No. 240 (2005) 6.

[15] R Hudec, 'GATT Dispute Settlement after the Tokyo Round: An Unfinished Business', (1980) 13 *Cornell Journal of International Law* 145, 161.

[16] On the objectives of safeguards measures see generally: A Sykes, *The WTO Agreement on Safeguards: A Commentary* (Oxford, Oxford University Press 2006) Chapter 2; F Piérola, *The Challenge of Safeguards in the WTO* (Cambridge, Cambridge University Press 2014) Chapter 2; Y-S Lee, *Safeguard Measures in World Trade: the Legal Analysis* (3rd edn, Cheltenham, Edward Elgar 2014) Chapter 1.

[17] Section 201 Trade Act of 1974 [Pub L 93-618, 88 Stat 1978].

[18] Note the decline of three US industries (lamb meat, wheat gluten, and line pipe) after they had received protection in the form of safeguards: D Ryan, 'The Effects of Section 201 Safeguards on US Industries', (2013) 44 *Georgetown Journal of International Law* 249, 264–310.

allowing the industry to continue production in a protected environment, such a policy ends up having an anti-adjustment bias—it does nothing either to induce the industry to shrink or to transform itself to meet the reality of a new and more competitive economic environment.[19]

Indeed, protection can encourage industries to invest in lobbying rather than restructuring, further reducing the possibility of industries being able to compete.[20]

Another argument is that while aggregate economic welfare is traditionally believed to increase as a result of trade liberalization, the increase in economic welfare need not be uniform. In such cases safeguard measures are seen as a tool for the redistribution of wealth.[21] As before, however, where society decides that there ought to be limitations on the aggregate increase of welfare when losses may be acutely felt by a group of individuals, the use of safeguard measures is not the most effective method to redistribute economic gains. Direct aid to affected individuals would be a more efficient method of redistribution than protection that is considered 'an exceptionally clumsy method of redistribution'.[22]

It would seem, therefore, that the economic arguments in favour of safeguards are not entirely convincing. However, irrespective of the potential economic benefits of safeguard measures to the economy (or lack thereof) this is not the only motivation for their use. Political economy arguments can help to understand the importance of using or including safeguards in trade agreements in order to gain political support for the proposed trade agreement, or a broader liberalizing policy.[23]

b. Political economy arguments for the use of safeguard measures

Drawing on insights from political economy, two potential advantages to the inclusion of an escape clause in a trade agreement can be identified.[24] First, escape clauses have been linked to minimizing dangers of contracting parties withdrawing from a trade agreement when under domestic pressure (the 'safety valve' argument). Second, escape clauses may increase the likelihood of parties granting concessions at the negotiation stage by virtue of a legitimate and temporary opt-out in the case of emergency (the 'contractarian' position).[25]

[19] CP Bown and R McCulloch, 'Trade Adjustment in the WTO System: Are More Safeguards the Answer?', (2007) 23(3) *Oxford Review of Economic Policy* 415, 416.

[20] A Sykes, *The WTO Agreement on Safeguards*, n. 16, 51, though, note problems with this position at 56.

[21] Ibid., 56. Once again, this is not a wholly satisfactory argument, 58–9. Though, note former Director General Lamy's criticism of the lack of measures at the domestic level to compensate those who have suffered from the impact of trade liberalization: BBC News, 'Trade Boss Criticises Financial Mess', 30 May 2008 <http://news.bbc.co.uk/1/hi/business/7425027.stm> accessed 15 March 2015.

[22] A Sykes, 'Protectionism as a "Safeguard": A Positive Analysis of the GATT "Escape Clause" with Normative Speculations', (1991) 58 *University of Chicago Law Review* 255, 272.

[23] J Stiglitz, 'Dumping on Free Trade: The US Import Trade Laws', (1997) 64(2) *Southern Economic Journal* 402, 407.

[24] See also, F Piérola, *The Challenge of Safeguards in the WTO*, n. 16, 85–98.

[25] A Sykes, *The WTO Agreement on Safeguards*, n. 16, 59–72.

The 'safety valve' argument is centred on the scope of protectionist pressures from domestic groups on policy makers in the face of a sudden or unexpected change in circumstances.[26] Where concessions have been made, safeguard measures allow domestic industries to petition for protection from the State through administrative processes.[27] By providing a 'safety valve' from these pressures, it is hoped that industries will content themselves with engaging in a rule-based process rather than direct lobbying. It has been observed that this is based on the premise that protection received from administrative bodies will be less harmful to free trade than legislative protection.[28] There is scope for this as safeguard measures are temporary in nature; however, it is unclear that where access to legislative protection remains, those industries will not target both administrative and legislative options where their resources allow it.[29] Nonetheless, the safety valve argument has been an influential one, viewed by a Swiss representative at the Uruguay Round as the key objective of Art. XIX; the GATT system was to function as 'part of the liberalization machinery, of which [Art. XIX] is in a sense the "safety valve"'.[30]

The contractarian position, put forward by Alan Sykes, offers an interesting account for the existence of safeguard measures. First, he draws parallels between a safeguards clause and comparable *force majeur* clauses in contracts; the cost of temporary protection by one party is less than the cost of withdrawal from the agreement *in toto*.[31] He concludes that negotiators are more likely to agree to concessions if they are aware of a temporary 'opt out' where the political cost of complying with obligations becomes overwhelming.[32]

In attempting to encourage liberalization each of these theories acknowledges the challenges that safeguards measures face, searching an acceptable point on a spectrum between the general benefits of free trade and protecting individuals or industry from unexpected import surges. They focus on the international plane, and in particular, the GATT/WTO system, tending toward the economically liberal end of the spectrum, accepting the benefits of trade for the parties concerned.[33] The tensions at the heart of safeguard measures are thus viewed through the prism of the traditional liberal/protectionist conflict.[34] This approach is helpful

[26] Similar in effect to a *rebus sic stantibus* provision, F Piérola, *The Challenge of Safeguards in the WTO*, n. 16, 87.

[27] Chapter 3.C(4).

[28] A Sykes, *The WTO Agreement on Safeguards*, n. 16, 59.

[29] Ibid., 60–1.

[30] Communication from Switzerland (5 October 1987) GATT Doc MTN.GNG/NG9/W/10, para. 4.

[31] In essence, an efficient breach. A Sykes, 'Protectionism as a "Safeguard": A Positive Analysis of the GATT "Escape Clause" with Normative Speculations', n. 22, 259.

[32] Ibid.

[33] So-called 'GATT-think' which has been described as a form of enlightened mercantilism: K Bagwell and R Staiger, 'GATT-Think', *Columbia University Economics Discussion Paper Series*, no. 0102-39 (March 2002), 43–4 applying Paul Krugman's observations of negotiating tactics at the GATT level.

[34] This is to be expected given the public choice theory basis for these political economy arguments which presupposes a 'policy market-place' and two broad objectives by the policy consumers within the market, either protection or liberalization. A Sykes, 'Protectionism as a "Safeguard": A Positive Analysis of the GATT "Escape Clause" with Normative Speculations', n. 22, 272.

though it can be limited, failing to appreciate the strength of safeguard measures from a domestic perspective within a value-oriented narrative based not on self-interested or short-sighted protectionism but instead on shared understandings of fairness and society's duty to the disenfranchised.

2. Safeguard measures as an expression of fairness

Customarily safeguard measures are distinguished from other TDIs insofar as they are not based on a response to 'unfair' behaviour. Nonetheless, fairness still underpins the popular motivation for safeguard measures. 'Unfair' acts such as subsidies and dumping are classified as unfair due to the perception that they are a form of 'cheating'. This is based on an understanding of trade relations as a game with specific rules, where those who commit certain acts[35] are viewed to be unfairly advantaging themselves.[36]

At times 'cheating' language is utilized when safeguard measures are introduced, the US safeguard measures on steel were a clear example of this. Introducing temporary safeguard measures on steel imports, President George W. Bush stated:

> I take this action to give our domestic steel industry an opportunity to adjust to surges in foreign imports, recognizing the harm from 50 years of foreign government intervention in the global steel market, which has resulted in bankruptcies, serious dislocation, and job loss. We also must continue to urge our trading partners to eliminate global inefficient excess capacity and market-distorting practices, such as subsidies.[37]

In December of the following year, announcing the suspension of the safeguard measures, he again returned to the 'fair play' issue: 'I strongly believe that America's workers can compete with anyone in the world as long as we have a fair and level playing field.'[38]

In this regard, safeguard measures are not distinguished in their purpose from other TDIs. This view of their role is to enforce the rules of the game, to encourage 'fair play' in international trade. However, this approach is contingent on other activities that are deemed unfair (subsidies or other forms of government intervention). Instead, there is another conception of fairness underpinning safeguard measures: one focussed on the outcomes or trade liberalization rather than the way that trade is conducted.

[35] These acts are not necessarily prohibited: dumping per se, for example, is not prohibited by the covered agreements.

[36] This has been classified as a breach of the Golden Rule, 'rules-of-the-game' fairness. S Suranovic, 'A Positive Analysis of Fairness with Applications to International Trade', (2000) 23(3) *The World Economy* 294.

[37] President Announces Temporary Safeguards for Steel Industry, 5 March 2002, Statement by the President <http://georgewbush-whitehouse.archives.gov/news/releases/2002/03/20020305-6.html> (accessed 15 March 2015).

[38] President's Statement on Steel, 4 December 2003, Statement by the President <http://georgewbush-whitehouse.archives.gov/news/releases/2003/12/20031204-5.html> (accessed 15 March 2015).

Safeguard measures are underpinned by competing conceptions of fairness, what Franck considered procedural fairness and distributive justice.[39] One might characterize the first as the fairness of process and the second as the fairness of outcomes. Safeguard measures represent a battleground over the type of fairness that should be prioritized. On the one hand, as discussed above, they can serve to encourage fair play (i.e. fairness of process). Alternatively, they can serve to protect people from the unpredictable damage associated (rightly or wrongly) with the functioning of the market. Just as the welfare state implies a duty to provide aid to those who have been harmed by the functioning of the market, so safeguard measures serve to protect domestic industries and workers from certain unexpected changes in the market.[40] This view of the market is an important element in modern discourse on the relationship between the market and society.[41] Susan Strange vividly described the strength of the market and its unpredictability (and that unpredictability's attendant consequences) when she stated:

> [States'] failure to manage the national economy, to maintain employment and sustain economic growth, to avoid imbalances of payments with other states, to control the rate of interest and the exchange rate is not a matter of technical incompetence, nor moral turpitude nor political maladroitness. It is neither in any direct sense their fault, nor the fault of others. None of these failures can be blamed on other countries or on other governments, they are, simply, the victims of the market economy.[42]

In this view safeguard measures are initiated in order to protect domestic industry from unforeseen import surges, granting industry and workers a temporary reprieve as they either enhance their competitiveness or reallocate resources into different, more viable sectors.[43] It recognizes that while freer trade ought to increase overall welfare, the gains from liberalization may not be evenly spread across society. Safeguards can offer the perception of fairness of outcomes to the liberal project,

[39] T Franck, *Fairness in International Law and Institutions* (Oxford, Oxford University Press 1997) 7.

[40] The Beveridge Report ('Social Insurance and Allied Services', Report by Sir William Beveridge, November 1942 HMSO) which is credited with initiating the welfare state in the United Kingdom. It stated that the objectives of welfare included: 'Abolition of want requires, first ... provision against interruption and loss of earning power ... Abolition of want requires, second, adjustment of incomes, in periods of earning, as well as interruption of earning, to family needs ...' (paras 12 and 13).

[41] See: Chapter 3.B(3), Chapter 6.B and D.

[42] S Strange, *The Retreat of the State* (Cambridge, Cambridge University Press 1996) 14.

[43] Something that President Bush accepted in his statements on the steel safeguards: 'The U.S. steel industry wisely used the 21 months of breathing space we provided to consolidate and restructure. The industry made progress increasing productivity, lowering production costs, and making America more competitive with foreign steel producers. Steel producers and workers have negotiated new groundbreaking labor agreements that allow greater flexibility and increase job stability. The Pension Benefit Guaranty Corporation has guaranteed the pensions of eligible steelworkers and retirees and relieved the high pension costs that burdened some companies. My jobs and growth plan has also created more favorable economic conditions for the industry, and the improving economy will help further stimulate demand.' President's Statement on Steel, 4 December 2003, n. 38.

minimizing the harm to those negatively affected by the reduction of trade barriers. Though the economic evidence does not support this view, it still enjoys an important position in the discourse and thus social construction of the market and its relation to the State.[44]

The danger, however, is that by encouraging protection to protect the 'losers' of the trade bargain, the entire project is undermined. A concern over ensuring just results from trade may, if unchecked, raise levels of protection and minimize the gains from free trade (exactly the concerns raised by the materially focussed economic analysis discussed earlier).

3. Reconciling outcome-based fairness and the gains from trade

The desire to cushion the impact of liberalization on workers and industry can fall into conflict with the belief in the overall merits of free trade, and the best way to encourage the development of the market. A system that permits the protection of workers from self-confessed competitive imports risks undermining the trading system. In order to reconcile outcome-based fairness with the potential gains from trade, safeguard measures must be understood in a way that neither ignores requirements of fairness, nor unduly harms the benefits from trade. The key point is that the concerns are built upon the economic arguments but not dependent upon them: it is the use of the arguments within the social setting that configures the relationship here.

In light of this need to reconcile these two positions, the use of safeguard measures has been curtailed: as actors attempt to encourage their own interpretation of their proper role and the 'correct' balance between these values they attempt to mould the regulation of safeguard measures to support their approach. As discussed in the previous chapter, one of the most obvious ways for 'actors' to pursue their preferences is to embed their conception of the correct role of safeguard measures in the international agreements themselves.[45] This not only relates to the text of the agreement (Art. XIX GATT and Agreement on Safeguards) but also by determining the conditions for their use, as well as their temporary nature. In this way, globalized actors encourage their own conception of where the line is to be drawn between protection and liberalization in the face of uncertain economic changes: this has broader consequences than for safeguard measures, it is a core element in how a member approaches the role of private and public power in the market.

In the case of safeguard measures, the US has been the principal determinant of their place within the larger international trade regime. This is not to say that the US maintains a static position on the proper interpretation and role of safeguards. The State itself is subject to its internal influences: in this instance, the interpretation of the proper use of safeguard measures has been one of the key

[44] Chapter 3.B and Chapter 6.D. [45] Chapter 3.C(1).

battlegrounds between liberal and protectionist actors within the US political system.[46]

The next section will examine how the US has sought to project its conception of the proper role of safeguard measures onto the international trading system, and in turn, onto the legal systems of other members, by embedding its normative preferences within the GATT and Agreement on Safeguards. The apparent success of this instrumental use of law will be challenged, identifying other causal influences that explain how it is that the US has lost control over how safeguards are understood.

C. The Development of Article XIX GATT and the WTO Agreement on Safeguards

This section examines the way in which the instrumental use of international law by the US, motivated by domestic battles, helps to explain the way in which WTO law has developed. Specifically, the focus is on the most visible of all forms of instrumental influence: the crystallization of norms within a treaty thereby embedding normative preferences in the international trade system. This section will show how, as the US developed an understanding of how safeguard measures should be used, it applied its conception of them onto the GATT and then the WTO Agreement on Safeguards (AoS).

This section examines key moments in the development of safeguard measures and the importance of the US approach to their application. It analyses how the US's determination of the proper role for safeguards in a trading system has influenced their development at both domestic and international levels. While safeguard measures are underpinned by an understanding of outcome-oriented fairness, the US's concerns not to undermine liberal trade relations have had a formative influence on them. It will then examine how the US continued in projecting its understanding of safeguard measures and the consequences of such a projection on the development of the legal regime of safeguards. Rather than examining the development of the law on safeguard measures through the lens of progressive panel and Appellate Body reports, this section acknowledges multiple causes in a globalized context, drawing attention to the mutually constitutive interaction between domestic and international legal activity.

Safeguards are especially appropriate for such an examination as their regulation spans both international and domestic systems. At the international level there exist agreements between trading States; originally these were in bilateral agreements but were soon incorporated into the multilateral trading system, under the GATT. Since 1994, there has been further development of the disciplines in the Agreement on Safeguards. Domestically, trade laws implement a regime for the use of safeguard measures, determining who may initiate an investigation into whether

[46] Themselves contestations over values rather than interests: Chapter 3.B(1).

a safeguard is warranted, under what circumstances, when a safeguard may be applied, and for how long. The US system was originally the most developed, however, in the past decades others members have brought into force their own laws providing for the imposition of safeguard measures.

1. The US origins of safeguard measures

The earliest escape clause was introduced in the US–Mexico Reciprocal Trade Agreement 1942[47] negotiated under the authority of the Trade Agreements Act of 1934 which had delegated considerable trade policy powers from the Congress to the Executive.[48] The act outlined a trade programme targeted at liberalization that was to become US policy following the Smoot-Hawley debacle.[49] As the Executive negotiated bilateral agreements with its trading partners and reduced tariffs on a range of products,[50] Congress became increasingly concerned with the impact of such measures.[51] Taking the escape clause present in the US–Mexico Reciprocal Trade Agreement 1942 as its security against the harm caused by overeager negotiators, Congress required President Truman to include such escape clauses in all future agreements and to set up a procedure for safeguard petitions.[52] In return, Congress granted continuing authority under the Reciprocal Trade Agreements programme for the negotiation of new agreements.[53]

Under the US petition procedure, industry petitioned the Tariff Commission (later to become the US International Trade Commission) for relief in response to serious injury (or threat thereof) caused by tariff concessions. The Tariff Commission would then decide according to its own requirements whether the claim merited a recommendation of relief. The Tariff Commission used a 'four point test': that (1) as a result of unforeseen circumstances, and (2) obligations incurred under an Agreement, (3) there is an increase in imports, that (4) threatened or caused

[47] This agreement had been negotiated as part of a warming of US–Mexico relations. In essence, to reward Mexican entry into the Second World War earlier in the year, the US eased its restrictions on the exportation of Mexican oil to the US: L Zorrilla, *Historia de las Relaciones entre México y los Estados Unidos de América 1800–1958* (Mexico, Porrua 1965) 495.

[48] Chapter 474 sec 1, 48 Stat 943 (1934).

[49] The 1930 Act that raised tariffs on US imports in order to protect domestic industries (in particular the farming industry) and arguably sparked the rising levels of protectionism during the interwar period: IM Destler, *American Trade Politics* (4th edn, Washington DC, Institute for International Economics 2005) 11–12.

[50] D Sarooshi, 'Sovereignty, Economic Autonomy, the United States, and the International Trading System', (2004) 15(4) *European Journal of International Law* 651, 660 citing D Beane, that 'between 1934 and 1945 the US entered into 32 bilateral trade agreements with 27 countries, granting tariff concessions on 64 per cent of dutiable imports and reducing tariff rates to an average of 44 per cent'.

[51] Subjected to pressure from constituents and representing specific geographic areas, congressional members customarily engage in furthering a more protectionist stance than the membership of the Executive: R Brewster, 'The Domestic Origins of International Agreements', (2003) 44(2) *Virginia Journal of International Law* 1, 32.

[52] Acknowledged in Executive Order No. 9832, signed 25 February 1947.

[53] W Murayama, 'The Evolution of the Escape Clause—Section 201 of the Trade Act of 1974 as Amended by the Omnibus Trade and Competitiveness Act of 1988', (1989) *Brigham Young University Law Review* 393, 400.

serious injury to a domestic industry.[54] An affirmative decision (or tie) would be passed to the President who could then act upon it with broad discretion (including, if so desired, not at all).[55] This granted a right under US law for industry to request action in response to the result of an agreement entered into between the importing and exporting States. As a matter of domestic law, it led to an agency determination capable of incurring the responsibility of the State under a trade agreement. Whilst domestic industry lobbies Congress, this system permitted a direct channel from industry to the Executive via a quasi-judicial administrative body. As a result, the greater voice for domestic producers and convergent interests of an increasingly resurgent Congress in matters of trade policy, resulted in the relaxation of the strict domestic safeguard disciplines so as to best accommodate the two increasingly protectionist factions.

The resulting Trade Agreements Extension Act 1951 was a victory (from an internal perspective) for the protectionist tendencies in the US system.[56] It placed the petitioning system on a statutory footing and relaxed many of the requirements of the escape clause for domestic industries. As will be discussed below, the requirement that the increase in imports be the result of 'unforeseen developments' was removed and the causation requirements for demonstrating an injury lessened.[57] However, before this change took place the multilateral rules on safeguards had already been modelled on the US's earlier approach.

2. Crystallizing preferences under the GATT 1947: Article XIX

Article XIX GATT 1947 was based very closely on the aforementioned escape clause in the US–Mexico Reciprocal Trade Agreement of 1942.[58] Largely identical, Art. XIX.1(a) reads:

> If, as a result of unforeseen developments and of the effect of the obligations incurred by a contracting party under this Agreement, including tariff concessions, any product is being imported into the territory of that contracting party in such increased quantities and under such conditions as to cause or threaten serious injury to domestic producers in that territory of like or directly competitive products, the contracting party shall be free, in respect of such product, and to the extent and for such time as may be necessary to prevent or remedy such injury, to suspend the obligation in whole or in part or to withdraw or modify the concession.

The Havana Charter also contained a safeguard clause based on the US–Mexico provision, though it relaxed some of the prerequisites for the initiation of safeguards.[59] The inclusion of a safeguards clause was non-negotiable as the US was

[54] See Y-S Lee, *Safeguard Measures in World Trade: the Legal Analysis*, n. 16, 227.
[55] Executive Order No. 9832, para. 2. [56] [Ch 141 sec 10, 65 Stat 75].
[57] T Stewart, *The GATT Uruguay Round: A Negotiating History Vol II* (The Hague, Kluwer Law International 1993) 1733.
[58] Ibid., 1720.
[59] Article 40 Havana Charter, Final Act of the United Nations Conference on Trade and Employment (April 1948) UN Docs E/Conf. 2/78, though in the view of Stewart, 'Since 1947, the

required to include such a clause in all its new trade agreements.[60] However, the clear transplant of the US provision to the GATT must have been viewed as an assurance that other States would approach the use of safeguard measures in a similar way to the US.

This formulation of a safeguards clause displays key elements that are at the heart of safeguard measures even today: their temporary nature, the requirement that domestic producers suffer injury (or are threatened by injury), and the 'emergency' nature of safeguards requiring a connection to 'unforeseen developments'.

While the text of Art. XIX did not change, the domestic provisions upon which it was based did.[61] In the US the application of the requirements by the USICT were more rigorous. John Jackson identified the problem: 'This means that industry groups within the United States who seek escape-clause relief find that in many circumstances they are not eligible under US law for that relief, although they might well be eligible for such relief if the GATT language were the applicable legal standard.'[62] This divergence would eventually be lessened with the introduction of the Agreement on Safeguards. It once again took the example of following the domestic provisions of US safeguards law and incorporated it into a distinct situation.[63]

3. Crystallizing preferences at the WTO: The Agreement on Safeguards

In the years that followed the provisional application of the GATT, the US had witnessed many changes to its own safeguards legislation as a result of internal battles, reflecting the changing circumstances of international trade in which the US found itself.[64] In the 1970s, confronted by international economic disorder and progressive competition, partly from the EC but more importantly Japan,[65] Congress pushed for a safeguard system that would provide protection for domestic industries in light of this new competition and curtail the President's powers to override determinations of the US International Trade Commission ('USITC').

The current petitioning procedure is a remnant of this time, found in ss 201–4 Trade Act 1974.[66] A domestic industry[67] may petition the USITC to conduct an investigation into whether 'an article is being imported into the United States in such increased quantities as to be a substantial cause of serious injury, or the threat

contracting parties have generally interpreted GATT Article XIX in a manner consistent with the revisions made at the Havana Conference.' T Stewart, *The GATT Uruguay Round*, n. 57, 1720.

[60] T Stewart, *The GATT Uruguay Round*, n. 57, 1772; Y-S Lee, *Safeguard Measures in World Trade: the Legal Analysis*, n. 16, 227.

[61] J Jackson, *The World Trading System* (2nd edn, Cambridge MA, MIT Press 1997) 181.

[62] Ibid., 182.

[63] Uruguay Round Agreements Act, Statement of Administrative Action, H.Doc 103-316 (I), 4298.

[64] n. 54. [65] S Strange, *The Retreat of the State*, n. 42, 21–2.

[66] [Pub L 93-618, 88 Stat 1978].

[67] By means of an 'entity, including a trade association, firm, certified or recognized union, or group of workers, which is representative of an industry', 19 USC §2252(a)(1).

thereof, to the domestic industry producing an article like or directly competitive with the imported article'.[68] Despite the relaxation of certain requirements, receiving a positive determination from the USITC is still a difficult goal to achieve. Since the 1988 Omnibus Trade and Competitiveness Act amendment, domestic industries must now also show how they intend to adapt to competitive pressures if relief is to be granted.[69] This includes whether or not they will focus their resources on improving competitiveness or instead focus on a separate area of business.

Once a petition has been lodged, the USITC conducts a detailed investigation. Where three or more of the six Commissioners vote in favour of a determination of serious injury (or threat thereof), they pass their recommendations on to the President. The President then has a wide range of considerations to factor in (from national security to trade diversion),[70] and an even wider range of actions available to him from the list found in the Act, including the broad catchall 'any other action ... which the President considers appropriate and feasible'.[71]

The Agreement on Safeguards follows the tradition of Art. XIX and once again uses US legislation as its model. During the Uruguay Round the US representative at the Working Group preparing the Agreement on Safeguards stated somewhat coyly:

> The purpose of this paper is not to advocate that the specific procedures of the United States be incorporated into a safeguards agreement or that the United States experience readily lends itself to use by other contracting parties. This paper is presented more for the purpose of demonstrating how one country has defined injury in its national trade law and developed a transparent process for making injury determinations consistent with Article XIX.[72]

The resulting Agreement on Safeguards, however, does incorporate the US position. With the exception of certain procedural requirements (which are more detailed under US law), the WTO Agreement on Safeguards is overtly modelled on the ss 201–4 system.[73]

4. Structural adjustment assistance: A failure to embed norms?

One notable difference between US law and the WTO Agreement on Safeguards is the lack of an obligation to ensure a plan for structural adjustment at the time of petitioning. The Agreement on Safeguards, unlike US legislation, lacks any requirement for a structural adjustment plan.

The Agreement on Safeguards makes reference to structural adjustment but offers no more than an exhortation. There are four references to adjustment in the Agreement on Safeguards. In the preamble it states the general importance of

[68] 19 USC §2251(a).
[69] [Pub L 100-418, 102 Stat 1107].
[70] 19 USC §2253(a)(2).
[71] 19 USC §2253(a)(3)(i).
[72] Communication from the United States (3 March 1988) GATT Doc MTN.GNG/NG9/W/13, 1. Note also the presumption of consistency with Art. XIX.
[73] Uruguay Round Agreements Act Statement of Administrative Action, HR Doc 103-316. Note similar references in more recent Statements: United States–Korea Free Trade Agreement Implementation Act, Statement of Administrative Action, HR Doc 3080, 23.

structural adjustment: '*Recognizing* the importance of structural adjustment and the need to enhance rather than limit competition in international markets.' The remaining references are in Arts 5.1, 7.1, and 7.4. Article 7 is concerned with the duration of safeguard measures and uses structural adjustment as one of the motivations for the use of safeguards. They are to be applied only so long as is necessary to either 'prevent or remedy serious injury and to facilitate adjustment'.[74] As specific time-frames are then included, this provision, like the preamble, appears to provide a context for their use rather than a specific obligation.

Article 5.1 is, on its face, more demanding as it states that a 'Member shall apply safeguard measures only to the extent necessary to prevent or remedy serious injury and to facilitate adjustment'. The panel in the *Korea–Dairy* case, however, was not convinced.[75] It held:

> We wish to make it clear that we do not interpret Article 5.1 as requiring the consideration of an adjustment plan by the authorities, as the European Communities asserts. The Panel finds no specific requirement that an adjustment plan as such must be requested and considered in the text of the Agreement on Safeguards. Although there are references to industry adjustment in two of its provisions, [Arts 5 and 7] nothing in the text of the Agreement on Safeguards suggests that consideration of a specific adjustment plan is required before a measure can be adopted. Rather, we believe that the question of adjustment, along with the question of preventing or remedying serious injury, must be a part of the authorities' reasoned explanation of the measure it has chosen to apply. Nonetheless, we note that examination of an adjustment plan, within the context of the application of a safeguard measure, would be strong evidence that the authorities considered whether the measure was commensurate with the objective of preventing or remedying serious injury and facilitating adjustment.[76]

While developing countries pushed for structural adjustment to be included as a requirement in the Agreement on Safeguards during the Uruguay Round,[77] the US was unhappy with its inclusion as a formal requirement.[78] Given that US law already requires that a plan for adjustment be presented at the same time as a petition for relief, it might seem odd that it would not push for an internationalized version of this commitment.[79]

When safeguards are examined through the lens of competing values (the belief in economic gains through liberalization and outcome-based fairness), US reticence becomes representative of an understanding that though values can be projected, there still remains scope for differing interpretations. In the US, structural adjustment plans are arranged by industry in the first instance as it demonstrates

[74] Article 7.1 AoS.

[75] *Korea—Definitive Safeguard Measure on Imports of Certain Dairy Products*, Panel Report (21 June 1999) WT/DS98/R ('*Korea–Dairy Panel*').

[76] *Korea–Dairy Panel*, para. 7.103.

[77] Brazil in particular, Communication from Brazil, (25 May 1987) GATT Doc MTN.GNG/NG9/W/3. The 1990 Draft of the Agreement on Safeguards contained Art. 15 permitting the use of adjustment assistance in lieu of border measures. This provision did not survive to the final version, however. (Negotiating Group on Safeguards, 'Draft Text by Chairman' (31 October 1990) GATT Doc MTN.GNG/NG9/W/25/Rev.3.)

[78] T Stewart, *The GATT Uruguay Round*, n. 57, 1775.

[79] 19 USC §2252(a)(2)(a).

how it plans to adapt to changing conditions, either by enhancing competitiveness or by orderly contraction. The underlying values of the US system, such as a desire for the free action of companies and a generalized dislike of government intervention ensures that structural adjustment serves as a tool to provide long-term solutions to industry.[80] Where a member takes a separate view, inclined more toward government intervention or dirigisme, structural adjustment could be guided by governmental advice or direction. Though structural adjustment would still be part of the process for enacting safeguard measures, the role of government would be central—something contrary to the policy of the US in the rest of its negotiations on the Agreement on Safeguards. From its position, it could well be that requirements for structural adjustment programmes might risk encouraging other members to prioritize governmental action over market-driven adjustments.

D. Legal Change and Unexpected Outcomes

The previous section outlined two clear projections by the US of its own understanding of the proper definition of safeguard measures. The focus has so far been on the largely domestic origins of the international obligations on safeguard measures, and particularly the internal US disputes that encouraged policy direction at the GATT/WTO. The subsequent instrumental use of US domestic law as a model for Art. XIX, and then later, the Agreement on Safeguards would encourage us to think that US aims were achieved.

This has not been the case, however. As identified before, the interplay between causal influences is complex, and accounts based on one (here instrumental) are incomplete. In this case, US law and the international regime for safeguards have either diverged (over the GATT years) or come into open conflict (in the case of the WTO Agreement on Safeguards).

The following sections study the behaviour of the US in responding to the consequences of these divergences as a way of understanding the development of safeguard measures. While the US was successful in using its own model of law for the international safeguard regime, it failed to synchronize its own law and the applicable international regime. During the GATT years a notable divergence took place, while since 1995 the US has yet to successfully defend the legality of a safeguard measure before the Appellate Body.

The reasons behind these divergences are distinct in each period (the GATT years and the WTO era). However, the constitutive and systemic influences of the institutions of the dispute settlement system in interpreting the meaning of Art. XIX and the Agreement on Safeguards were important in both. By helping to mould the adjudicative system of the WTO, the US undermined its attempt to embed its norms in the regulation of safeguard measures, going so

[80] See: D Sarooshi, 'Sovereignty', n. 50, 656; Chapter 6.C.

far as to open itself to influence from the international system that it had sought to avoid.

1. The 'unforeseen developments' clause

This section traces the application of a specific clause in Art. XIX GATT, the 'unforeseen developments' clause. The application and interpretation of this clause has been emblematic of the tensions underlying safeguard measures, both within the US system as well as at the GATT/WTO level. The traditional explanations have, however, focussed on instrumental and systemic accounts of how law functions. This section will draw attention to the interplay between these, and the final constitutive influence, to offer an alternative explanation for the surprising development of the law in this area.

a. The origins and rationale of the 'unforeseen developments' clause

Article XIX:1(a) GATT reads:

> If, *as a result of unforeseen developments and of the effect of the obligations incurred* by a contracting party under this Agreement, including tariff concessions, any product is being imported into the territory of that contracting party in such increased quantities and under such conditions as to cause or threaten serious injury to domestic producers in that territory of like or directly competitive products, the contracting party shall be free, in respect of such product, and to the extent and for such time as may be necessary to prevent or remedy such injury, to suspend the obligation in whole or in part or to withdraw or modify the concession.[81]

The 'unforeseen developments' clause is central as it represents the element of uncertainty for which Art. XIX was the insurance. This clause serves two key purposes: first, in the context of the original GATT negotiations, it provided a safety net for States entering into unprecedented tariff reductions where the results of certain concessions may not have been possible to calculate accurately; second, the unforeseen developments clause serves to guide the calculation for an increase in imports. Under Art. XIX, a requirement for the invocation of a safeguard measure is an increase of imports. This raises the question of how the increase is to be calculated. What point in time should be used as the starting point for the increase in imports? The 'unforeseen developments' clause requires that the increase in imports be both the result of unforeseen developments but also 'of the obligations incurred' under the GATT. This suggests using the most recent tariff binding as the point from which to increase the import surge.[82] If this clause is ignored, however, there is no clear point from which to calculate.[83] Yet,

[81] Article XIX GATT (emphasis added).

[82] Confirmed in *Argentina—Safeguard Measures on Imports of Footwear*, Report of the Appellate Body (14 December 1999) WT/DS121/AB/R ('Argentina–Footwear Appellate Body') para. 91.

[83] A Sykes, 'The Safeguards Mess: A Critique of WTO Jurisprudence', (2003) 2(3) *World Trade Review* 261, 266.

despite having a clear place in the agreement[84] as well as an important purpose, the very application of the unforeseen developments clause has been the subject of considerable debate.[85]

As discussed, the inclusion of the 'unforeseen developments' criterion has its origins in the United States—Mexico Reciprocal Trade Agreement of 1942, while a subsequent Executive Order required the inclusion of escape clauses in any trade agreement the US was to enter into, including the GATT.[86]

As a matter of US law, however, the escape clause was altered. The Trade Agreements Extension Act 1951 removed the 'unforeseen developments' requirement from the domestic requirements for a positive determination by the Tariff Commission in response to the perception that it was too difficult to obtain relief.[87] It has not been part of the criteria under US law since. Similarly, neither the EU's current regulations,[88] nor those prior to the entry into force of the Agreement on Safeguards required 'unforeseen developments' as a cause of an increase in imports.[89]

1951 was not only the year the 'unforeseen developments' clause was removed from US legislation but was also the year it came before a GATT Working Group. This case was an important indicator of the problems facing the GATT system: its diplomatic approach to the dispute at hand. This case also foreshadowed a problem with crystallizing norms in treaty provisions: the divergence arising from a change in the domestic provision while the international rule stayed the same.

b. The Hatters' Fur *case: A brief overview*

The *Hatters' Fur* case[90] is the only dispute arising from the GATT system over the meaning and scope of the 'unforeseen developments' clause. *Hatters' Fur* arose from the grant of concessions by the US on certain types of women's fur felt hats. Following a change in the fashion, imports into the US from Czechoslovakia

[84] It is an established rule of international law that a treaty should be interpreted 'in good faith and in accordance with the ordinary meaning to be given to the terms of the treaty in their context and in light of their object and purpose' (Art. 31(1) VCLT 1969); *United States—Standards for Reformulated and Conventional Gasoline*, Report of the Appellate Body (29 April 1996) WT/DS2/AB/R, 17; *Territorial Dispute Case* (Libyan Arab Jamahiriya/Chad) (Judgment) [1994] ICJ Rep 6, para. 41.

[85] P Mavroidis, *Trade in Goods* (Oxford, Oxford University Press 2007) 366, fn 101.

[86] Executive Order No. 9832.

[87] T Stewart, *The GATT Uruguay Round*, n. 57, 1731. This would appear to be at variance with the position that the further from the 1947 tariff bindings one got, the easier it became to comply with the 'unforeseen developments' criterion; A Sykes, 'The Safeguards Mess', n. 83, 265.

[88] Council Regulation (EC) No 260/2009 [31.3.2009 L84/7]. Council Regulation (EC) No 625/2009 [17.7.2009 L185/1] relates to safeguard measures applied to goods from non-WTO members.

[89] Council Regulation (EEC) No 288/82 of 5 February 1982 on common rules for imports [1982] OJ L35/1 (repealed); Council Regulation (EC) No 3285/94 of 22 December 1994 on the common rules for imports and repealing Regulation (EC) No 518/94 [1994] OJ L349/53 (repealed).

[90] *Hatters' Fur Case*, Report on the Withdrawal by the United States of a Tariff Concession under Art. XIX of the General Agreement on Tariffs and Trade (27 March 1951) CP/106.

increased to such an extent that the US, invoking Art. XIX, withdrew its concessions. The Working Group[91] took the position that:

> ... the term 'unforeseen development' should be interpreted to mean developments occurring after the negotiation of the relevant tariff concession which it would not be reasonable to expect that the negotiators of the country making the concession could and should have foreseen at the time when the concession was negotiated.[92]

The Working Group continued, noting the peculiarities of the fashion industry and its propensity to change.[93] It concluded that changing fashions in and of themselves could not constitute 'unforeseen developments', the implicit reasoning being that it would be reasonable for a negotiator to expect that there would be a change in the circumstances of the industry in the foreseeable future.[94] The issue was therefore, '*the degree to which* the change in fashion affected the competitive situation, could not reasonably be expected to have been foreseen by the United States authorities'.[95]

This sets out a two-stage approach: first, there must be a development which could not reasonably have been foreseen at the time of the concession negotiation, and second, if a development was reasonably foreseeable then it is necessary to examine the extent, gravity, or length of the development. Where beyond the reasonable expectation in the first stage then the development can be termed 'unforeseen'. This raises a host of questions that were to lie dormant until after the entrance into force of the Agreement on Safeguards in 1995. During the intervening years, no other contentious case arose over this provision at the international level.

c. *The* Hatters' Fur *case: Systemic interpretations*

The traditional account of *Hatters' Fur* was that it 'read out' of the GATT the 'unforeseen developments' clause by virtue of its lax interpretation,[96] suggesting that the *Hatters' Fur* report is indicative of 'the fact that this particular clause [i.e. the "unforeseen developments" requirement] is too ambiguous and equivocal to create objective legal criteria'.[97]

However, the *Hatters' Fur* case does not, on the face of it, confirm the inoperability of the 'unforeseen developments' clause. *Hatters' Fur* posits an

[91] The form of dispute settlement used under the GATT (1947–95) was, particularly in the earlier years (that is 1947–78), largely consensual in nature, hence the use of Working Groups rather than panels. On the shift after 1978: R Hudec, 'The New WTO Dispute Settlement Procedure: An Overview of the First Three Years', (1999) 8 *Minnesota Journal of Global Trade* 1, 4.

[92] *Hatters' Fur* case, para. 9.

[93] 'change is the law of fashion', ibid., para. 10.

[94] This is the position taken by the panel in *United States—Safeguard Measures on Imports of Fresh, Chilled or Frozen Lamb Meat from New Zealand and Australia* (16 May 2001) WT/DS177/R, WT/DS178/R, para. 7.24.

[95] Ibid., para. 12 (emphasis added).

[96] J Jackson, *The World Trading System*, n. 61, 187; *Korea—Definitive Safeguard Measure on Imports of Certain Dairy Products*, Panel Report (21 June 1999) WT/DS98/R ('*Korea–Dairy Panel*') p. 171, fn 425; *Argentina–Footwear Panel*, para. 865.

[97] YS Lee, 'Destabilization of the Discipline on Safeguards', (2001) 35(6) *Journal of World Trade* 1241.

examination of what negotiators could reasonably be expected to have foreseen at the time of tariff concessions and an objective determination of the extent of the change.

While it is the case that there was a lack of further use of the 'unforeseen developments' clause in safeguard measures, this is indicative of the general lack of international oversight of safeguard measures due to the limitations of dispute settlement during the GATT years.[98] While this provision of Art. XIX may have had a limited constraining or enabling influence, this was characteristic of the GATT system as a whole: hence the desire to move to a more formal, rule-based system in the WTO era.[99] Further, the opportunities for actors to stimulate a challenge over this provision were limited in the GATT years that saw the dwindling use of safeguard measures over the four decades following *Hatters' Fur*.[100]

This helps to explain the inconsistency between the proposition that the international perception was that a standard interpretation of Art. XIX in *Hatters' Fur* could be so easy as to lead to *de facto* automatic compliance whilst in the US it was felt necessary to remove the requirement from legislation in order to relax the stringent obligations under the Trade Acts.[101]

While the Working Group produced a viable resolution, at the domestic level the influence from groups that desired a greater willingness on the part of the State to protect their industry (or the industry of their constituents) led to a relaxation of the legal requirements for an affirmative petition, thus channelling their aims through legislative amendment. However, the Tariff Commission applied the domestic legislation so strictly that the possibility of negative GATT determinations was of secondary concern: if a claim survived the US petitioning procedure, it was likely to survive GATT scrutiny.[102]

The groups that had desired a greater degree of protection through safeguard measures were not successful, however; the US International Trade Commission (the Tariff Commission's successor) still applied strict standards and as the President could negotiate his own Voluntary Export Restraints with trading partners. VERs are 'gentleman's agreements' that restrict imports but escape domestic and international scrutiny by virtue of their informal nature with trading partners.[103] As a result, VERs were often used as a 'second-best' solution.[104] Thus, Art. XIX was not subject to further controversy, not because of any change in the line of

[98] n. 91. [99] J Jackson, *The World Trading System*, n. 61, 109ff.

[100] Compare twenty-four Art. XIX measures in force in 1991 to 284 Voluntary Export Restraints which serve the same purpose: T Stewart, *The GATT Uruguay Round*, n. 57, 1726.

[101] n. 57. [102] n. 62 and corresponding text.

[103] Discussed further in Section E.

[104] Between 1943 and 1951 only one petition was found to merit safeguard relief by the Tariff Commission (T Stewart, *The GATT Uruguay Round*, n. 57, 1731), from 1951–58 ten industries out of eighty-seven petitions received protection (1732), three out of twenty-eight petitions were successful under the 1962 Trade Expansion Act (1736), nineteen industries received some sort of relief out of sixty-two petitions under the Trade Act of 1974 (1737), with the 1988 Omnibus Trade and Competitiveness Act still setting the requirements for successful petitions particularly high (1738).

jurisprudence at the GATT but because domestic legal systems, especially that of the US, did not give rise to such a claim.

Another argument put forward for the decline in the use of the 'unforeseen developments' clause is that it was designed specifically for the unique circumstances surrounding the GATT, but that as the years passed and subsequent rounds were completed, this clause no longer became applicable in any meaningful way.[105] This does not explain, however, the existence of a comparable clause in the previous US–Mexico Reciprocal Trade Agreement 1942 where, while concessions were made, the reduction of tariffs was not as dramatic as that in the first GATT round.[106]

The traditional view of the *Hatters' Fur* case was influential and when the new Agreement on Safeguards came into force the general view was that the 'unforeseen developments' clause was not legally operative.[107] This assumption, based on a *post hoc* rationalization of *Hatters' Fur* ignored the instrumental influences from US actors and did not take into account the innovations of the new WTO agreements and their constitutive influence on safeguards law.

The limitation that the US found in its first attempt to embed norms in an international agreement was, in part, corrected by the US's (likely unintentionally) influence in undermining the 'unforeseen developments' clause. As many States did not yet have developed safeguard systems, the US's served as an influential model. The GATT Contracting Parties began to treat the 'unforeseen developments' clause as if it were not there, following their domestic practice in removing it from the legal requirements of the implementation of a safeguard measure.[108]

The first attempt by the US to set its preferences within the international regime appeared to have had a limited success; safeguards were not largely used and where they were, they mimicked the US's own domestic requirements rather than Art. XIX. While the US was a key player in undermining the use of Art. XIX, its motivation was routed in the divergence between its own law and the GATT system. Internationally safeguard measures were barely regulated, permitting States to apply a range of interpretations of how safeguards should be used. Yet, within the US, a successful petition under the ss 201–4 system was particularly difficult.[109]

[105] A Sykes, 'The Persistent Puzzles of Safeguards: Lessons from the Steel Dispute', (2004) 7(3) *Journal of International Economic Law* 523, 528.

[106] 1947 saw '45,000 tariff concessions affecting $10 billion of trade' <http://www.wto.org/English/thewto_e/whatis_e/tif_e/fact4_e.htm> (accessed 13 February 2015).

[107] Either as a result of its drafting and subsequent interpretation, n. 97, or as part of a conscious bargain: M Bronckers, 'Nondiscrimination in the World Trade Organization Safeguards Agreement: A European Perspective', in K Bagwell, G Bermann, and P Mavroidis (eds), *Law and Economics of Contingent Protection in International Trade* (Cambridge, Cambridge University Press 2014), 369, fn 15.

[108] While Japanese law included the 'unforeseen developments' clause, Japan did not, in fact, initiate any safeguard investigations or subsequent measures until the WTO era; N Komuro, 'Japan's Safeguard Law and Practice', (2001) 35(5) *Journal of World Trade* 851.

[109] n. 104.

The negotiations over an Agreement on Safeguards as part of the Uruguay Round offered a new opportunity. The new WTO system was not going to be hobbled by a weak dispute settlement system, and from the US's perspective, the domestic model for the WTO Agreement on Safeguards was relatively stable, having not been substantively amended since 1988.[110] The dual failures of a change in domestic legislation leading to divergence and a failure of international oversight appeared to have been resolved.

Though the US succeeded in embedding its normative preferences in the Agreement on Safeguards, it failed to take into account the consequences of other achievements during the Uruguay Round: in this instance, the Dispute Settlement Understanding and its effects in both constituting and constraining the panels and Appellate Body.

2. The 'unforeseen developments' clause in the WTO era: Instrumental expectations

The Agreement on Safeguards marked one of the great successes of the Uruguay Round. A clear rule-set to deal with safeguards and bring them back into the multilateral fold had been a priority for some time.[111] Failure to address this had been one of the great disappointments of the Tokyo Round. The WTO Agreement on Safeguards achieved a great deal: a clearer set of rules for the use of safeguards, prohibition of 'grey-area' measures (and providing a limited life span for those existing at the time), and more besides. This led to an increase in the use of safeguard measures by members and a rekindling in the interest of their application and the legal disciplines to be applied.

While the US had once again succeeded in using its legislation as the model, it was to suffer a series of defeats at the Appellate Body. Contrary to the vocal criticism of the Appellate Body's interpretation of the Agreement on Safeguards and Art. XIX,[112] it is argued that a better explanation of these decisions lies not in the incompetence or empire-building of the Appellate Body but rather as a consequence of the complex multi-causal influences at play, specifically through the creation of the new dispute settlement system.[113]

[110] Omnibus Trade and Competitiveness Act 1988 [Pub L 100-418, 102 Stat 1107].

[111] Preamble to the Agreement on Safeguards: 'Recognizing the need to clarify and reinforce the disciplines of GATT 1994, and specifically those of its Article XIX (Emergency Action on Imports of Particular Products), to re-establish multilateral control over safeguards and eliminate measures that escape such control.'

[112] A 'series of wooden, largely useless and often logically incoherent decisions that simply underscore the deficiencies of the treaty text without clarifying them in the least'. A Sykes, 'The Fundamental Deficiencies of the Agreement on Safeguards: A Reply to Professor Lee', (2006) 40(5) *Journal of World Trade* 979, 993.

[113] Amongst the debates see: Y-S Lee, 'Not Without a Clue: Commentary on "the Persistent Puzzles of Safeguards"', (2006) 40 *Journal of World Trade* 385; J Greenwald, 'WTO Dispute Settlement: An Exercise in Trade Law Legislation?', (2003) 6(1) *Journal of International Economic Law* 113; A Sykes, 'The Persistent Puzzles of Safeguards: Lessons from the Steel Dispute', (2004) 7(3) *Journal of International Economic Law* 523; P Rosenthal and J Beckington, 'Dispute Settlement Before the World Trade Organization in Antidumping, Countervailing and Safeguard

Though the US succeeded in using its domestic safeguards law as the model for Art. 2.1 Agreement on Safeguards, it failed to anticipate the consequences of a separate though parallel projection: embedding certain values in the institutional workings of the new dispute settlement system. The new DSU and its attendant methodology are central in understanding the position taken by the Appellate Body in the *Korea–Dairy* and the *Argentina–Footwear* reports. This has had a lasting impact on the review of safeguard determinations at the WTO level with numerous negative determinations passed on the legality of safeguard measures since and none surviving Appellate Body scrutiny.

a. *The Agreement on Safeguards and the 'unforeseen developments' clause*

Article 2.1 Agreement on Safeguards sets out the conditions for the use of safeguards as follows:

> A Member may apply a safeguard measure to a product only if that Member has determined, pursuant to the provisions set out below, that such product is being imported into its territory in such increased quantities, absolute or relative to domestic production, and under such conditions as to cause or threaten to cause serious injury to the domestic industry that produces like or directly competitive products.

Largely modelled on s. 201 Trade Act 1974, it replicated the lack of 'unforeseen developments' or 'obligations incurred' requirements.

The difference between the wording of Art. XIX and Art. 2.1 Agreement on Safeguards arose during two separate disputes raised by the EU against Korea and Argentina. Amongst the claims of the EU was that the investigating authorities in Korea and Argentina had not fulfilled their obligations under Art. XIX by showing that the increase in imports was a result of 'unforeseen developments'. The respondents' claims can be divided into three separate threads.

First, it was argued that the Agreement on Safeguards contained the full set of disciplines relating to the use of such measures and compliance with it thus fulfilled the requirements under the GATT.[114] Second, that where a conflict exists between the GATT and the Agreement on Safeguards, it is to be resolved in favour of the Agreement, as per the Interpretative Note to the WTO Agreement.[115] Third, engaging with the possibility of the validity of the 'unforeseen developments' clause, that the increase in imports could not have been foreseen.[116] The EU, for its part, submitted that the obligations under the covered agreements were part of a 'single undertaking' and as such were cumulative in nature. The entirety

Actions: Effective Interpretation or Unauthorized Legislation?', speech delivered at a conference presented by the Trade and Customs Law Committee of the International Bar Association, 'Developments in WTO Law', Geneva, Switzerland, 20 and 21 March 2003, 1. Note the balanced position taken in F Mueller, 'Is the General Agreement on Tariffs and Trade Article XIX "Unforeseen Developments Clause" Still Effective Under the Agreement on Safeguards?', (2003) 37(6) *Journal of World Trade* 1119.

[114] *Korea—Definitive Safeguard Measure on Imports of Certain Dairy Products*, Panel Report (21 June 1999) WT/DS98/R (*'Korea –Dairy Panel'*), para. 7.33.

[115] WTO Agreement Annex 1a.

[116] *Argentina–Footwear Panel*, para. 848.

of both Art. XIX and the Agreement were to be applied.[117] In the context of the Argentinean case, the EU also pointed out that as Argentina had pursued a conscious policy of liberalization over the period of 1989/1990, an increase in imports could not be 'unforeseen' for the purposes of Art. XIX.[118]

The *Korea–Dairy* panel in this case took an approach in line with academic opinion at the time. It interpreted the text so as to avoid conflict and proceeded to examine the text of Art. XIX:1 'based on the ordinary meaning of the terms',[119] concluding that the 'unforeseen developments' clause did not create any specific obligations but was instead explanatory.[120] The panel elucidated the purpose of Art. XIX in light of the historic commitments made in 1947 and in doing so, cited both the *Hatters' Fur* dispute (confirming its undermining of the 'unforeseen developments' clause) as well as (via Art. XVI:1 of the WTO Agreement) forty-eight years of State practice.[121] It concluded that Art. XIX contained no obligation with reference to the 'unforeseen developments' clause.[122]

The *Argentina–Footwear* panel reasoning was somewhat distinct, citing Art. 11.1(a) of the Agreement on Safeguards which stipulates the requirement to enact safeguard measures in compliance with Art. XIX 'applied in accordance with Agreement [on Safeguards]'.[123] The panel concluded that Art. XIX and the Agreement on Safeguards were 'intrinsically linked' and that Art. XIX was to be read in light of the 'subsequently negotiated and much more specific provisions of the Agreement on Safeguards'.[124] The 'unforeseen developments' clause was then read in light of the object and purpose of the Agreement on Safeguards; the Agreement intending (as per its Preamble) to 'clarify and reinforce' the disciplines found in Art. XIX.[125]

The 'unforeseen developments' clause fit into the panel's analysis by virtue of two conceptual exercises. First, it posited that the omission of the 'unforeseen developments' clause in the Agreement on Safeguards was an intentional, express omission. There was no detailed examination of negotiating histories, instead the panel based its position on the speculation of the mind-set of negotiators at the time.[126] Second, a distinction was drawn between the provisions in the Agreement on Safeguards in light of its aim to reassert control over the multilateral system of safeguards; on the one hand the tightening of disciplines (e.g. elimination and restriction of VERs) and on the other hand, the relaxing of disciplines (e.g. flexibility over compensation actions).[127] By making the omission of the 'unforeseen developments' clause an intentional alteration the panel was free to include it in the latter category. In this manner, the panel could view the omission of the 'unforeseen developments' clause as part of the new provisions in the Agreement on Safeguards designed to make it easier to apply safeguard measures, echoing the motivations in 1951 for the omission of the 'unforeseen developments' requirement under US

[117] *Korea–Dairy Panel*, para. 7.36. [118] *Argentina–Footwear Panel*, para. 847.
[119] *Korea–Dairy Panel*, paras 7.37–7.39. [120] Ibid., para. 7.45.
[121] Ibid., p. 171 fn 425, and para. 7.46. [122] Ibid., para. 7.48.
[123] Article 11.1(a) Agreement on Safeguards.
[124] *Argentina–Footwear Panel*, para. 8.56. [125] Ibid., para. 8.62.
[126] Ibid., para. 8.65. [127] Ibid., para. 8.63.

law.[128] While paying lip-service to the limits on adding to or diminishing rights or obligations under the covered agreements[129] it still concluded that 'conformity with the explicit requirements and conditions embodied in the Agreement on Safeguards must be sufficient for the application of safeguard measures within the meaning of Article XIX of GATT'.[130]

b. The influence of the DSU and its attendant methodology

The appeal of the *Korea–Dairy* and *Argentina–Footwear* reports to the Appellate Body gave it the opportunity to demonstrate the ideational shift that took place in 1995. In doing so, the Appellate Body opened itself to criticism as it sought to enhance its own legitimacy. The Appellate Body has been criticized for these reports, especially on the application of the 'unforeseen developments' clause.[131] Yet the object here is not to question the validity of the legal reasoning in the reports themselves on this point, but rather to understand why and what this says about how the Appellate Body sought to develop the law on this point.

The Appellate Body's response to these disputes was released almost simultaneously and the relevant passages were essentially the same. In particular, it took issue with the panels' approach by stressing the need to give meaning and effect to all provisions in the text[132] and reversed the panels' findings that the 'unforeseen developments' clause created no legal obligation.[133] The Appellate Body also took the opportunity to clarify the aim of this interpretation; that is, in line with the object and purpose of the Agreement on Safeguards, to reassert control over the multilateral disciplines on safeguards.[134] This is useful in clarifying the position of the 'unforeseen developments' clause during the intervening years. By stressing the need to reassert control over the safeguard system the clear implication is not that the 'unforeseen developments' clause had been legally inoperative but instead that a suitable enforcement method was lacking.[135]

[128] It is unfortunate that the panel did not provide further detail as the assumption may well have been correct: M Bronckers, 'Nondiscrimination in the World Trade Organization Safeguards Agreement: A European Perspective', n. 107, 369: 'some people, including myself, thought that part of this grand bargain was that the "unforeseen developments" requirement of Article XIX had been dropped'.

[129] A requirement under Art. 3.2 DSU.

[130] *Argentina–Footwear Panel*, para. 8.67.

[131] A 'legal error' in the view of Mavroidis, *Trade in Goods* (2nd edn, Oxford, Oxford University Press 2013) 623 fn. 29.

[132] *Korea—Definitive Safeguard Measure on Imports of Certain Dairy Products*, Report of the Appellate Body (14 December 1999) WT/DS98/AB/R ('*Korea–Dairy Appellate Body*') para. 82

[133] Ibid. [134] Ibid., para. 88

[135] The lack of a non-State enforcer of the covered agreements, such as the Commission in the EU results in a lack of disputes in areas where many States have potentially violated the WTO rules (the 'glass house' problem). See C Zimmermann, 'Rethinking the Right to Initiate WTO Dispute Settlement Proceedings', (2011) 45(5) *Journal of World Trade* 1057.

The traditional view that the *Hatters' Fur* dispute interpreted the 'unforeseen developments' clause in such a lax way so as to, *de facto*, remove it from the text is an approach based on the examination of only one side of the picture. It is, by itself, an unsatisfactory position as it fails to explain *how* this has happened when the text of the report is far from being so clear. Not only does the text of *Hatters' Fur* not support such a dismissive application but even if it were to, it need not extinguish the legal requirements, no matter how easy compliance may be. States do not ignore making claims because they suspect that the other side has likely satisfied the requirements, and dispute settlement bodies cannot skip over required steps by assuming that the respondent has complied.

Instead, the reason for this period of non-application stems from the practice of the members and the systemic influence on their actions of their own domestic law. By removing the 'unforeseen developments' requirement from US law (the most developed 'escape clause' action system at the time) it set a precedent for others to follow. The strict domestic interpretation of these requirements by quasi-judicial bodies such as the USITC and the lack of willingness on the part of the executive (in the US system) resulted in a situation where claims simply did not arise, as they failed to encourage the use of a safeguard. This was not, however, due to the elimination of the 'unforeseen developments' clause as a matter of international law.

Conversely, the 'reintroduction' of the 'unforeseen developments' requirement following the Appellate Body's decisions in *Korea–Dairy* and *Argentina–Footwear* is a result of the new legal settlement at the WTO, in particular the DSU's constitutive and systemic influence on the Appellate Body: constitutive, in that it required a textual approach to interpretation by the Appellate Body as a keystone of its institutional legitimacy and systemic in that it was constrained by the binding nature of the WTO obligations at hand (in this instance, Art. 3.2 DSU).

The result of the domestic (predominately US) influence on a strictly limited scope of action for the WTO dispute settlement system and its textual focus has led to an inability to ignore a textual provision by interpreting it away. Criticisms of the Appellate Body's position in these cases, arguing that too rigorous an application of Art. XIX and the Agreement on Safeguards undermines the 'safety valve' purpose of the provisions,[136] miss the broader imperatives that drive the Appellate Body. This is its concern with prioritizing its own legitimacy. Highlighting the Appellate Body's focus on a 'textual' approach (even where considerably more complex) to maintain its legitimacy, Weiler argues:

> On the whole the legitimation strategy practised by the Appellate Body (whether express or implicit) has been one of hermeneutic prudence and institutional modesty with a keen eye on balancing internal and external legitimacy. The almost obsessive attempts of the

[136] A Sykes, 'The "Safeguards Mess" Revisited—A Reply to Professor Jones', (2004) 3(1) *World Trade Review* 93, 95–6.

Appellate Body to characterize wherever possible the normal wide-ranging, sophisticated, multifaceted and eminently legitimate interpretations of the Agreement as 'textual' resulting from the ordinary meaning of words is another manifestation of the internal-external legitimacy paradigm.[137]

Such interpretative responses are a shield against vocal opposition.[138] For the time being, a dispute settlement system that seeks to legitimize itself appears to be more important to the actors involved than the potential effect of strict legal criteria on the use of safeguard measures. Indeed, for all the criticism that the Appellate Body has engaged in 'judicial activism' there are those that hold the view that it has given content to the provisions of the Agreement on Safeguards in line with its purpose.[139]

This is not to argue that the Appellate Body did not reduce or extend the scope of the Agreements but instead stresses its need to justify such an act to its constituents. For example, the position taken by the Appellate Body that safeguard measures ought to be extraordinary measures has been described as 'an exercise in policy-making' rather than 'even-handed interpretation'.[140] The Appellate Body justifies its position by grounding its statement in the text of Art. 11.1(a) of the Agreement on Safeguards and the title of Art. XIX GATT which specifically states that safeguard measures are to be emergency actions. 'Thus, Article XIX is clearly, and in every way, an extraordinary remedy.'[141] Indeed, to criticize the Appellate Body in this instance for 'policy-making' is to hold the view that there is a clear identifiable rule that can be applied mechanically: it is a systemic understanding of law as a body of rules rather than as a process subject to the behaviour of different actors pursuing different goals.

If our concern is to understand why the law has developed as it has done, whether or not the Appellate Body engages in 'policy-making' is less important than the issue of how dispute settlement bodies behave in light of the constitutive influence of the DSU. The behaviour of the panels and Appellate Body is influenced by the norms embedded in the DSU that in turn has to be examined in light of the objectives of a number of globalized actors, including the dispute settlement bodies themselves.

In the field of safeguard measures it would appear that the US has enjoyed limited success in embedding norms at the international level. The consequences of the attempt to develop GATT and then WTO law in its favour extend beyond

[137] JHH Weiler, 'The Rule of Lawyers and the Ethos of Diplomats: Reflections on the Internal and External Legitimacy of WTO Dispute Settlement', (2001) 35(2) *Journal of World Trade* 206.

[138] For an overview of the typical concerns: I Fergusson and L Sek, 'World Trade Organization: Issues in the Debate on US Participation', CRS Report for Congress, Order Code RL32918, updated on 9 June 2005.

[139] D McRae, 'What is the Future of WTO Dispute Settlement', (2004) 7(1) *Journal of International Economic Law* 3, 6.

[140] J Greenwald, 'WTO Dispute Settlement: An Exercise in Trade Legislation?', (2003) 6 *Journal of International Economic Law* 113.

[141] *Argentina—Safeguard Measures on Imports of Footwear*, Report of the Appellate Body (14 December 1999) WT/DS121/AB/R, paras 93–4.

the international plane. As is clear, the regulation of safeguard measures takes place at both domestic and international levels, and the relationship between them is continuous.

The next section outlines how the systemic influence of the dispute settlement system has encouraged the US to change its own administrative practices in light of developing WTO law. Identifying the impact that the development on safeguards law has at the domestic level is important for two reasons: first, it stresses the mutually constitutive and bi-directional causal relationship between domestic and international law, especially at the WTO which is inherently transjurisdictional as a site of globalized legal development; second (and the focus of Section 4), the change in domestic practice also has a role to play in understanding the continuing development of the legal regulation of safeguard measures and the resort to other (perhaps non-compliant) agreements to control imports.

3. The alteration of practice in the US's administrative bodies

In the US, as is the case with most members, administrative bodies are given considerable responsibilities for governing the internal application of WTO rules. In the US this is primarily the competence of the Department of Commerce ('DoC') and the USITC. However, while the US has attempted to insulate itself, international pressures still invariably influence its domestic practice.[142]

If we continue to trace the application of the 'unforeseen developments' clause following the 1999 Appellate Body reports in *Korea–Dairy* and *Argentina–Footwear*, we see how the US found its own safeguard investigations challenged (*inter alia*) on the basis that there had been no 'unforeseen developments' analysis.

In the 2000 *US–Wheat Gluten* dispute, the US claimed that it was not required to conduct a separate investigation into whether or not the safeguard measures it imposed on EU products was a response to an increase in imports that resulted from 'unforeseen developments'.[143] Perhaps unsurprisingly, the Appellate Body did not agree and ruled against the US. The following year, in *US–Lamb,* the US argued that there was no requirement in the USITC report to include a separate section or conclusion on the existence of 'unforeseen developments'[144] claiming that the requirement was met where the existence of 'unforeseen developments' could be inferred from the factual evidence in the

[142] Section 102(a) Uruguay Round Agreements Act of 1994 [Pub L 103-465, 108 Stat 4809]. See P Reed, 'Relationship of WTO Obligations to US International Trade Law: Internationalist Vision Meets Domestic Reality', (2006) 38 *Georgetown Journal of International Law* 209; J Jackson, 'Status of Treaties in Domestic Legal Systems: A Policy Analysis', (1992) 86(2) *American Journal of International Law* 310.

[143] *United States—Definitive Safeguard Measures on Imports of Wheat Gluten from the EC*, Report of the Appellate Body (22 December 2000) WT/DS166/AB/R ('*US–Wheat Gluten*') para. 37.

[144] *United States—Safeguard Measures on Imports of Fresh, Chilled or Frozen Lamb Meat From New Zealand and Australia*, Report of the Appellate Body (1 May 2001) WT/DS177-178/AB/R ('*US–Lamb*') para. 13.

report.[145] As the Appellate Body noted, the position taken by the US may have been influenced by the fact that the USITC report was published before the Appellate Body had released its *Korea–Dairy* and *Argentina–Footwear* reports. Nonetheless, it found against the US.

However, in the *US–Steel* dispute,[146] prior to introducing safeguard measures on steel products the USTR requested that the USITC produce a report on whether the increase in imports was the result of 'unforeseen developments'.[147] As was made clear during the ensuing litigation, the USITC was not required as a matter of domestic law to take such an analysis and yet a report was requested to ensure WTO compliance. The issues that arose in the *US–Steel* case was not the lack of a proper report (as in *US–Wheat Gluten* and *US–Lamb*) but the level of analysis that the USITC undertook.[148]

While the US accepts that 'it is no longer of the view that it is unnecessary to demonstrate the existence of unforeseen developments',[149] given US restrictions on the applicability of WTO obligations, one must assume that this refers to an obligation existing under international law and not domestic law.[150] However, the costs of not adapting to the newly enforced requirements at the international level pressure the State into complying and changing its procedures when possible, irrespective of its own view on the binding nature or otherwise of international obligations. Whether or not, in the case of US practice, this application of the unforeseen developments requirement will become codified in US legislation or become administrative practice is unclear, though the trend appears to be toward an acceptance of the international obligation, as evidenced in the recent US safeguard cases, indicating the strong systemic influence of the WTO dispute settlement system.[151]

In spite of the supposed 'reading out' of Art. XIX from the GATT, safeguards have not disappeared from use. What is the case, is that they are not frequently used, certainly not as frequent as AD/CVDs or indeed the more recently fashionable form of protection: local content requirements.[152]

As the next section shows, however, this reticence to use safeguards, or at least the lack of Appellate Body involvement, does not the stop the law on safeguard measures from developing. As actors continue to mould the use of safeguards in a way that coincides with their interests, they stimulate the development of WTO law. The consequence of the Appellate Body's interpretative method in restricting the freedom to apply safeguard measures has led members to avoid scrutiny

[145] Ibid., para. 67.

[146] *United States—Definitive Safeguard Measures on Imports of Certain Steel Products*, Report of the Appellate Body (10 November 2003) WT/DS248-259/AB/R ('*US–Steel*').

[147] Ibid., para. 12. [148] Ibid., para. 330.

[149] *US–Lamb*, n. 144, fn 40. [150] n. 142.

[151] Note that the requirements to alter administrative practice are lesser than legislative amendment under the URAA system. See 19 USC § 3533(g).

[152] Raising concern over the use of local content requirements: T Cottier, 'The Common Law of International Trade and the Future of the World Trade Organization', (2015) 18(1) *Journal of International Economic Law* 3, 4.

through the WTO dispute settlement system and seek other avenues for import surge protection.

E. The Continuing Development of Safeguards Regulation at the WTO

Throughout the development of the legal regime for safeguard measures, 'grey-area' measures have been present.[153] Rather than viewing 'grey-area' measures as a threatening alternative to safeguard measures the view here is instead to view them as part of the wider picture of safeguards regulation. The value contestations that were identified earlier are continual, and do not depend on the narrow application of one specific measure. Instead, the fluid process of legal development results in continued engagement with instruments that serve the purposes of actors.

Thus, contrary to the customary view of 'grey area' measures as rising during the GATT years and falling under the Agreement on Safeguards, the picture is more nuanced. Rather than historical artefacts, 'grey-area' measures are part of the legal landscape of safeguards. Similarly, while the interpretations of the Appellate Body have been blamed for reading safeguards out of the WTO, in practice the legal regulation of safeguards continues to develop. Away from the narrow confines of the WTO dispute settlement system, the desire for the protection that safeguards offer has altered the practice of members and the institutions of the WTO.[154] This section examines four areas in which the legal activity in safeguard measures has continued: mutually agreed solutions which seek to control imports, bilateral commodity agreements, gentlemen's agreements over gold sales, and changes in dispute settlement practice.

1. A new generation of voluntary export restraints?

We have identified the concern that the Appellate Body has applied the Agreement on Safeguards too strictly, or at least, inconsistently.[155] It has found each safeguard measure before it in violation of the Agreement on Safeguards and/or Art. XIX GATT.[156] If it is felt that there is a systemic bias against safeguard measures,

[153] EM Hizon, 'The Safeguard Measure/VER Dilemma: The Jekyll and Hyde of Trade Protection', (1994–95) 15 *Northwestern Journal of International Law & Business* 105, 107.

[154] Both as a matter of formal law under Art. 31(3)(b) Vienna Convention on the Law of Treaties 1969 (23 May 1969) 1155 UNTS 331, and Art. 2(1)(j) Vienna Convention on the Law of Treaties between States and International Organizations or between International Organizations (1986) 25 ILM 54, and more generally.

[155] A Sykes, 'The Safeguards Mess: A Critique of WTO Jurisprudence', n. 195, 262; K Jones, 'The Safeguards Mess Revisited: the Fundamental Problem', (2004) 3 *World Trade Review* 83, 86; Y-S Lee, 'Destabilization of the Discipline on Safeguards', n. 199, 1245.

[156] *Korea–Dairy Appellate Body, Argentina–Footwear Appellate Body, US–Steel, United States—Definitive Safeguard Measures on Imports of Circular Wielded Carbon Quality Line Pipe From Korea*, Report of the Appellate Body (15 February 2002) WT/DS202/AB/R, *US–Lamb*, and *US–Wheat Gluten*.

members may feel that there is no point in using them. At the same time, the influence of panel and Appellate Body reports on the administrative procedures of the membership may in turn restrict their application where it is felt that the rules are stringent, if unclear. If even more requirements are imposed as a result of negative determinations at the WTO level (such as the requirement of a specific 'unforeseen developments' determination), domestic petitioning procedures are less likely to grant relief. The 'unforeseen developments' clause was just one example of a number of requirements required by the Appellate Body. The need to demonstrate the causal relationship between the 'unforeseen developments' and the increase in imports, as well as other tests have reduced the appeal of using Art. XIX compliant measures.[157]

However, by examining the regulation of safeguard measures as part of a globalized legal process driven by various causal influences, we can see how the restrictive scope for their introduction has encouraged members to pursue other forms of import control. In light of these restrictions, actors have continued to pursue their objectives through other means which in turn alters the WTO system over time. In this way law responds to these pressure as practice changes.

'Grey area' measures are a key part of this discussion. While the Agreement on Safeguards claimed to eliminate them, the results are less clear. Indeed, even early on in the WTO's life, the question of whether 'grey area' measures might still be introduced was live. At the Safeguards Committee, the EU asked the US directly how it squared the provisions of the Trade Act 1974 that permit the negotiation of 'grey area' measures with the prohibition of such agreements under the Agreement on Safeguards.[158] The US responded cautiously, claiming:

> Article 11:1(b) does not prohibit agreements, but rather prohibits so-called grey area and other measures not taken in conformity with the provisions of Article XIX and in accordance with the Agreement (e.g., not based on a serious injury determination). Indeed, Article 5:2 specifically authorizes a Member applying restrictions 'to seek agreement with respect to the allocation of shares in the quota with all other members having a substantial interest in supplying the product concerned.' Moreover, Article 11:1(b) itself specifically provides, in a footnote that: 'An import quota applied as a safeguard measure in conformity with the relevant provisions of GATT 1994 and the Agreement may, by mutual agreement, be administered by the exporting Member.'

Thus, the mere negotiation of limits is not per se a violation of Art. 11. Under US safeguard law, the President may negotiate agreements only after receiving a report from the ITC containing an affirmative injury determination. Any agreement negotiated would comply with all requirements and limitations contained in the Safeguards Agreement.[159]

[157] See the concerns in A Sykes, 'The Safeguards Mess', n. 155.

[158] Sections 202(e)(4)(a) and 203(a)(3) Trade Act 1974.

[159] Committee on Safeguards, 'Replies to Questions Posed by the European Communities Concerning the Notification Provided by the United States of Laws and Regulations under Art 12.6 of the Agreement' (23 April 1996) G/SG/W/126, second question.

The US went on to state that while this may be the case, to the best of the reporters' knowledge, no such agreement had been concluded. This is no longer the case (if indeed it ever was) as new 'grey area' measures are concluded.

2. Mutually agreed solutions for the restriction of imports

Mutually Agreed Solutions ('MAS') represent the resolution of a dispute between two members.[160] In many ways they constitute the preferred method of dispute settlement under the DSU: they are negotiated, consensual, and present a lower cost for the WTO community than litigation.[161] For long running disputes which are complicated by entrenched political positions, negotiated settlements may be the only likely long-term resolution available.

One such highly publicized example is the result of the softwood lumber dispute between Canada and the US. Since 1982 the US and Canada have been engaged in numerous legal battles over Canada's subsidization of softwood lumber and the US's response in the form of AD/CVDs. This dispute has played out in domestic, bilateral, regional, and multilateral forums[162] and was the subject of such politicization that the conclusion of the most recent Softwood Lumber Agreement was linked to a vote of confidence in the Canadian Parliament.[163]

In 2006, a MAS was notified to the WTO that included the conclusion of a new Softwood Lumber Agreement ('SLA 2006').[164] The previous Softwood Lumber Agreement (1996) had already been criticized for its inconsistency with the Agreement on Safeguards.[165] Whilst nominally designed to resolve a dispute over anti-dumping duties,[166] the SLA 2006 maintains the principal elements that would classify it as a 'grey area' measure; it is discriminatory as it applies only to softwood lumber from Canada (in violation of Art. 2(2) Agreement on Safeguards), prevents the US from initiating s. 201 investigations (or using other applicable trade defence instruments), and sets out export

[160] See in particular: Arts 1.1, 3.5, 3.6, 3.7, and 4.3 DSU.

[161] W Alschner, 'Amicable Settlements of WTO Disputes: Bilateral Solutions in a Multilateral System', (2014) *World Trade Review* 1, 5.

[162] See: C Charmody, 'International Decisions—Softwood Lumber Dispute (2001–2006)', (2006) 100 *American Journal of International Law* 664; L Guglya, 'The Interplay of International Dispute Resolution Mechanisms: The Softwood Lumber Controversy', (2011) 2(1) *Journal of International Dispute Settlement* 175.

[163] Statement by the Prime Minister on the Softwood Lumber Agreement, 22 August 2006, available at <http://pm.gc.ca/eng/news/2006/08/22/statement-prime-minister-softwood-lumber-agreement> (accessed 15 March 2015).

[164] United States—Final Dumping Determination On Softwood Lumber From Canada, Notification of Mutually Agreed Solution, [2006] WT/DS264/29. The Notification also includes a copy of the SLA 2006.

[165] Y-S Lee, 'Revival of Grey-Area Measures?', (2002) 36(1) *Journal of World Trade* 155.

[166] In this instance: *United States—Final Dumping Determination on Softwood Lumber from Canada—Recourse to Article 21.5 of the DSU by Canada*, Report of the Appellate Body (15 August 2006) WT/DS264/AB/RW.

charges for Canadian lumber exports to the US that go over a set price ($355 USD per thousand board feet).[167] It even includes a 'surge mechanism' to deal with sudden increases in imports to the US: the very situations that safeguard measures are designed to deal with (and in violation of Art. 11(1)(b) Agreement on Safeguards).[168]

The WTO structures do not appear suited to dealing with this type of 'grey area' measure as this agreement was reported to the DSB as part of the MAS to a dispute without opposition. Under the terms of the SLA 2006, neither party may raise a claim under either the WTO or NAFTA but rather settle disputes via arbitration at the London Court of International Arbitration.[169] Unless a third party is inclined to involve itself, it seems unlikely that the dispute settlement procedures within the WTO will be invoked before the termination of the agreement (currently 12 October 2015).[170]

As any MAS to a dispute must still conform to the requirements of the covered agreements,[171] the SLA 2006 has questionable grounds to claim WTO consistency. Indeed, it bears the hallmarks of what has been termed a 'MAS-', an agreement that would otherwise constitute a violation of WTO obligations between two members.[172] The exact legality of such measures is in question, in part dependent on whether one views WTO obligations as multilateral or bilateral: are members able to waive claims for violations of obligations owed to each other, or does the impact of such violations on third parties give them grounds to raise a claim themselves?[173] In either case, it should be noted that even if obligations under the covered agreements are viewed as bilateral in nature, the imposition of import controls on goods between members may nonetheless affect the rights of other members through consequential changes in trade flows.[174]

The increasing use of MAS, in a number of forms, and the attention paid to them may well help to clarify the legal situation over time. Whether such an outcome produces optimal outcomes for those concerned with the functioning of the wider system is an open question.

[167] Articles V, VII, and VIII SLA 2006. [168] Article VIII SLA 2006.

[169] Article XIV SLA 2006. On the legal effect of such a provision: A Alvarez-Jiménez 'Mutually Agreed Solutions under the WTO Dispute Settlement Understanding: An Analytical Framework after the Softwood Lumber Arbitration', (2011) 10(3) *World Trade Review* 343.

[170] Article 1. Agreement between the Government of Canada and the Government of the United States of America Extending the Softwood Lumber Agreement between the Government of Canada and the Government of the United States of America, as Amended, Washington DC (23 January 2012).

[171] Article 3(5) DSU. [172] W Alschner, n. 161, 12.

[173] On this discussion: J Pauwelyn, 'A Typology of Multilateral Treaty Obligations: Are WTO Obligations Bilateral or Collective in Nature?', (2003) 14(5) *European Journal of International Law* 907; C Charmody, 'WTO Obligations as Collective', (2006) 17(2) *European Journal of International Law* 419.

[174] Note the raft of safeguard investigations initiated by members as a result of US safeguards that in turn (allegedly) caused increases in imports in a numerous other markets. For example, Commission Regulation (EC) No 1694/2002 of 27 September 2002 imposing definitive safeguard measures against imports of certain steel products [L261, 28/09/2002 P. 0001–0123].

3. Bilateral commodity agreements

If there is one area where the control of irregular import/export flows is frequently called for, it is in the area of commodities. The effect of volatile prices can have wide-felt repercussions from countries whose primary export is a commodity to those whose industries are dependent on commodities as inputs in the manufacturing process.[175] Most recently, commodity prices have once again drawn attention as within an eight-year period States have gone from facing inflationary pressures from rising prices in energy and food, to economic instability in light of plunging oil prices.[176]

The demand for instruments that are capable of protecting minority groups that are disproportionately affected by price fluctuations has encouraged the conclusion of 'grey area' measures in the form of quasi-commodity agreements, as well as stimulated the call for legal reform of the Agreement on Agriculture.[177]

There exist a number of multilateral commodity agreements, though bilateral agreements differ in a number of ways.[178] On their face, bilateral commodity agreements which have as their objective price stabilization and/or compensation for exporters, but pose a potential challenge to (at a minimum) Art. XI GATT, Art. XIX GATT, and Art. 11(2) Agreement on Safeguards. In the context of agricultural goods, they may also violate the prohibition on 'grey area' measures under Art. 4 Agreement on Agriculture.[179]

The Commonwealth Secretariat has reported on the recent increasing misuse of commodity agreements, turning them into de facto 'grey area' measures in a wide range of product areas from steel, wine, textiles, and automobiles amongst others.[180] It should be noted, however, that many of the agreements identified such as the Russia steel agreements were concluded with (then) non-WTO members.[181] As such, their legality is likely less problematic than presented.[182] Nonetheless, there is scope for concern: the GATT makes provision for commodities with Art. XXXVIII(2) encouraging members to conclude 'international arrangements' for

[175] What the EU terms 'critical raw materials'. See the recent report of the Ad hoc Working Group on defining critical raw materials, 'Report on Critical Raw Materials for the EU' (May 2014) available at <http://ec.europa.eu/enterprise/policies/raw-materials/files/docs/crm-report-on-critical-raw-materials_en.pdf> (accessed 15 March 2015).

[176] P Lamy, *The Geneva Consensus: Making Trade Work For All* (Cambridge, Cambridge University Press 2013) 68–70.

[177] The results have been limited though progress is being made: Ministerial Conference, *Public Stockholding for Food Security Purposes Ministerial Decision of 7 December 2013,* WT/MIN(i3)/38 WT/L/913 (2013).

[178] Multilateral agreements overseen by International Organizations cover (*inter alia*) sugar, cocoa, tropical timber, and coffee. See: P Mavroidis, *Trade in Goods* (2nd edn, Oxford, Oxford University Press 2013) 351–5.

[179] Agreement on Agriculture (15 April 1994) LT/UR/A-1A/2 <http://docsonline.wto.org>

[180] R Grynberg et al., 'Bilateral Commodity Agreements—New Generation Grey-Area Measures? A Scoping Study', in V Qalo (ed.), *Bilateralism and Development: Emerging Trade Patterns* (London, Cameron May 2008).

[181] For example, the now defunct Agreement between the European Community and the Russian Federation on trade in certain steel products (26/10/2007) OJ L300 of 17/11/2007, p. 51.

[182] Y-S Lee, *Safeguard Measures in World Trade*, n. 16, 165–72.

access to, and stability of, commodity markets of particular interest to developing members[183] and Art. XX(h) as a general exception for international commodity agreements ('ICAs').[184]

The requirements of Art. XX(h) are not entirely clear, however at a minimum they appear to require the following elements: they should be open to participation by interested exporting and importing members,[185] be notified as commodity agreements to the WTO membership,[186] and function on a non-discriminatory basis.[187] The more general requirements, developed from the proposed principles set out in the Havana Charter have been accepted by many international commodity organizations with it being suggested that these have become part of 'international commodity law and policy'.[188]

Bilateral commodity agreements do not appear to adhere to the most basic principles of either Art. XX(h) or the *chapeau*: they are discriminatory and are not open to all interested parties. In part this is exactly because their purpose is not to control the fluctuations of commodity prices at a global level per se but rather, restrict imports into the markets of members whose own industry is incapable of responding to the competitive pressures of other trading partners so as to protect a subsection of society. Such agreements mark a rejection of the requirements under the Agreement on Safeguards and Art. XIX for import controls as set out and instead highlight the pursuit by actors of another instrument to pursue similar goals but within a nominally distinct legal regime (i.e. the regulation of commodities and not import surge relief). Such behaviour places pressure on the institutions of the WTO and its membership to adapt. While their legality is unclear, they play a key

[183] Article XXXVIII(2) GATT 1994.

[184] While Art. XI:2(b) excludes the prohibition of quantitative restrictions in the case of commodities, this is only insofar as the restrictions are 'necessary to the application of standards or regulations for the classification, grading or marketing of commodities in international trade'. The necessity requirement relates directly to the question of minimum marketing or quality standards rather than controls on trade flows of the commodity in question. See Background Note by the Secretariat, 'Relevant Provisions in the General Agreement and MTN Agreements and on Relevant Uruguay Round Proposals' (2 February 1990) GATT Doc DPG/W/6, 3.

[185] See Art. 60, Havana Charter 1948; Art. 1(2) Agreement Establishing a Common Fund for Commodities (concluded 27 June 1980) 1538 UNTS 3; though a Revised Draft Modalities for Agriculture (6 December 2008, TN/AG/W/4/Rev.4) suggested altering this in the case of agricultural commodities, at para. 95: 'an understanding will be reflected in the Agreement on Agriculture that the term "arrangements" [in Art. XXXVIII GATT taken with Art. XX(h) GATT] covers both commodity agreements of which all interested producing and consuming countries are parties; and agreements of which only commodity-dependent producing countries are parties.' It is unclear whether this reflects a changing view of the traditional requirement that both exporters and importers are to be involved in any international commodity agreement.

[186] Article XX(h) GATT, supported by the panel in *European Communities—Import Regime for Bananas, Panel Report* (18 January 1994) 34 ILM (1995) 180, 53.

[187] If justified under Art. XI:2 GATT, Art. XIII clearly requires non-discrimination. Where the member argues for an Art. XX(h) GATT exception, the chapeau of Art. XX GATT also demands: 'Subject to the requirement that such measures are not applied in a manner which would constitute a means of *arbitrary or unjustifiable discrimination between countries where the same conditions prevail*, or a disguised restriction on international trade ...' (emphasis added).

[188] KUR Khan, *The Law and Organisation of International Commodity Agreements* (The Hague, Martinus Nijhoff 1982) 71.

role in encouraging legal change, especially in the context of increasing attention to commodity price fluctuations in agriculture.[189]

4. Gentlemen's agreements and restrictions on gold sales

The third example where actors have begun to pursue forms of 'grey area' measures, challenging the Art. XIX/Agreement on Safeguards regime is in the field of 'gentlemen's agreements'. One example is the case of the Central Bank Gold Agreements ('CBGAs').[190] In light of concerns over the historic low price of gold in the 1990s and the openly announced auctions of gold by certain European States (primarily the United Kingdom), the CBGAs were intended to 'stabilise' the gold market. The increase in the price of gold since 2007 has allayed some of these concerns, yet the relevant States and international organizations have maintained the gold sale regime.

The CBGAs are informal agreements between the Central Banks of the Eurozone states, the United Kingdom, Sweden, Switzerland, and the European Central Bank restricting sales of gold. Under the CBGAs sales are restricted as follows: 400 tonnes annually from 1999, 500 tonnes annually from 2004, 400 tonnes annually and no more than 2,000 tonnes over the 2009–2014 period and 2014–19.[191] The objective is to avoid one State selling a sufficient quantity of gold at once which would have the negative effect (from central banks' viewpoint) of reducing the price of gold.

The agreement is not limited to these States; the IMF has stated that in the event of a sale of its gold reserves it would be subject to existing or future CBGAs.[192] While it has not signed the 2009 CBGA, agreement was reached whereby the IMF's intended sale of 403 tonnes of gold 'can be accommodated within' the agreed restrictions.[193] As is usual for a 'grey area' measure, the agreement is an informal 'gentleman's agreement' between central banks and not States or international organizations. That these agreements are not legally binding is no barrier to potential challenge, in the context of non-violation complaints the panel in the *Japan–Film* dispute stated:

> [A] government policy or action need not necessarily have a substantially binding or compulsory nature for it to entail a likelihood of compliance by private actors in a way so as to

[189] P Lamy, *The Geneva Consensus: Making Trade Work For All* (Cambridge, Cambridge University Press 2013) 68–70.

[190] Also known as the Washington Agreements on Gold after the first agreement's conclusion at the annual IMF meeting in Washington DC in 1999. A copy of the text of the 'agreements' can be found as a joint press release at <http://www.ecb.europa.eu/press/pr/date/1999/html/pr990926.en.html> for the 1999 agreement, <http://www.ecb.europa.eu/press/pr/date/2004/html/pr040308.en.html> for the 2004 agreement, <http://www.ecb.europa.eu/press/pr/date/2009/html/pr090807.en.html> for the 2009 agreement, and at <http://www.ecb.europa.eu/press/pr/date/2009/html/pr090807.en.html> for the 2014 agreement (all accessed 15 March 2015).

[191] Ibid.

[192] Committee to Study Sustainable Long-Term Financing of the IMF, Final Report 31 January 2007 available at <http://www.imf.org/external/np/oth/2007/013107.pdf> (accessed 15 March 2015).

[193] CBGA 2009, para. 3.

nullify or impair legitimately expected benefits within the purview of Article XXIII(1)(b). Indeed, it is clear that non-binding actions, which include sufficient incentives or disincentives for private parties to act in a particular manner, can potentially have adverse effects on competitive conditions of market access. For example, a number of non-violation cases have involved subsidies, receipt of which requires only voluntary compliance with eligibility criteria.[194]

The acts of central banks are clearly attributable to the members involved, irrespective of their independence from executive interference.[195] Like the bilateral commodity agreements referred to above, the CBGAs do not involve importing (i.e. purchasing) members, are discriminatory in their function and purpose and are not reported to the WTO membership. Insofar as any member might claim the agreements as falling under Art. XX(h), this seems an untenable position. More convincingly, it could be argued that the exception under Art. XX(c) applies, 'relating to the importations or exportations of gold or silver'.[196] However, as with the other VERs discussed above, the obligations under the chapeau of Art. XX still apply: the restriction of these cannot be 'applied in a manner which would constitute a means of arbitrary or unjustifiable discrimination between countries where the same conditions prevail, or a disguised restriction on international trade'.[197]

These brief examples serve to demonstrate how the Agreement on Safeguards did not conclusively eliminate 'grey area' measures. Rather, members test the limits of the oversight safeguards system by pursuing alternative instruments that have a similar effect. The objectives pursued through such instruments are not eliminated through either specific treaty provision or negative Appellate Body reports. Nor is their use a binary choice: members still use safeguard measures, where the practice has changed is their unwillingness to challenge such measures at the Appellate Body. Rather than signalling a reduction of oversight, members have moved the regulation of safeguards measures to the Safeguards Committee as an alternative form of dispute settlement.

5. Dispute settlement through the Safeguards Committee

An increase in 'grey area' measures has been matched by a subtle increase in the number of provisional safeguards and investigations.[198] Faced by such challenges, the Safeguards Committee has begun to the respond to the demands of the

[194] *Japan—Measures Affecting Consumer Photographic Film and Paper*, Panel Report (31 March 1998) WT/DS44/R, para. 10.49.

[195] *United States—Sunset Review of Anti-Dumping Duties On Corrosion-Resistant Carbon Steel Flat Products From Japan*, Report of the Appellate Body (15 December 2003) WT/DS244/AB/R, para. 81. Article 4(1) Articles on Responsibility of States of Internationally Wrongful Acts (2001) GAOR 56th Session Supp 10, 43, though the question of attribution of acts of the ECB to the EU and/or its member states may well be more complex: see generally, Draft Articles on Responsibility of International Organizations (2011) GAOR 66th Sess., Suppl. 10, Doc. A/66/10, 54.

[196] Article XX(c) GATT.

[197] Chapeau, Art. XX GATT.

[198] Committee on Safeguards, 'Minutes of the Regular Meeting Held on 22 October 2012' (8 March 2013) G/SG/M/42, noted at para. 50.

membership, serving as a forum for the resolution of disputes and, potentially, a site for rule elaboration.

In light of the Appellate Body's strict application of the Agreement on Safeguards, members have become reluctant to raise disputes through the traditional dispute settlement system. Where they do, they do not appear willing to appeal.[199] The need to resolve disputes arising from the introduction of safeguard measures has not disappeared, however. Instead, members have begun to prioritize less formal dispute settlement procedures through the Safeguards Committee. Such a practice was recently welcomed in a joint statement of ten members including Canada, the EU, Japan, and the US which highlighted the concerns of an 'emerging and serious disregard of multilateral rules'.[200] In particular, the members raised issues of good faith use of safeguards: especially the use of provisional measures with only a cursory investigation (in one instance only four days long) and a lack of efficient notification (required under Art. 12.1 Safeguards Agreement).[201]

Facing these changing conditions, the Committee has become a focal point for resolving disputes, 'a good forum to discuss conformity of safeguard measures with the rules'[202] as part of the Committee's mandate under Art. 13 Safeguards Agreement to monitor implementation of the Agreement.[203] Moving beyond dispute settlement, it has also been suggested that the Committee engage in the process of identifying best practice through a sub-group, thus clarifying the scope of the procedural requirements under the Safeguards Agreement that are lacking (and widely considered the reason for numerous disputes in this area).[204]

It is interesting to note the role the Committee has played in encouraging the effective use of safeguards within a context of economic crises and rigorous legal requirements. Specifically, the focus has been on encouraging compliance with transparency and due process obligations (in particular notifications), and questioning not only safeguards investigations themselves but also legislation of members. Beyond these seemingly neutral methods of oversight, the Committee has become a focal point for members to identify what they perceive of as incompatible behaviour. India has been singled out for its fondness for safeguard measures,[205] while Russia has been criticized for failing to uphold the commitments it made prior to accession.[206] These are not legal criticisms in the strict sense but forms of social pressure and shaming that rest upon a legal framework.[207]

[199] For example *Dominican Republic—Safeguard Measures on Imports of Polypropylene Bags and Tubular Fabric* (31 January 2012) WT/DS415/R.

[200] Committee on Safeguards, 'Systemic Concerns with Certain Safeguard Proceedings', Joint Statement from Australia; Canada; the European Union; Japan; Korea; New Zealand; Norway; Separate Customs Territory of Taiwan, Penghu, Kinmen, and Matsu; Singapore; and the United States (5 October 2012) G/SG/W/226.

[201] Ibid.

[202] Committee on Safeguards, 'Minutes of the Regular Meeting Held on 22 October 2012' (8 March 2013) G/SG/M/42, para. 61.

[203] Ibid., para. 69. [204] Ibid., para. 70.

[205] Committee on Safeguards, 'Minutes of the Regular Meeting Held on 28 April 2014' (26 September 2014) G/SG/M/45, paras 30–1.

[206] Ibid., para. 90. [207] See: Chapter 2.D(4)(A).

As a consequence of the reticence to use the formal dispute settlement system, legal regulation of safeguard measures continues to develop, albeit away from the Dispute Settlement Body and instead within the Safeguards Committee. This presents its own challenges, particularly in light of the 'grey area' measures that were discussed earlier. Further, how the 'new' dispute settlement processes of the Safeguards Committee will respond is unclear: while diplomatic resolution of disputes has its advantages, it raises problems for how we are to identify the law and how it develops in a more informal (and less public) setting.

F. Concluding Remarks

The regulation of safeguard measures is characterized by its multi-jurisdictional nature and the range of causal influences at play. Rather than focusing on the narrow application of the rules on safeguards, the aim here has been to place them within their wider context. In doing so, a number of insights can be drawn from what is often considered a sterile area of trade law consigned to stasis or redundancy in the face of misguided Appellate Body reports.

First, the regulation of safeguards offers lessons on how embedding norms in treaty provisions plays out in practice. By attempting to influence the intersection between domestic and WTO law, the US has sought to project its understanding of the role of safeguards in trading relations. This visible and seemingly successful method of pursuing objectives (the crystallization of norms as treaty obligations) suffered here from two notable weaknesses. One, where the US's domestic legal regulation of safeguard measures and their petitioning procedures changed over time, the international obligations required adjustment to avoid dissonance and, two, the US's influence on how the Appellate Body takes decisions, its method of adjudication, had a crucial influence on the way in which the law developed at both the WTO and within the US. Just as the GATT period failed to enforce a strict rule-based dispute settlement system, at the WTO dispute settlement is inherently bound to an approach that claims textuality as mandated by the DSU as its *cri de coeur*. Its influence on US practice indicates that the causal strength of the WTO as a system is capable of wearing down the barriers which implementing legislation would otherwise maintain.

The second interesting development has been the continued pursuit of 'grey area' measures by actors. The underlying demands that safeguard measures seek to satisfy continue to exist even where the proximate instrument to do so may not be preferable. As an actor-driven process, other agreements are concluded, at times of dubious legality. Yet this questionable compliance with the WTO obligations itself triggers developments in WTO law and practice: the use of mutually agreed solutions, raising agricultural safeguards as a central issue in trade talks, and the focus on the Safeguards Committee. All of these shifts in how members control imports are stimulated through the complex interaction of causal influences.

Safeguard measures have provided a useful starting point. This case-study is, however, limited in certain respects: the influence of the US on the development of safeguard measures and their use over the years is not typical of all GATT/WTO instruments, nor is the conspicuous use of crystallizing norms as treaty obligations. The next case study offers a more complex but also fruitful example for a number of reasons: sanitary and phytosanitary ('SPS') measures have been developed in different locations, primarily the US and EU, though increasingly at international standards bodies and associations of private actors; the regime for their application involves bodies other than the WTO at the international level; and underpinning the ways in which SPS measures are understood and judged are competing epistemological approaches, bringing legal analysis and scientific reasoning into conflict.

5

Sanitary and Phytosanitary Measures

A. Introduction

This chapter examines the legal regulation of sanitary and phytosanitary ('SPS') measures at the WTO. As part of a globalized legal process, the law on SPS measures at the WTO has developed through a number of trans-jurisdictional influences. The different ways in which globalized actors' interests and values are expressed and then altered between domestic and international levels makes it an especially interesting example.

SPS measures are necessary tools for members to respond to the potentially harmful effects of increased cross-border trade in goods that may have a deleterious impact on human, animal, or plant life or health. Their regulation is of particular interest, as it exists at the intersection between domestic and international planes, the public and private spheres, and political and scientific decision-making. Whereas the law on safeguard measures came principally from the US, a number of other legal traditions have had a particular influence on the regulation of SPS measures at the WTO. This chapter examines how the transposition of domestic and international regulatory positions to the WTO has created a space in which a number of causes exert their influence over the development of SPS law. What is of particular interest is how the discussions relating to SPS measures align with the influences on their legal regulation: instrumental concerns over the ability of members to introduce measures to protect their population and biosphere; systemic concerns over the appropriate standard of review in SPS cases; and constitutive concerns over the nature of scientific reasoning in regulatory and legal decision-making.

Specifically, this chapter examines the development of SPS measures in two contentious areas: the distinction between risk assessment and risk management, and the regulation of private standards at the WTO. The debates surrounding SPS measures are in each instance focussed on a specific conception of how law functions and how it develops. The three principal strands of debate that arise in these areas: the limitations on the ability of members to pursue policies to protect their populations; the appropriate standard of review for the examination of SPS measures; and the ways in which types of knowledge are used, each relate to a concern with how law develops from a specific perspective (instrumental, system, and constitutive respectively). Understood as part of a pluralist global process, each of these debates represents a concern over the nature of SPS regulation (and indeed, international regulation more broadly) and decision-making in a globalized world.

The chapter proceeds in three parts. First (Section B), SPS measures are briefly introduced, identifying the central points of contention and their use in world trade. The history of their development is examined through the experiences of the US, EU, and on the international plane, the Codex Alimentarius Commission ('Codex'). By identifying the underlying contestations that take place in each specific sphere, Section C examines the distinction between risk assessment and risk management in the *Beef–Hormones* dispute, understanding both the background and result of the legal dispute as part of a clash between competing conceptions of how legal decision-making should function. Section D examines the way in which the law on SPS measures develops through non-judicial institutions, where the systemic influence of the WTO Agreement restricts potential rule-making—here examining the possible regulation of private SPS standards through the SPS Committee.

B. The Use of SPS Measures and their Underlying Values

As international trade is liberalized, both by quantity and by sector, more goods travel across the world. While the traditional consensus is that increased trade in both goods and services benefits the parties involved, there are potential dangers involved, and not only those connected to the uneven distribution of gains, as was the case in the previous chapter. As agricultural goods are traded more widely and produced more intensively, the potential risks to human, animal, and plant life or health pose potentially complex challenges for a global system interested in increasing trade flows.[1] Combine this with other factors such as greater demands by the public for health protection and improved detection and management techniques, and the relationship between trade and health becomes critical.[2] The WTO attempts to balance the legitimate objectives of members as they protect the health of humans, plants, and animals with concerns over

[1] For example, concerns over the connection between intensive farming methods and drug-resistant pathogens: recent studies indicate concerns over the prevalence of multidrug-resistant Staphylococcus aureus ('MRSA') in intensively farmed livestock within the US: A Waters et al., 'Multidrug-Resistant Staphylococcus aureus in US Meat and Poultry', (2011) 52(10) *Clinical Infectious Diseases* 1227–30, 1230. The EU has also echoed similar concerns: Joint Scientific Report of ECDC, EFSA and EMEA on Meticillin Resistant Staphylococcus Aureus (MRSA) in Livestock, Companion Animals, and Food, EFSA-Q-2009-00612 (EFSA Scientific Report (2009) 301, 1–10) and EMEA/CVMP/SAGAM/62464/2009.

[2] The Food and Agriculture Organization ('FAO') and World Health Organization ('WHO') report *Food Safety Risk Analysis: A Guide for National Food Safety Authorities* (FAO 2006) 1–4, cites increasing volume of international trade, expanding international and regional bodies and resulting legal obligations, increasing complexity of food types and geographical sources, intensification and industrialization of agriculture and animal production, increasing travel and tourism, changing food-handling patterns, changing dietary patterns and food-preparation preferences, new food-processing methods, new food and agricultural technologies, increasing resistance of bacteria to antibiotics, and changing human/animal interactions with potential for disease transmission.

unjustifiable restrictions on trade such as overtly burdensome regulation or import bans.[3]

The GATT 1947 made provision for trade restrictions where 'necessary to protect human, animal or plant life or health'.[4] The Agreement on the Application of Sanitary and Phytosanitary Measures developed a clearer set of disciplines in this area at the WTO level.[5] Building on the Tokyo Round Agreement on Technical Barriers to Trade[6] and the experiences of the negotiators in the Uruguay Round in other fields, the SPS Agreement was negotiated as part of the wider negotiations on agriculture.[7] The final agreement regulated all SPS measures, defined as any measure:

(a) to protect animal or plant life or health within the territory of the Member from risks arising from the entry, establishment or spread of pests, diseases, disease-carrying organisms or disease-causing organisms;
(b) to protect human or animal life or health within the territory of the Member from risks arising from additives, contaminants, toxins or disease-causing organisms in foods, beverages or feedstuffs;
(c) to protect human life or health within the territory of the Member from risks arising from diseases carried by animals, plants or products thereof, or from the entry, establishment or spread of pests; or
(d) to prevent or limit other damage within the territory of the Member from the entry, establishment or spread of pests.[8]

Despite the potentially wide and controversial scope of such measures, the SPS Agreement had a comparatively smooth transit through the Uruguay Round as part of the negotiations in the field of agriculture.[9] Both the EU and US had, or were developing, particularly influential models of SPS protection. However, at the time of negotiations, there appeared little to indicate the intense confrontations that would arise in the years after 1994.

Numerous areas of disagreement over the use of SPS measures have been highlighted since 1995. Of these, some of the most intractable have been the role of science in the decision-making of panels and the Appellate Body,[10] interference of

[3] Acknowledged by the Appellate Body as the 'shared, but sometimes competing, interests of promoting international trade and of protecting the life and health of human beings'. European Communities—Measures Concerning Meat and Meat Products, Report of the Appellate Body (16 January 1998) WT/DS26/AB/R and WT/DS48/AB/R ('*EC–Hormones Appellate Body*'), para. 177.

[4] Article XX(b) GATT 1947.

[5] Agreement on the Application of Sanitary and Phytosanitary Measures (15 April 1994) LT/UR/A-1A/12 <http://docsonline.wto.org> ('SPS Agreement').

[6] Terminated on 1 January 1996 following decision of the WTO and GATT Committees on Technical Barriers to Trade (20 October 1995) TBT/M/50. Superseded by the Agreement on Technical Barriers to Trade (15 April 1994) LT/UR/A-1A/10 <http://docsonline.wto.org> ('TBT Agreement').

[7] A similar position to that taken in the drafting of the North American Free Trade Agreement (concluded 17 December 1992, entered into force 1 January 1994) 32 ILM 289, 605 ('NAFTA') where Chapter 7 couples 'Agriculture and Sanitary and Phytosanitary Measures'.

[8] SPS Agreement, Annex A(1). [9] See below, Section B(1).

[10] For example E Fisher, *Risk Regulation and Administrative Constitutionalism* (Oxford, Hart Publishing 2010); E Fisher, 'Beyond the Science/Democracy Dichotomy: The World Trade Organization

the WTO in the regulatory autonomy of its members (including debates over what constitutes an SPS measure),[11] and over whether the WTO is the proper place to debate issues related to SPS measures more broadly.[12] These debates emphasize the different causal influences on the development of the law: constitutive, systemic, and instrumental respectively.

SPS measures differ from other forms of protection examined in this book in one key respect: the principal debate over SPS measures is not over their aims or objectives but rather how they are used. The protection of human, animal, or plant life or health is not controversial: who decides what the risks are and on what basis that decision is taken *is*.[13] The development of the law on SPS measures is thus tied to governance questions as part of a globalized legal process.

Questions over the place of SPS measures in international trade and who is to regulate them come from various sources. SPS measures present a complex challenge to examining the development of law through a globalized process: unlike safeguard measures, which have largely developed between two jurisdictions (the US and the WTO), SPS measures at the WTO level are the result of debates across the EU and US with the Codex exerting a subtle influence in the background.[14]

Sanitary and PhytoSanitary Agreement and Administrative Constitutionalism', in C. Joerges and E. Petersmann (eds), *Constitutionalism, Multilevel Trade Governance and Social Regulation* (Oxford, Hart Publishing 2006); R Howse, 'Democracy, Science, and Free Trade: Risk Regulation on Trial at the WTO', (2000) 98 *Michigan Law Review* 2329; M Echols, *Food Safety and the WTO: The Interplay of Culture, Science and Technology* (London, Kluwer 2001); J Peel, 'Risk Regulation Under the WTO SPS Agreement: Science as an International Normative Yardstick?' Jean Monet Working Paper 02/04, June 2004; J Scott, *The WTO Agreement on Sanitary and Phytosanitary Measures: A Commentary* (Oxford, Oxford University Press 2009) Chapter 3; M E Footer, 'Post-normal Science in the Multilateral Trading System: Social Science Expertise and the EC–Biotech Panel', (2007) 6(2) *World Trade Review* 281.

[11] J Peel, 'A GMO by Any Other Name ... Might Be an SPS Risk!: Implications of Expanding the Scope of the WTO Sanitary and Phytosanitary Measures Agreement', (2007) 17(5) *European Journal of International Law* 1009; R Quick and A Blüthner, 'Has the Appellate Body Erred? An Appraisal and Criticism of the Ruling in the WTO Hormones Case', (1999) *Journal of International Economic Law* 603.

[12] These can range from providing a critique of the *EC–Biotech* (*European Communities)—Measures Affecting the Approval and Marketing of Biotech Products*, Panel Report (26 September 2006) WT/DS291,292,293/R) panel's restrictive approach to 'non-WTO' materials in M Young, 'The WTO's Use of Relevant Rules of International Law: An Analysis of the Biotech Case', (2007) 56 *International and Comparative Law Quarterly* 907, to advocating the removal of disputes with an environmental element from the WTO: Adelphi Consult, Friends of the Earth Europe and Greenpeace, 'Is the WTO the Only Way? Safeguarding Multilateral Environmental Agreements from International Trade Rules and Settling Trade and Environment Disputes Outside the WTO' (2005).

[13] This debate is a proxy for a much larger process of contestation taking place within all levels of international regulation today: are decisions taken on the basis of democratic pressures and/or checks, accepting that such a process will not always be based on the best evidence but rather influenced by the opinions of the majority? Or is technical expertise to be prioritized, potentially at the cost of accountability? In the face of complex problem solving and challenges to governance, should the priority be on increasing accountability and limiting any 'democratic deficit' at the cost of effectiveness or encouraging technocratic modes of governance?

[14] The EU and US play pivotal roles in determining the scope and nature of international regulation, particularly in areas where technical expertise is prized. See generally, D Drezner, *All Politics is Global: Explaining International Regulatory Regimes* (Princeton, Princeton University Press 2007).

The following sections outline: first, the relative ease with which the negotiating parties came to consensus over the SPS Agreement; second, the shifts in the EU's approach to SPS regulation over the past two decades; third, a similar brief examination of the US's tradition in regulating SPS issues; and fourth, an account of the Codex's role as an interested actor creating a role for itself through mutual legitimation with the WTO. It is suggested that each system has developed in light of different concerns faced at different times. Rather than viewing the interaction in terms of US versus EU or domestic versus international, the focus is on the different legal influences interacting under different conditions at the WTO.

1. Negotiations on the SPS Agreement

The negotiations on agriculture during the Uruguay Round were some of the most complex. Within this wide area, the SPS Agreement passed through with relative ease. Linking SPS regulation with negotiations on agriculture was seen as necessary: the former essential to ensure that the gains made by the latter would not be undermined. The US submission in this area made clear the general approach:

> The broad array of policy instruments [in the negotiations on agriculture] is categorized into four subsets: import access, export competition, internal support and sanitary and phytosanitary measures. The United States proposal calls for reform in all four areas, and these reforms should be viewed as *integral parts of a comprehensive package and not as four separate proposals*. Our comprehensive proposal is designed to guide agricultural production and trade toward a market oriented system governed by strengthened and more operationally effective GATT rules and disciplines and to integrate agriculture fully into the GATT.[15]

While tensions existed over the EC position with regard to certain issues (agricultural subsidies in particular), negotiations over SPS regulation did not attract the same level of animosity. It is striking that one of today's most contentious agreements would have betrayed so little of the future disagreements at the negotiation stage.

There was broad agreement that the general position should be based around a requirement for scientific justification. The more controversial issues related instead to the treatment of developing countries, the scope of measures more stringent than the international standard, and the extent to which non-scientific concerns might be used to justify measures.[16] More broadly, however, the submissions of diverse members such as those in the Cairns group, the EC, the Nordic countries, the US, and Brazil were all met with general agreement in discussion.[17]

[15] Submission of the United States on Comprehensive Long-Term Agricultural Reform (25 October 1989) GATT Doc MTN.GNG/NG5/W/118 (emphasis added).

[16] T Stewart, *The GATT Uruguay Round: A Negotiating History Vol I* (The Hague, Kluwer Law International 1993) 201.

[17] Respectively: Communication from the Cairns Group (2 October 1989) GATT Doc MTN. GNG/NG5/W/112; Submission of the European Communities on Sanitary and Phytosanitary Regulations and Measures (20 December 1989) GATT Doc MTN.GNG/NG5/W/146; Submission of the Nordic Countries on Some Elements in a Comprehensive Long-Term Agricultural Reform

It is also telling that the Working Group on the SPS Agreement was the only negotiating group in agricultural negotiations to successfully produce a draft by the 20 November deadline in 1990, further indicating general consensus.[18]

To tackle the concern that developed members might be required to lower their level of health protection, both the US and EC agreed on the core principle of scientific justification of SPS measures, balancing it with the use of international standards and harmonization as a means to ensure both uniformity and an avenue to maintain their own desired level of protection. Indeed, this was not a novel position: Codex had already advertised its transition to science-based analysis for the determination of risk, and such an approach was largely established in the US.[19] The package gained widespread support amongst members.[20] Indeed, the final agreement, even in light of considerable public attention, was little altered from the 1992 draft.[21]

The role of scientific justification did not cause great disagreement: the text in the draft produced by the SPS working group on 20 November 1990, referred to 'generally accepted scientific principles' while other issues such as 'genuine consumer concern' were bracketed.[22] Questions over consumer concerns were side-lined and did not appear in the final draft, nor did the concerns raised by both Japan and Korea over their cultural traditions relating to goods which could be effected by the liberalization of agricultural produce.[23] The focus on scientific justification rather than cultural or political reasoning was a response to fears over 'trading down' levels of SPS protection in developed members rather than intentionally excluding any other 'non-scientific' justification. Note the response to an Austrian proposal that any question over the legitimacy of a measure should be referred first through the appropriate international scientific body (one of the Three Sisters: Codex, World Organization for Animal Health, or International Plant Protection Convention) before going through the dispute settlement system at the WTO.[24] In rejecting such an approach: 'It was further observed that sanitary and phytosanitary measures were not based only on science, but on a risk assessment which also took account of potential economic damage.'[25]

Programme (December 1989) GATT Doc MTN.GNG/NG5/W/143; Submission of the United States on Comprehensive Long-Term Agricultural Reform (25 October 1989) GATT Doc MTN. GNG/NG5/W/118. While a member of the Cairns Group, Brazil also provided its own specific views: Statement by Brazil on Special and Differentiated Treatment (2 October 1989) GATT Doc MTN.GNG/NG5/W/108.

[18] T Stewart, n. 16, 200; Negotiating Group on Agriculture: Working Group on Sanitary and Phytosanitary Regulations and Barriers, 'Draft Text on Sanitary and Phytosanitary Measures' (20 November 1990) GATT Doc MTN.GNG/NG5/WGSP/7.

[19] See below, Sections B.2(b)–(c).

[20] The Cairns Group being an exception to this: T Stewart, n. 16, 201.

[21] T Stewart, n. 16, 41.

[22] Negotiating Group on Agriculture, n. 18.

[23] T Stewart, n. 16, 188ff.

[24] Note by Secretariat, 'Summary of the Main Points Raised at the Fifth Meeting of the Working Group on Sanitary and Phytosanitary Regulations and Barriers' (19 March 1990) GATT Doc MTN. GNG/NG5/WGSP/W/13.

[25] Ibid., 2–3.

Given the lack of controversy surrounding the negotiation of the SPS Agreement it is surprising that it be the subject of so much debate today. The primary reason for such a development is the process of contestations *since* the conclusion of the SPS Agreement. Pollack and Shaffer offer a lucid account of this process, having conducted a detailed analysis of the motivations and mechanics of the transatlantic dispute over genetically modified organisms in the food chain.[26] They argue:

> . . . that the very different approaches to GMO regulation that we observe between the US and the EU, were not determined in any straightforward way by either the institutions, the political culture or the interest-group configurations present on either side of the Atlantic. It was *not* inevitable that US regulators would adopt a product-based approach to GMO regulation, nor was it obvious from the outset that the EU would adopt the strict, politicized, and highly precautionary system that emerged over the course of the 1990s. The best explanation for the observed transatlantic differences, we believe, is multi-causal, lying in the ability of interest groups to capitalize on preexisting cultural and institutional differences, with an important role played by contingent events such as the European food safety scandals of the 1990s.[27]

In their account, Pollack and Shaffer examine the role of the WTO as a space that offers opportunities for co-operation where bilateral and transnational US–EU attempts have failed.[28] Yet, the WTO itself is one of a host of actors which have their own interests and motivations (committees and dispute settlement organs, for example) as well as those which share a close relationship with the WTO such as the Codex. The motivation for, and results of, these processes of contestation are thus felt across a globalized regulatory space.

To illustrate this point, the following section identifies some key features of experiences of SPS regulation in the EU, US, and Codex. The aim is to identify the differing motivations and influences on how risk-assessment procedures are understood in each system, tracing their interaction at the WTO.

2. Experiences in SPS Regulation: The European Union, United States, and the Codex

Differing debates within the EU and the US over the nature of SPS regulation have subsequently set the scene for a transatlantic dispute at the WTO. The purpose here is to highlight the different concerns that arise from the law–science interface within administrative governance at the EU and US, identifying how the different legal systems exert both systemic and constitutive influences on these actors at the WTO. This in turn influences how the debates progress at the international level. The section then turns to the role of Codex in contributing to the discussion, and

[26] M Pollack and G Shaffer, *When Cooperation Fails: The International Law and Politics of Genetically Modified Foods* (Oxford, Oxford University Press 2009).

[27] Ibid., 11. While the development of SPS measures is multi-causal as Pollack and Shaffer argue, it is not multi-causal in the sense of a number of individual causes but rather multi-causal in the sense of resulting from the interaction between multiple causal influences.

[28] Ibid., Chapter 3.

its role in how the WTO law on SPS measures has developed. Rather than focussing on the instrumental use of law by the US and EU at the WTO to pursue their goals, limited by the systemic influence of WTO law on their action, this chapter emphasizes the role that these influences play while also acknowledging two key factors: the constitutive influence of WTO law on Codex and its subsequent engagement with the WTO, and the role of the institutions of the dispute settlement system in filtering these influences.

a. The European Union

SPS regulation at the European level is as an attempt to balance the maintenance of a single market dependent on the free movement of goods and services with the concerns of the Member States and their polities.[29]

Within the EU, the move from national regulation of SPS measures to EU-wide regulation of food safety took place in response to some very public and damaging food crises in the late 1980s and 1990s.[30] Though competence to act in this area was granted under the Single European Act in 1986 (and extended under the Maastricht Treaty in 1992), it was not until a series of crises (most notably BSE) that the EU dramatically changed its system for regulating food safety.[31] Whereas the EU had previously encouraged greater autonomy for the Member States, it now centres much regulation at the EU level with a subsidiary role for national regulatory agencies.

The European Food Safety Authority ('EFSA') focuses exclusively on the scientific analysis of risk ('risk assessment') rather than the determination of the appropriate level of risk for a society ('risk management'), which is left to other Union institutions.[32] EFSA co-ordinates and co-operates with the national regulators of the Member States in an attempt to ensure wider consistency and transparency of scientific assessment,[33] and is charged with providing 'scientific advice and scientific and technical support for the Community's legislation and policies in all fields which have a direct or indirect impact on food and feed safety. It shall provide independent information on all matters within these fields and communicate on risks.'[34] In matters of food and feed safety, the EFSA works with the Commission and Member State representatives via the Standing Committee on the Food Chain

[29] Competing conceptions over non-discrimination and market access play a role within this discussion: E Reid, 'Risk Assessment, Science and Deliberation: Managing Regulatory Diversity under the SPS Agreement?', (2012) *European Journal of Risk Regulation* 535, 543–4.

[30] It is an interesting characteristic that food safety has tended to develop in response to crises: E Fisher, 'Food Safety Crises as Crises in Administrative Constitutionalism', (2010) 20 *Health Matrix* 55.

[31] For an account on the BSE crisis: E Fisher, *Risk Regulation and Administrative Constitutionalism*, n. 10, Chapter 2, for other crises: R Löfstedt and D Vogel, 'The Changing Character of Regulation: a Comparison of Europe and the United States', (2001) 21 *Risk Analysis* 399.

[32] For a more detailed account of risk assessment and risk management: Section C, below.

[33] See Strategy for Co-operation and Networking Between the EU Member States and EFSA, MB 19.12.2006 – 6a Strategy for co-operation and networking.

[34] Council Regulation (EC) No 178/2002, Art. 22(2).

and Animal Health (chaired by a member of the Commission).[35] In the case of potential food or feed crises within the EU, Member States may act to restrict certain products though must inform the Commission immediately[36] while where the Member State is unable or unwilling to act, the Commission can act under its own authority.[37] Member State authorities are expected to examine the scientific evidence, though EFSA is involved where necessary.[38]

At first sight, this would appear to be an unremarkable development in European integration: competences progressively transferred to the European level are then matched by increasing institutional developments for those competences to be exercised effectively.[39] However, EFSA only conducts risk assessment; risk management is carried out by the committee relationship between Commission and Member States. This allows the political organs of the EU to produce 'outcomes with little relation to scientific findings, allowing Member States to block approvals even if EFSA has not found a significant risk'.[40] While the hope was that deference would be given to the EFSA on the basis of its expertise and requirement to apply the precautionary principle, this has not been the case.[41]

There are some notable differences in the regulation of food safety over other matters falling within EU competence. Of particular note is the criticism arising from the handling of the BSE crisis which was not only concerned with a question of technical capacity but also over legitimacy of decision-makers taking actions that could potentially have a wide-ranging impact on populations.[42] In a European context this criticism has added weight as the EU is, and has been for decades, attempting to tackle a profound existential challenge: the so-called 'democratic deficit', the distance between populations and decision-makers.[43]

In response to these criticisms the EU system permits wide-ranging political inputs into its decision-making process in determining appropriate levels of protection for food safety. Scott describes the authorization process for GMOs at the EU as 'involving actors across different levels of government, from the local to the European' and structured so that it 'establishes a role for political and expert actors'.[44] While the influence of public opinion is limited, the continual presence

[35] Ibid., Art. 58(1). [36] Ibid., Art. 50(2). [37] Ibid., Art. 53.

[38] See the non-binding: Standing Committee on the Food Chain and Animal Health (section Toxicological Safety) 2.2; Modus operandi for the management of new food safety incidents with a potential for extension involving a chemical substance (January 2006).

[39] Recent increasing co-operation on fiscal policy within the Eurozone is a paradigmatic example. See Treaty on Stability, Co-ordination, and Governance in the Economic and Monetary Union (concluded 2 March 2012) T/SCG/en 1.

[40] N Krisch, *Beyond Constitutionalism: The Pluralist Structure of Postnational Law* (Oxford, Oxford University Press 2010) 216, fn. 125.

[41] G Skogstad, 'Contested Accountability Claims and GMO Regulation in the European Union', (2011) 49(4) *Journal of Common Market Studies* 895, 903–4.

[42] J Peel, 'Risk Regulation Under the WTO SPS Agreement', n. 10, 36.

[43] European Parliament Resolution on the democratic deficit (1988) OJ C 187/229; A Follesdal and S Hix, 'Why There is a Democratic Deficit in the EU: A Response to Majone and Moravscik', (2006) 44(3) *Journal of Common Market Studies* 533.

[44] J Scott, 'European Regulation of GMOs: Thinking About "Judicial Review" in the WTO', Jean Monnet Working Paper 04/04 (2004) 2–3.

of political actors opens the process to greater influence by motivated and well-organized actors.

The primary EU legislation in the area of food law further enshrines the position of the consumer as central to food regulation:

> Food law shall pursue one or more of the general objectives of a high level of protection of human life and health and the *protection of consumers' interests*, including fair practices in food trade, taking account of, where appropriate, the protection of animal health and welfare, plant health and the environment.[45]

The focus on consumer interests is buttressed by incorporating the precautionary principle,[46] inclining the system towards a more conservative approach to authorizing novel agricultural technologies.[47] Recourse to the precautionary principle is designed to strengthen the legitimacy of regulators in the eyes of a population that had serious concerns in light of the crises of the 1990s.[48]

The EU system is not simply constituted with an instinctive bias towards conservative policies regarding novel technologies in agriculture. Were Member States free to restrict feed and food products simply on the basis of consumer interests or their perceived concerns over certain issues, without scientific basis, the internal market would be fundamentally threatened. And so, while EFSA was born out of a desire to assuage the concerns of European citizens and support the vertical relationships of the European Union (that is to say, the relationship between citizen, Member State, and Union institutions), these priorities must find an accommodation with the principal purpose of the European Union: the internal market.[49] Thus, debates over the legitimacy of certain institutions within the EU spark a parallel debate over the ability of Member States to exert their influence over decision-makers in SPS matters in a way that will not undermine the free movement of goods.[50]

It has fallen to the judicial branches of the European Union to balance the inbuilt caution within the EU's food safety regime. While political influences have numerous points of entry in the decision-making process, once the decision has been made the courts have given short shrift to any argument made that might then undermine the free movement of goods within the EU. It may seem self-serving for European courts to defer to the decisions of the EU institutions

[45] Council Regulation (EC) No 178/2002, Art. 5(1) (emphasis added).

[46] Ibid., Art. 7(1), also, Art. 191 Treaty on the Functioning of the European Union ('TFEU') [2010] OJ C83/47.

[47] Where the process involved in making a good is relevant in a way that it is not under US law. See C Hanrahan, 'Agricultural Biotechnology: The US–EU Dispute', Congressional Research Service Reports (2010) Paper 69, p. 4.

[48] R Löfstedt, 'The Swing of the Regulatory Pendulum in Europe: From Precautionary Principle to (Regulatory) Impact Analysis', (2004) 28(3) *The Journal of Risk and Uncertainty* 237, 252–3.

[49] Article 26(2) TFEU: 'The internal market shall comprise an area without internal frontiers in which the free movement of goods, persons, services and capital is ensured in accordance with the provisions of the Treaties'.

[50] On the need to find an accommodation: K Vignarajah, 'Reconciling Free Trade and Safe Trade: New Paradigms for Regulating Imports in the Twenty-First Century', (2009) 43(4) *Journal of World Trade* 771.

where scientific uncertainty exists (in the case of beef hormones, for example)[51] while at the same time giving less leeway to Member States that wish to introduce trade restrictions on the basis of limited scientific evidence as was the case with Danish restrictions on additives in foodstuffs[52] or restrictions on British beef post-BSE.[53] Peel identifies the key difference when reviewing decisions based on unclear scientific evidence: 'these preconditions are reviewed more lightly in the case of Community measures, where the countervailing considerations of internal market regulation are less salient'.[54]

The European system is not only influenced by EU-level debates but also by those within specific Member States. Unlike the US system described below, the EU is comprised of a larger number of smaller agricultural producers and more limited space for agricultural development. Combined with a cultural concern over the mechanization in the agricultural industry, sections of the EU have been more cautious in the reception of novel agricultural technologies.[55] It is not that the European model is risk-averse (note the consumption of unpasteurized cheeses), rather that it is averse to novel technologies in agricultural production, or at least those that are not identifiable as being part of either a food tradition or culture within that society.[56]

The regulation of SPS measures within the EU has been a story of crisis response and institution building. Behind these developments exists a multi-layered process of contestation, setting the terms and priorities for the EU's food and feed safety policy. Across Europe, preoccupations over the EU's capacity to protect the health of the citizenry have had to find an accommodation with countervailing concerns over the legitimacy of EU decision-makers and the continued success of the internal market. At a more local level, the specific structure of the agricultural industry within the EU and the cultural outlook of its communities have resulted in a cautious approach to novel technologies in food production.[57] This can be contrasted with the US experience that has been informed by drastically different internal priorities.

b. The United States

The US regulation of SPS measures is conducted by administrative agencies with considerable discretion and autonomy. Administrative agencies are the key players in determining which products might or might not constitute a risk to human animal or plant life or health within the US, and the regulation of SPS measures

[51] Case T-13/99 *Pfizer Animal Health SA v Council of the European Union* [2002] ECR II-03305.
[52] Case C-192/01 *Commission v Denmark* [2003] ECR I-9693, para. 29.
[53] Case C-393/01 *France v Commission* [2003] ECR I-5405.
[54] J Peel, 'Risk Regulation Under the WTO SPS Agreement', n. 10, 47.
[55] M Pollack and G Shaffer, *When Cooperation Fails*, n. 26, 73ff. [56] Ibid.
[57] This is not universal amongst EU Member States. See poll commissioned by British Science Association and cited by The Guardian indicating a rise of people not concerned by GM crops from 17 per cent in 2003 to 25 per cent in 2012: 'Public concern over GM food has lessened, survey shows', The Guardian, Friday, 9 March 2012.

part of a wider set of issues that US administrative law faces in its constitutional system. For instance, unlike the EU system, the US process is more insulated from political influences during the process of regulating SPS risks. Determinations take place outside of the charged political sphere and, importantly, do not incorporate the EU approach of considering consumer interests in determining what course of action to take. Nor is the precautionary principle, now viewed as a principle of EU law, treated in a similar manner in the US where its application is more limited.[58]

Further, the cultural outlook in the US vis-à-vis food safety (also the result of national processes of contestation) is less hostile to technological developments in agri-business. Pollack and Schaffer refer to the relative comfort with which the US population views the use of science and technology in food production as a result of numerous factors including: a large-scale agricultural industry developing after mechanization; no genuine limitation on space that may be used for arable pastoral land; and (until recently) the lack of highly publicized failings by the key regulators involved in assessing and determining SPS risks.[59]

While the EU has been attempting to tackle issues of scientific evidence in legal decision-making more recently, US courts have been confronted with questions over the relationship between law and science since the 1960s,[60] while judicial review of the actions of administrative agencies also have a longer pedigree.[61] While the EU system was influenced by debates relating to questions of legitimacy, competence, and integrity of the single market, the US system has been informed by other considerations. The most obvious of these is the distinct constitutional settlement that serves as a backdrop: the US federal legal system has a highly developed and nuanced jurisprudence engaging with the appropriate levels of judicial oversight of administrative agencies as bodies exercising delegated powers.[62]

The deference shown to the decisions of agencies under US law by the judiciary is of particular relevance here. US courts have been wary not to review the actions of agencies in detail under the *Chevron* doctrine.[63] Under the *Chevron* doctrine, in instances of delegated executive authority, both agency and courts are to abide by

[58] On the pedigree of the precautionary principle under US law: N Ashford, 'The Legacy of the Precautionary Principle in U.S. Law: The Rise of Cost-Benefit Analysis and Risk Assessment as Undermining Factors in Health, Safety and Environmental Protection', in N de Sadeleer (ed.), *Implementation of the Precautionary Principle: Approaches from the Nordic Countries, the EU and the United States* (London, Earthscan 2007).

[59] M Pollack and G Shaffer, *When Cooperation Fails*, n. 26, 43ff and 73. This may change with the introduction of wider preventative obligations in food safety for the FDA under ss 101–16, Food Safety Modernization Act 2011 [Pub L 111-353, 124 Stat 3885].

[60] J Peel, 'Risk Regulation Under the WTO SPS Agreement: Science as an International Normative Yardstick?' Jean Monnet Working Paper 02/04, 20.

[61] The cornerstone of modern US administrative law dates to the Administrative Procedure Act 1946 [Pub L 79-404, 60 Stat 237].

[62] See generally, S Breyer, R Stewart, and C Sunstein (eds), *Administrative Law and Regulatory Policy* (6th edn, New York, Aspen 2006); S Breyer, 'Judicial Review of Questions of Law and Policy', (1986) 38 *Administrative Law Review* 363; and A Scalia, 'Judicial Deference to Agency Interpretations of Law', (1989) *Duke Law Journal* 511.

[63] *Chevron U.S.A. Inc. v Natural Resources Defense Council, Inc.*, 467 U.S. 837 (1984).

Congress' intent where it is clear. Where Congress' intent under the delegating legislation is not clear the agency's interpretation of the legislation (and thus its duties and how it carries them out) is to be deferred to so long as it is not unreasonable.[64] In practice this creates a hierarchy of authority: Congress' wishes are to be given priority where clear; failing that, where its instructions are unclear (intentionally or inadvertently)[65] the agency's judgment is to be given priority. Only where the agency acts unreasonably is the judiciary to review its acts.[66]

Here we can see the priority given to Congress as the political fountainhead of the agency's legitimacy. In this context, judicial restraint in reviewing agency interpretations is part of the courts' desire to support the premise at the heart of the US constitutional bargain: that it is for the courts to interpret and review where necessary but it is for the political branches of government (i.e. Congress and the executive) to exercise powers on behalf of the people. In this context, accountability is to be best achieved where there is active or potential political oversight. Agencies, which derive their powers from legislation and exercise executive authority are closer to the politically accountable elements of government: '[w]hile agencies are not directly accountable to the people, the Chief Executive is'.[67] Whereas the EU's priorities were to establish a legitimate framework for the relationships between citizen, Member State, and Union Institutions, the US approach is designed to 'foster democratic values by ensuring that policy decisions are being made by politically responsible bodies'.[68] It is concerned with ensuring legitimacy of decision-making via horizontal balances (i.e. between the branches of government and the exercise of their powers through delegation).

Just as the EU courts became involved in a compromise between the integrity of the internal market and the desire to ensure the legitimacy of the Union institutions in health matters, so the US courts have had to accommodate the relative autonomy of the agencies with a genuine need to ensure appropriate outcomes in their decision-making. The *Benzene* decision is the landmark case in this area, with the Supreme Court encouraging the use of scientific evidence as the basis for decisions on potential areas of risk regulation.[69] The result has been widespread, encouraging a decision-making process by agencies focussing on standard setting and the prioritization of scientific evidence.[70] This approach, taken up by the US handbooks on risk assessment, is an attempt to counter the autonomy that courts

[64] Ibid., 842–4. [65] Ibid., 865–6.

[66] Editorial, 'Justifying the Chevron Doctrine: Insights from the Rule of Lenity', (2010) 123 *Harvard Law Review* 2043, 2043–4.

[67] *Chevron U.S.A. Inc. v Natural Resources Defense Council, Inc*, n. 63, 865.

[68] 'Justifying the Chevron Doctrine: Insights from the Rule of Lenity', (2010) 123 *Harvard Law Review* 2043, 2063. This has been strengthened by the Supreme Court's opinion in *Coeur Alaska, Inc. v Southeast Alaska Conservation Council*, 557 US 1 (2009) in which the Court retreated from previous opinions that had served to undermine Chevron deference, notably *United States v Mead Corp.*, 533 US 218 (2001).

[69] *Industrial Union Department v American Petroleum Institute*, 448 US 607 (1980) ('Benzene'), 656.

[70] 'Standard setting was increasingly being understood as primarily an analytical process in which there was little role for professional judgement, deliberation or administrative policy choice.' E Fisher, *Risk Regulation and Administrative Constitutionalism*, n. 10, 116.

grant agency decisions with the need to ensure that they do not exercise authority in an unfettered manner.[71]

c. *Codex Alimentarius Commission*

The US and EU are not the only members with diverse experiences of regulating SPS measures. The aim here has been to offer an illustrative example, in particular in light of the *Beef Hormones* dispute which will be discussed below. Clearly, there are a number of different experiences that have had a direct impact on litigation at the WTO, Japan being the most obvious example. Japan's concern over food security as a net importer (an anxiety entrenched in the post-war period) as well as its related regulatory approaches offering peace of mind to the population (incorporated in the concept of '*anzen-anshin*') has developed a distinct relationship with SPS regulation.[72] To depict Japan as crudely protectionist in matters of agriculture as a result of rent-seeking influences is to identify *a* proximate cause and not the underlying causes of Japan's legal regulation and their interface with the WTO. Similar analyses can be offered of other members active in SPS regulation such as Australia, Argentina, or Russia. One of the aims here, however, is to move away from a single level analysis and instead view the interacting actors as part of a globalized legal space. One such actor, central to the discussions in this chapter, is not a WTO member but an international organization: Codex.

Codex has its origins in post-war attempts to improve standard setting and recognition in food standards. In particular, the economic integration efforts within Europe spurred on the earlier Codex Alimentarius Austriacus, then Codex Alimentarius Europeaus, and then later the truly multilateral Codex Alimentarius Commission under the auspices of the FAO in 1961.[73] From the earliest days of international standard setting in the field of food, the use of scientific evidence was present, with the 1950 FAO/WHO Expert Committee on Nutrition identifying the problems posed by introducing legislation without scientific basis.[74]

Over the 1961–95 period, Codex demonstrated both the strengths and weaknesses of pre-emergence global governance.[75] Decision-making was principally consensus based and a 'gentlemen's club' atmosphere prevailed.[76] Away from the public eye, Codex could pursue its work in a less contentious environment.

[71] National Research Council, *Risk Assessment in the Federal Government: Managing the Process* (National Academy Press 1983), *National Research Council, Science and Judgment in Risk Assessment* (National Academy Press 1994).

[72] T Yamaguchi, 'Social Imaginary and Dilemmas of Policy Practice: The Food Safety Arena in Japan', (2014) 45 *Food Policy* 167; R D Smith, 'Food Security and International Fisheries Policy in Japan's Postwar Planning', (2008) 11(2) *Social Science Japan Journal* 259.

[73] See Codex Secretariat, *Understanding the Codex Alimentarius* (3rd edn, FAO 2006), 6–9.

[74] World Health Organization, techn. Rep. Ser. (1950) 16, p. 24.

[75] That is, before emerging economies such as Brazil and China began to assert themselves effectively in multilateral negotiations.

[76] M Burkard, 'The Ractopamine Dispute in the Codex Alimentarius Commission', (2012) *European Journal of Risk Regulation* 610, 611.

Consensus, however, can lend itself to dominance by powerful participants, and the limitations on the technical capacity of many members restricted their ability to engage with the standard setting process in which they were nominally participants.[77]

The change came with the entry into force of the SPS Agreement. Standard setting at Codex had been useful, encouraged, and effective but the SPS Agreement added a further dimension: Codex standards were to have legal effect insofar as a standard based on an international standard (including Codex standards) was presumed to comply with the relevant obligations under the SPS Agreement and GATT.[78] Debates at Codex took on increased relevance as their outcomes could have a direct impact on how members could legitimately regulate to protect human, animal, and plant health or safety. Indeed, heated discussions at Codex in the early 1990s over the regulation of growth hormones in beef, for example, become more contentious as the legal import of such standards was strengthened.[79]

We recall that the WTO was to resolve difficult questions over food safety (for example) by requiring scientific justification for measures, and that Codex had gone through a similar change following (*inter alia*) earlier debates over the use of hormones in beef production. Yet the interaction between Codex and the WTO was mutually constitutive: the WTO legitimated Codex as a global regulator, while Codex refashioned itself as the embodiment of science-based procedures in setting food standards. Winickoff and Bushey's examination of this process demonstrate how since 1995, 'the Codex transitioned from a largely invisible standard-setting body to a global regulatory agency, enshrining an authoritative discourse of "risk analysis".'[80] Science was to resolve the difficult debates in SPS regulation, and Codex was to play a central role in embodying the scientific turn in international regulation (strongly encouraged by a post-*Benzene* US).

The Codex seeks to depict itself as a value-neutral depoliticized body intent on decision-making through scientific rational processes: note, the *Principles for the Risk Analysis of Foods Derived from Modern Biotechnology* which specifically do not address 'environmental, ethical, moral and socio-economic aspects of the research, development, production and marketing of these foods'.[81] The increased political attention stemming from its legal relevance has strained the consensus-based model of decision-making at Codex: if a standard is going to have legal consequences for a member, abstaining in the Codex vote is insufficient, and so the superficially divisive politics of majority voting could take hold.[82] In an attempt to respond to this development, Codex has sought to

[77] An imbalance that Art. 11 TBT Agreement seeks to correct in part.

[78] Article 3(2) SPS Agreement. See further n. 97 and accompanying text.

[79] For example Report of the Nineteenth Session of the Joint FAO/WHO Codex Alimentarius Commission (1991) Alinorm 91/40.

[80] D E Winickoff and D M Bushey, 'Science and Power in Global Food Regulation: The Rise of the Codex Alimentarius', (2010) 35(3) *Science, Technology, & Human Values* 356, 358.

[81] Section 2(7) CAC/GL 44-2003 (adopted 2003, amendments 2008, 2011).

[82] For one such dispute: M Burkard, n. 76.

encourage greater participation by developing members, capacity building and transparency.[83]

What transpires is a mutually reinforcing and yet challenging relationship between Codex and the WTO. As Winickoff and Bushey identify:

> Just as the WTO addressed problems of legitimacy in the legal/economic order by identifying a common trust in scientific rigor and existing international expertise, so too the Codex addressed difficult questions regarding the role of science in regulatory process through legitimation received from the WTO. In effect, the SPS negotiators and the trading regime had to produce the very science-based agency it had identified as its foundation.[84]

Yet, the mutual benefits have also brought challenges: first, the subsequent political interest in Codex has placed pressure on its ability to identify as an apolitical and objective standard setting institution, while, second, the Codex's entrenchment of the strict scientific basis for risk assessment has distorted the way in which such processes are understood at the WTO and within the membership. It is this second challenge which will create added complications when we return to the *EC–Beef Hormones* dispute.

3. Decision-making and models of knowledge

Unlike safeguard measures, where a number of competing theories exist for their use, debates surrounding SPS measures are instead concerned with what constitutes a *legitimate* SPS measure. Sanitary and phytosanitary measures encompass a range of different regulatory acts with different objectives. There are those whose objective is the protection of certain plants[85] or animals,[86] some measures concern protecting human health and safety as well as other biological factors (for example, the EU's position over the potential risk of genetically modified organisms in the food chain).[87] There are other measures, however, the objective of which is specifically the protection of human health and safety.[88] With a potentially wide range of distinct measures falling under regulation of the SPS Agreement and their

[83] Report of the Fifty-First (Extraordinary) Session of the Executive Committee of the Codex Alimentarius Commission (2003) Alinorm 03/25/2, 4.

[84] D E Winickoff and D M Bushey, n. 80, 362.

[85] *Japan—Measures Affecting Agricultural Products*, Report of the Appellate Body (22 February 1999) WT/DS76/AB/R.

[86] *Australia—Measures Affecting Importation of Salmon*, Report of the Appellate Body (20 October 1998) WT/DS18/AB/R.

[87] *European Communities—Measures Affecting the Approval and Marketing of Biotech Products*, Panel Report (26 September 2006) WT/DS291,292,293/R ('EC – Biotech').

[88] For example, those challenged in: *European Communities—Measures Concerning Meat and Meat Products*, Report of the Appellate Body (16 January 1998) WT/DS26/AB/R and WT/DS48/AB/R ('*EC–Hormones* Appellate Body'); *European Communities—Measures Concerning Meat and Meat Products (Hormones) Complaint by the US*, Panel Report (18 August 1997) WT/DS26/R/USA ('*EC–Hormones* Panel (US)'); and *European Communities—Measures Concerning Meat and Meat Products (Hormones) Complaint by Canada*, Panel Report (18 August 1997) WT/DS48/R/CAN ('*EC–Hormones* Panel (Canada)').

potential impact on trade, the key disputes over how SPS measures are to be regulated have instead been concerned with deciding the criteria of validity for such measures. Put simply, how are they to come to that decision?

While the original hope was that science would serve as a value-neutral yardstick with which to determine which measures were genuine and which were protectionist, practice has been more complex. As decision-making takes place in the shadow of the legal structures and cultures in place, the different influences of law inspire different concerns over the ability of the SPS 'sound science' bargain to provide the certainty expected.

For example, there are serious questions over the nature of scientific evidence, how to use minority evidence, and what to do in the absence of evidence. These concerns relate to the core role that law has in determining the way in which decision-makers are to understand evidence. One such intervention on this point is an examination of the role of 'post-normal science' in decision-making. Footer describes post-normal science as 'science for policy, which embraces a situation where scientific uncertainty and value issues are commonplace, where objectivity is not possible, where prediction and control are limited, and where society and politics have a key role to play'.[89] We see here the difficulties presented by a 'sound science' approach in areas where scientific evidence is lacking or the complexities of the object of study render scientific examination in this model of limited use. It is a concern over how our current legal rules prioritize one way of thinking about what constitutes a proper scientific method over other methods. This is the nexus between scientific positivism and legal formalism, a concern that crude accounts of what 'the science says' are as useful as 'what the text says' in a given instance. The SPS Agreement encourages an epistemology which in turn shapes how we investigate the subject of this legal regulation.

An interrelated concern is over the inability of members to use WTO law instrumentally in order to restrict imports where a population is particularly hostile to certain products. This is framed as a choice between 'science' on one hand and 'democracy' on the other (though it could equally be distinguished on the basis of expertise or populism). In essence, this is a concern over the ways in which law can be used for a purpose: limiting protectionism, or acknowledging consumer concerns.[90]

In her work on administrative constitutionalism, Fisher disagrees with the fundamental premise of the science/democracy dichotomy arguing that at the national level such decisions are routinely taken by administrative agencies that are neither elected nor subject to popular oversight.[91]

[89] M E Footer, 'Post-normal Science in the Multilateral Trading System', n. 10, 285.

[90] On EU consumer concerns: Special Eurobarometer 341/73.1, 'Biotechnology' available at <http://ec.europa.eu/public_opinion/archives/ebs/ebs_341_en.pdf> (accessed 6 August 2015).

[91] E Fisher, *Risk Regulation and Administrative Constitutionalism*, n. 10, 180–5. In a similar vein: A Arcuri, 'Food Safety at the WTO after "Continued Suspension": a Paradigm Shift?', in A Antoniadis, R Schütze, and E Spaventa (eds), *The European Union and Global Emergencies: A Law and Policy Analysis* (Oxford, Hart Publishing 2011).

Viewing the debate surrounding regulation of risk as symptomatic of the debate surrounding the appropriate use of technical information and expertise within a system that requires such skills in areas of complex regulation, Fisher reframes the debate, distinguishing between two different models of decision-making in risk regulation. In the first, the 'Rational-Instrumental' paradigm, agencies are given very strict specific instructions with legislators viewing their role instrumentally, applying rules, and following the guidance set down for them in the legislation. This approach reconciles the legislature that is democratically legitimate and a public administration that is not. 'Public administration may not be democratic, but it can be structured to ensure the efficient pursuit of goals generated by the democratic process.'[92] Such an approach is premised on restricting the autonomy of administrative decision-makers to ensure the primacy of democratic institutions, giving agencies a series of 'discrete analytical tasks'.[93] This presents problems as the science related to risk necessarily contains uncertainties and value judgments must be made.

The second paradigm Fisher suggests is the 'Deliberative-Constitutive' model. In this approach administrative agencies are given considerable leeway in how they come to their decision, 'granting to public administration substantial and ongoing problem-solving discretion in relation to particular issues'.[94] This gives agencies greater scope to exercise authority in a way that the legislators may not have foreseen or, more importantly, may not have wanted. Most usefully, it encourages open deliberation and discourse that in turn, it is hoped, provides better outcomes.[95]

In raising these issues and reframing the debate, Fisher attacks the caricature of science as value neutral and precise as opposed to political decision-making or judicial interpretation as unhelpful and harmful.[96] She further indicates how such a dichotomy strengthens the conceptual divide between trade and non-trade areas of regulation, a divide that may serve only to undermine an accurate understanding of how the WTO does and should work. Instead the key debate is over the way in which administrative bodies reach decisions and if the method chosen produces the best outcomes and satisfies the preoccupations of the polity in question. Yet, these other narratives are relevant, the key point is that they speak to different expectations and concerns with how SPS regulation effects actors (whether consumers, policy-makers, or risk-regulators).

The picture drawn of SPS regulation thus far is a complicated one. Competing motivations, institutions, and epistemologies all feeding into a heavily contested area of law. The following sections examine the development of specific issues in SPS regulation at the WTO to analyse how these competing influences play out. Part C traces the interpretation and usage of the term 'risk assessment' at the

[92] E Fisher, *Risk Regulation and Administrative Constitutionalism*, n. 10, 28.
[93] Ibid., at 29. [94] Ibid., at 30.
[95] For one such account: C Sunstein, *Risk and Reason: Safety, Law, and the Environment* (Cambridge, Cambridge University Press 2002).
[96] E Fisher, *Risk Regulation and Administrative Constitutionalism*, n. 10, 16ff.

WTO, specifically through the *EC–Beef Hormones* dispute as a way of shedding light on how this area of law has developed in light of these influences.

C. The Distinction between Risk Assessment and Risk Management: Epistemological Conflicts

The SPS Agreement contains a simple yet powerful compromise between minimizing the trade distorting effects of SPS measures and the desire of members to maintain potentially higher standards of protection than the international standard. Article 3(2) states: 'Sanitary or phytosanitary measures which conform to international standards, guidelines or recommendations shall be deemed to be necessary to protect human, animal or plant life or health, and presumed to be consistent with the relevant provisions of this Agreement and of GATT 1994.' This allows members to use 'off the rack' standards and be confident in the knowledge that, so long as they are applied appropriately, their SPS controls will be presumed compliant.[97] However, should a member feel that the international standard is not sufficient for its needs, it can create its own 'bespoke' regulation. This comes at an additional cost,[98] as Art. 3(3) makes clear:

> Members may introduce or maintain sanitary or phytosanitary measures which result in a higher level of sanitary or phytosanitary protection than would be achieved by measures based on the relevant international standards, guidelines or recommendations, if there is a scientific justification, or as a consequence of the level of sanitary or phytosanitary protection a Member determines to be appropriate in accordance with the relevant provisions of paragraphs 1 through 8 of Article 5. Notwithstanding the above, all measures which result in a level of sanitary or phytosanitary protection different from that which would be achieved by measures based on international standards, guidelines or recommendations shall not be inconsistent with any other provision of this Agreement.

The requirements of Art. 5 are the focus of this section: 'Assessment of Risk and Determination of the Appropriate Level of Sanitary and Phytosanitary Protection',[99]

[97] It is possible to 'base' measures on an international standard but not incorporate it in such a way as to 'conform to' the international standard. In such cases, the measure does not enjoy the presumption of consistency that a measure conforming to the international standard would (*EC–Hormones Appellate Body*, para. 171). It has been questioned what advantage a member has in only 'basing' a measure on an international standard: J Pauwelyn, 'The WTO Agreement on Sanitary and Phytosanitary (SPS) Measures as Applied in the First Three Disputes: EC–Hormones, Australia–Salmon and Japan–Varietals', (1999) *Journal of International Economic Law* 641, 656.

[98] J Peel, 'Risk Regulation Under the WTO SPS Agreement', n. 10, p 60: 'unless a Member simply adopts the same risk regulatory measures as are recommended by international bodies or taken by other Member States, it will need to have sufficient technical capacity to be able to verify that there is an objective link between the scientific findings of a risk assessment and the measures it wishes to adopt.' In support Peel cites the concern of the FAO during the negotiations on the SPS Agreement: FAO paper submitted to the Working Group on Sanitary and Phytosanitary Regulations and Barriers, 'Technical Assistance in the Field of Plant Protection' (20 April 1990) GATT Doc MTN.GNG/NG5/WGSP/W/16.

[99] Title, Art. 5, SPS Agreement.

more commonly known as risk assessment and risk management. The distinction between these exercises, and its treatment at the hands of panels and the Appellate Body, can be understood as part of a four-way contestation: the US, the EU, Codex, and the institutions of the dispute settlement system itself. Each of these actors is motivated by their own legal strictures, yet the result at the WTO does not correspond to their preferred outcome.

The analysis of this section is in three stages: first, a brief examination of the distinction between risk assessment and risk management in risk regulation; second, an overview of the *EC–Hormones* litigation in this area, identifying the key causes for the panels' and Appellate Body's approach to the distinction;[100] and third, identifying key insights in the development of the law on risk assessment/risk management at the WTO in light of the interactions between the EU, US, Codex, and dispute settlement institutions of the WTO.

1. Approaches to distinguishing risk assessment from risk management

The distinction between risk assessment and risk management is a widespread one: the Codex maintains it,[101] as does the Cartagena Protocol[102] and numerous national regulatory systems including the EU, Australia, Japan, and the US.[103] As identified above, it became popular in the US as a result of domestic legal issues and increasingly spread to bodies such as the Codex and other members of the WTO.[104]

Risk assessment is defined by Codex as: 'A scientifically based process consisting of the following steps: (i) hazard identification, (ii) hazard characterization, (iii) exposure assessment, and (iv) risk characterization.'[105] It is a scientific process designed to identify and determine the level and nature of risk in a specific case.

Risk management is a different process, politically sensitive insofar as it is not restricted to science alone. Codex defines risk management as: 'The process, distinct from risk assessment, of weighing policy alternatives, in consultation with all interested parties, considering risk assessment and other factors relevant for the health protection of consumers and for the promotion of fair trade practices, and, if needed, selecting appropriate prevention and control options.'[106]

[100] Principally: *EC–Hormones (Appellate Body)*. *EC–Hormones Panel (US)*, *EC–Hormones Panel (Canada)*, n. 88, and *United States—Continued Suspension of Obligations in the EC–Hormones Dispute*, Panel Report (21 March 2008) 1WT/DS320/R ('*EC–Hormones Continued Suspension Panel (US)*'); *Canada—Continued Suspension of Obligations in the EC–Hormones Dispute*, Panel Report (21 March 2008) 1WT/DS321/R ('*EC–Hormones Continued Suspension Panel (Canada)*'); *United States—Continued Suspension Of Obligations In The EC–Hormones Dispute*, Report of the Appellate Body (16 October 2008) WT/DS320/AB/R ('*EC–Hormone Continued Suspension Appellate Body*').

[101] Codex Alimentarius Commission, *Procedural Manual* (17th edn, FAO 2007) 112.

[102] Articles 15–16, Cartagena Protocol on Biosafety to the Convention Biological Diversity (concluded 29 January 2000, entered into force 11 September 2003) 2226 UNTS 208.

[103] See generally: Food and Agriculture Organization & World Health Organization, *Food Safety Risk Analysis: A Guide for National Food Safety Authorities* (FAO 2006) 7.

[104] Section B.2. [105] Codex Alimentarius Commission, n. 101, 112. [106] Ibid.

It would appear to be a clear distinction: risk assessment serves as a scientific process undertaken by expert risk assessors who provide evidence to risk managers who then undertake decisions in light of policy choices and preferences tailored to the society in question. The appeal of such an approach is clear: risk specialists can be given instructions to provide quantitative or qualitative evidence for the levels of risk for certain hazards. This is done in a neutral scientific manner while leaving the risk management process to a distinct group of specialists who in turn can be given appropriate guidance over which criteria should be used to determine the appropriate level of protection for the SPS risk.[107]

Risk assessment is not a value neutral process, however. The view of science as a cold arbiter, concerned only with empirical data is not an accurate one in the context of risk regulation (or indeed more broadly).[108] There are various ways in which risk assessment is influenced by values and policy judgments. In the first instance, they point out how the first stage in the risk assessment process ('risk identification') already involves value judgments: 'A policymaker's perceptions and judgments are a function both of empirical observation and of the conceptual lenses used to view the evidence.'[109] Determining which risks we think require assessment is itself a value judgment.[110] Further, assumptions made over the way risk analysis is conducted in the face of uncertainty are again deeply influenced by value judgments: '[e]ven the trade off between mortality and morbidity (for example, pain associated with illness) involves tacit value judgments'.[111]

At a practical level also, the relationship between risk assessment and risk management is not as clear-cut as it might seem. It is common for risk managers to interact with risk assessors as SPS measures are tailored to the identified risk in order to achieve the desired level of protection for that member.[112] Thus, to distinguish between risk assessment and risk management in the manner identified so far is a *choice*, one that effects the way in which we think of science and the use of scientific knowledge in decision-making.[113]

Though common, within the WTO the distinction between risk assessment and risk management is not evident from the text. While the SPS Agreement defines risk assessment it makes no explicit mention of risk management.[114]

[107] The appeal of an allegedly neutral scientific method finds expression in a number of legally related areas: note the discussion in Chapter 2.C(1).

[108] D Winickoff, S Jasanoff, L Busch, R Grove-White, and B Wynne, 'Adjudicating the GM Food Wars: Science, Risk, and Democracy in World Trade Law', (2005) 30 *Yale Journal of International Law* 81, 93ff.

[109] Ibid., 94.

[110] This is another representation of the relationship between values and law discussed in Chapter 3.B(1): the determination of what should be subject to a form of regulation or, in this case, scientific analysis is the result of a process of contestation.

[111] Ibid.

[112] For a convenient diagram indicating the interactions between the risk assessment and risk management phases: L Gruszczynski, 'Risk Management Policies under the WTO Agreement on the Application of Sanitary and Phytosanitary Measures', (2008) 3(1) *Asian Journal of WTO & International Health Law and Policy* 261, 268.

[113] n. 91ff and accompanying text.

[114] Annex 1(A) para. 4 SPS Agreement, 'The evaluation of the likelihood of entry, establishment or spread of a pest or disease within the territory of an importing Member according to the sanitary

Article 5.1 sets out the core obligation as regards risk assessment: 'Members shall ensure that their sanitary or phytosanitary measures are based on an assessment, as appropriate to the circumstances, of the risks to human, animal or plant life or health, taking into account risk assessment techniques developed by the relevant international organizations.' Questions are raised, however, over the nature of the 'taking into account' provision with regards to other international organizations such as Codex. It is also unclear what factors should be taken into account in a risk assessment for it to comply with Art. 5.1. There is some guidance under the SPS Agreement: 'In the assessment of risks, Members shall take into account available scientific evidence; relevant processes and production methods; relevant inspection, sampling and testing methods; prevalence of specific diseases or pests; existence of pest- or disease-free areas; relevant ecological and environmental conditions; and quarantine or other treatment.'[115] Is this a closed list? Or is it merely indicative? If other factors are rejected, would they undermine the entirety of the risk assessment or simply be set aside? The precise scope of the risk assessment obligation is not as clear as it might have been hoped, especially in light of the differing cultures of risk regulation amongst both members and Codex.

The risk assessment obligations under the SPS Agreement were to become one of the key issues in the *EC–Hormones* dispute brought by Canada and the US over EU restrictions on the treatment of cattle with certain types of hormone and the sale of meat from any such cattle.[116] A key question with regard to the risk assessment/risk management distinction was whether the evidence examined as part of the EU's risk assessment complied with the requirements of Art. 5 SPS Agreement.[117] The panels[118] and Appellate Body approached this issue in part reflecting the debates relating to SPS measures within the EU, the US, as well as at the Codex. To further complicate matters, both the panels and Appellate Body

or phytosanitary measures which might be applied, and of the associated potential biological and economic consequences; or the evaluation of the potential for adverse effects on human or animal health arising from the presence of additives, contaminants, toxins or disease-causing organisms in food, beverages or feedstuffs.'

115 Article 5.2 SPS Agreement. In the case of risks to animal or plant life or health, 'Members shall take into account as relevant economic factors: the potential damage in terms of loss of production or sales in the event of the entry, establishment or spread of a pest or disease; the costs of control or eradication in the territory of the importing Member; and the relative cost-effectiveness of alternative approaches to limiting risks.' (Article 5.3 SPS Agreement.)

116 Primarily: Council Directive 81/602/EEC 31 July 1981 concerning the prohibition of certain substances having a hormonal action and of any substances having a thyrostatic action [1981] OJ L222/32, Council Directive 88/146/EEC of 7 March 1988 prohibiting the use in livestock farming of certain substances having a hormonal action [1988] OJ L70/16 and Council Directive 88/299/EEC of 17 May 1988 on trade in animals treated with certain substances having a hormonal action and their meat, as referred to in Art. 7 of Directive 88/146/EEC [1988] OJ L128/36. The hormones used were largely to encourage growth (though they also have applications for the fertility of cattle). See *EC–Hormones Panel* (*US*), II ('Factual Aspects').

117 Of particular importance for the EU's case was the use of reports of the European Parliament and opinions of the EC Economic and Social Committee (*EC–Hormones Panel* (*US*), paras 8.108–9).

118 In the first *EC–Hormones* dispute two panels were constituted (one for each claimant). However, as they are near identical and composed of the same panellists, for clarity the *EC–Hormones* (*US*) (*Panel*) will be used as the reference point unless otherwise specified.

sought to legitimate themselves in the eyes of the membership in light of the constitutive and systemic influence of the DSU and their own Working Procedures.[119]

2. The panels' interpretation of Article 5 SPS Agreement in the *EC–Hormones* litigation

The panels in *EC–Hormones* started by describing Art. 5 as relating to two separate sets of rights and obligations: those relating to risk assessment and those relating to risk management.[120] The panels interpreted Art. 5 as containing both risk assessment disciplines (Arts 5.1–5.3) and risk management disciplines (Arts 5.4–5.6).[121] For the panels it was self-evident that any process of risk regulation was divided in this manner and an examination of the risk procedures indicated by other international organizations such as Codex supported this.[122]

In dividing risk assessment and risk management, the panels chose to characterize the processes as fundamentally different. In general terms, the panel maintained 'that there is a distinction between *risk assessment* which is a *scientific* examination and *risk management* which involves social value judgments.'[123]

Risk assessment was identified as 'an assessment of risks is, at least for risks to human life or health, a scientific examination of data and factual studies; it is not a policy exercise involving social value judgments made by political bodies'.[124] Risk management, on the other hand, follows risk assessment whereupon 'a Member will need to decide, on the basis of its own value judgments, whether it can accept these risks. In so doing a Member sets its "appropriate level of sanitary protection". The determination and application of the appropriate level of protection by a Member is part of risk management.'[125]

In this manner, the panels contrasted the two separate processes: interpreting risk assessment as a mechanical process comprised of a series of clear decisions in the field of scientific investigation, followed by the application of the 'science' via risk management in order to achieve specific policy objectives.[126]

Consequently, the panels rejected the use of reports from political institutions: two reports of the EC Economic and Social Committee and four reports of the European Parliament on the basis that such reports 'evaluated' the scientific evidence and thus were part of the risk management process (and not eligible to contribute to the obligation to base measures on adequate risk assessment).[127] In addition they equated the requirement for a measure to be 'based on' a risk assessment under Art. 5.1 to being 'in conformity with' the conclusions of the scientific studies (i.e. the process of risk assessment).[128] These decisions, along with a focus on

[119] Canada's involvement in the dispute was supplemental and supportive of the US, raising its claim once the US had, and finalizing the dispute earlier with the completion of the EU–Canada Comprehensive Economic and Trade Agreement (available at <http://trade.ec.europa.eu/doclib/html/152806.htm>). For this reason, the US is the focus of the analysis.

[120] *EC–Hormones Panel* (*US*) para. 8.91. [121] Ibid., paras 8.95–6.

[122] Ibid., para. 8.103. [123] Ibid., para. 8.160 (emphasis in original).

[124] Ibid., para. 8.94. [125] Ibid., para. 8.160.

[126] What Fisher identifies as rational-instrumental: E Fisher, *Risk Regulation and Administrative Constitutionalism*, n. 10, 186.

[127] *EC–Hormones Panel* (*US*), para. 8.109. [128] Ibid., para. 8.117.

the evidence of appointed experts and a refusal to engage with broader principles or the difficulties associated with scientific uncertainty demonstrated the panels' view of risk assessment as a technical process restrained by the applicable legal rules and 'not to be complicated by scientific uncertainty or socio-political complexity'.[129]

The accounts offered for the approach taken by the panels at this stage has been explained in different ways: overreliance on the international standards of other international organizations (even where such standards had not been finalized),[130] choosing the US's approach to risk regulation as a model,[131] being influenced by its own frame of reference in determining the appropriate standard of review,[132] or apparent ignorance of the rules of treaty interpretation.[133]

These accounts overemphasize certain causal influences at the expense of others. Instead of focussing on the systemic influence of standards of review, or the constitutive influence of choices regarding the interpretation and use of scientific knowledge, the reports should be viewed as part of a multi-causal event with the panels' desire to self-legitimate in light of these competing influences as the centrepoint of the analysis. The Appellate Body, examined in the following section, has taken an equally interesting path.

3. The Appellate Body's response: Pursuing self-legitimation through deference and independence

The Appellate Body's response to the distinction drawn by the panels was clear: the panels had failed in their primary duty to interpret the SPS Agreement in light of the text as it stands.[134] By distinguishing the provisions of Art. 5 on the basis of risk assessment and risk management they had interpreted the text in a way that was inconsistent with the wording of the Agreement. The Appellate Body highlighted the lack of explicit provisions on risk management within the SPS Agreement: 'We must stress, in this connection, that Article 5 and Annex A of the SPS Agreement speak of 'risk assessment' only and that the term 'risk management' is not to be found either in Article 5 or in any other provision of the SPS Agreement.'[135] The Appellate Body's correction of the panels' application of the risk management/risk assessment distinction was only in part to correct the panels' interpretative method. The Appellate Body was also preoccupied by the panels' 'restrictive notion of risk assessment'.[136] The Appellate Body was

[129] E Fisher, *Risk Regulation and Administrative Constitutionalism*, n. 10, 187.

[130] Ibid., 186.

[131] Ibid., 189.

[132] M Du, 'Standard of Review Under the SPS Agreement After EC—Hormones II', (2010) 59 *International and Comparative Law Quarterly* 441, 442.

[133] *EC–Hormones (Appellate Body)* para. 181: 'The fundamental rule of treaty interpretation requires a treaty interpreter to read and interpret the words actually used by the agreement under examination, and not words which the interpreter may feel should have been used.' The unhelpful tone with which the Appellate Body overturns panel decisions has been criticized elsewhere: P Van Den Bossche, 'The WTO Appellate Body and Its Rise to Prominence', in G Sacerdoti, A Yanovich, and J Bohanes (eds), *The WTO at Ten: The Contribution of the Dispute Settlement System* (Cambridge, Cambridge University Press 2006) 316.

[134] *EC–Hormones (Appellate Body)*, para. 181.

[135] Ibid.

[136] Ibid.

particularly critical of the panels' desire to place within the realm of risk assessment under Art. 5.1 only factors that are subject to 'quantitative analysis by the empirical or experimental laboratory methods commonly associated with the physical sciences'.[137] Instead, the Appellate Body identified the type of risk to be examined under Art. 5:

> It is essential to bear in mind that the risk that is to be evaluated in a risk assessment under Article 5.1 is not only risk ascertainable in a science laboratory operating under strictly controlled conditions, but also risk in human societies as they actually exist, in other words, the actual potential for adverse effects on human health in the real world where people live and work and die.[138]

For the panels this would be counter-intuitive: the scientific basis for risk assessment is not dependent on the location of the analysis.[139] To contrast risk in a laboratory with risk in the 'real world' misunderstands the process of risk assessment that must necessarily take place under controlled conditions from which risk managers may then extrapolate. If, however, one takes a view that 'public administration is understood as a substantive institution engaging in ongoing problem solving through the exercise of flexible discretion based on deliberation and analysis'[140] then the Appellate Body's analysis coheres. It is a different way to understand risk assessment and the use of scientific knowledge, one which grants members greater freedom in their procedural (though not substantive) obligations.

A more deferential position was also taken by the Appellate Body's finding that for a measure to be 'based on' risk assessment for the purposes of Art. 5.1 the measure had to have a 'rational relationship' to the risk assessment.[141] Such a relationship was to be determined by the conclusions of the scientific evidence in the risk assessment and the implicit conclusions identifiable from the measure itself (as the panels had indicated) though not at the exclusion of all else.[142]

By rejecting the panels' interpretation of Art. 5 as being divided by risk assessment and risk management, the Appellate Body was not removing the risk management activities from the scope of the SPS Agreement but rather was incorporating them into a broader understanding of risk regulation that accepts qualitative and quantitative information in the analysis.[143] It has been suggested that the Appellate

[137] Ibid., para. 187. [138] Ibid.

[139] Viewing risk assessment in systemic terms, as a 'Weberian bureaucracy, a "transmission belt" that applies facts to specific legislative commands': E Fisher, 'Food Safety Crises as Crises in Administrative Constitutionalism', (2010) 20 *Health Matrix* 55, 62 (footnotes omitted).

[140] E Fisher, 'Food Safety Crises as Crises in Administrative Constitutionalism', n. 139.

[141] A Arcuri, 'Food Safety at the WTO after "Continued Suspension": a Paradigm Shift?', Rotterdam Institute of Law and Economics Working Paper Series, No 2010/04, 13. See also, J Scott, *The WTO Agreement on Sanitary and Phytosanitary Measures: A Commentary* (Oxford, Oxford University Press 2009) 104ff.

[142] *EC–Hormones* (Appellate Body) para. 193.

[143] In support of this interpretation and arguing for the existence of risk management disciplines in the SPS Agreement: L Gruszczynski, 'Risk Management Policies under the WTO Agreement on the Application of Sanitary and Phytosanitary Measures', (2008) 3 *Asian Journal of WTO & International Health Law and Policy* 261.

Body's decision in this case could reflect a choice between regulatory styles with the Appellate Body accepting the 'more deliberative nature of EU regulatory standard setting'[144] yet the picture is not quite so clear. This was not simply a choice between two options placed in front of the Appellate Body (a view based on the overemphasis of instrumental account of law). The choice here incorporated the Appellate Body's sensitivity to the expectation of the membership and the way in which it understood itself as an autonomous actor. This is particularly notable in the continuation of the dispute, at the compliance stage.

Questions over the appropriate interpretation of Art. 5 arose again when the EU raised claims against both the US and Canada for continuing to suspend WTO concessions despite the EU having complied (in its view) with the recommendations of the Dispute Settlement Body.

Citing the Appellate Body's criticism of the prior panel determinations, the panels accepted that the lack of reference to risk management provisions under Art. 5 specifically and the SPS Agreement more generally, meant that there could be no risk management components in the risk assessment process.[145] However, the Appellate Body implicitly supported the EU's submission that the panels had misunderstood the purpose of the Appellate Body's previous reasoning. Rather than excluding risk management factors per se the Appellate Body confirmed that its concern was at once with the panels' disregard for the text as it was but also the overly restrictive characterization of risk assessment:

> Therefore, in our view, the Panel's interpretation of 'risk assessment' resulted in the same 'restrictive notion of risk assessment' that the Appellate Body found to be erroneous in *EC – Hormones*. The Panel sought in this case to rewrite the Appellate Body Report in *EC – Hormones* and to re-establish the rigid distinction between 'risk assessment' and 'risk management' that the Appellate Body had rejected in that case.[146]

Making it abundantly clear that Art. 5 was not to be interpreted in such a fashion that would unduly restrict the factors that might be examined in complying with their obligations under Art. 5, the Appellate Body went further, strengthening its deferential stance in light of the appropriate standard of review. Rejecting either *de novo* review that would see the panels substituting members' determinations for their own scientific judgment or total deference that would give members such discretion as to undermine the obligation of the panels to provide an 'objective assessment', the Appellate Body clarified the position to be taken: '[T]he review power of a Panel is not to determine whether the risk assessment undertaken by a WTO Member is correct, but rather to determine whether that risk assessment is supported by coherent reasoning and respectable scientific evidence and is, in this sense, objectively justifiable.'[147] Such a stance grants considerable deference to

[144] E Fisher, *Risk Regulation and Administrative Constitutionalism*, n. 10, 189.
[145] *EC–Hormones Continued Suspension Panel* (*US*) paras 7.519–20. While there were two separate panels in this dispute also, as was the case in *EC–Hormones* they are near identical and so, for concision and clarity, references will be made to the panel constituted for the EC–US dispute.
[146] *EC–Hormones Continued Suspension* (*Appellate Body*), para. 542 (footnote omitted).
[147] Ibid., para. 590.

members in their risk assessments, allowing members greater freedom over defending their SPS measures.[148]

The interpretation of Art. 5 given by the Appellate Body is not simply a choice between options presented by either the EU or US approaches to risk. Instead, influenced by their interests as well as the Codex, the Appellate Body has pursued its own objectives as a constituted institution influenced by, yet separate to, those of the litigants at hand.

4. Intra-institutional contestations and the influence of the Dispute Settlement Understanding

The debate at the panels and Appellate Body over the appropriate definition of risk assessment under Art. 5 SPS Agreement is part of a challenge between alternative EU and US approaches to risk regulation, yet other influences abound: note the critical focus that the Appellate Body and the panels lent to the 'appropriate' interpretation of the text of Art. 5 and *their own* standard of review. While the alternative approaches of the US and EU may have inspired these bodies, they are only part of the process.

The Appellate Body and panels do not act in a normative vacuum. Though the EU and US attempt to use law instrumentally by raising claims to pursue their objective (in this specific example, to encourage a specific interpretation of Art. 5) they are not the only relevant actors; the Appellate Body and panels also pursue their own objectives, ones that do not necessarily run in tandem with the aims and objectives of the parties to the dispute. Nor are the EU and the US the only (or indeed principal) actors in determining the content of risk assessment: Codex has acted as a touchstone for the global shift towards a scientific basis for food safety, conceptualized in a particular systemic fashion, yet in a different legal framework, resulting in varied and divergent interpretations of risk-related concepts.

The previous chapter saw how the US's desire for the Appellate Body to be limited in its scope, instilling a textual fixation at the level of its constitutive document had unintended consequences for the interpretation of Art. XIX GATT. A similar though more complex process has taken place in this instance with the panels and the Appellate Body approaching the interpretation of Art. 5 not only through a lens of the paradigms on offer but also in light of their own legal framework. Constituted by the DSU, and constrained and enabled by its controls on their behaviour (including the consistent threat of DSB criticism), panels and the Appellate Body see their interests in maintaining their legitimacy as grounded in the direction they are given under the DSU. This finds form in this instance through a discourse on standard of review: in essence, a discussion

[148] S Cho, 'United States: Continued Suspension of Obligations in the EC–Hormones Dispute', (2009) 103(2) *American Journal of International Law* 299, 302; M Du, 'Standard of Review Under the SPS Agreement After EC–Hormones II', (2010) 59 *International and Comparative Law Quarterly* 441, 458.

over the *strength* of the systemic influence of the dispute settlement system on the membership.

a. *Panels as finders and assessors of facts*

For panels, Art. 11 DSU sets out their responsibilities as well as the appropriate standard of review to apply.[149] The Appellate Body confirmed this in *EC–Hormones*[150] and emphasized the key points in Art. 11:

> The function of Panels is to assist the DSB in discharging its responsibilities under this Understanding and the covered agreements. Accordingly, a Panel should make an objective assessment of the matter before it, including an objective assessment of the facts of the case and the applicability of and conformity with the relevant covered agreements, and make such other findings as will assist the DSB in making the recommendations or in giving the rulings provided for in the covered agreements. Panels should consult regularly with the parties to the dispute and give them adequate opportunity to develop a mutually satisfactory solution.[151]

The Appellate Body was at pains to emphasize the appropriate standard of review for panels: neither *de novo* nor total deference but instead an 'objective assessment' which involved considering evidence and making factual findings.[152] The concept of an 'objective assessment' is unclear and there has been considerable debate over its limits,[153] however, the role of the panel as fact-finder and fact-assessor has considerable conceptual weight.

The negotiating history of Art. 11 DSU shows serious concerns of the US over the level of deference that panels were to give national agency determinations.[154] In particular, the US was keen to have a form of *Chevron* deference[155] included in the DSU.[156] The concerns of other participants in the Uruguay Round over limiting the potential strength of panels in examining national measures lead to a deadlock[157] that was only resolved by accepting Art. 11 DSU as it now stands with a more restrictive standard of review under Art. 17.6 Anti-Dumping

[149] On the centrality of Art. 11 in the exercise of dispute settlement functions: *China—Measures Related to the Exportation of Rare Earths, Tungsten and Molybdenum*, Report of the Appellate Body (7 August 2014) WT/DS431-3/AB/R, para. 5.228.

[150] *EC–Hormones (Appellate Body)* para. 116.

[151] Ibid., underlining in original.

[152] Ibid., para. 133.

[153] R Becroft, *The Standard of Review in WTO Dispute Settlement: Critique and Development* (Cheltenham, Edward Elgar 2012) 50–2. Note the contours of the standard of review are informed by the substantive agreement in question: *US—Countervailing Duty Investigation on Dynamic Random Access Memory Semiconductors (DRAMS) from Korea*, Report of the Appellate Body (27 June 2005) WT/DS296/AB/R, 184.

[154] Indicated in interviews conducted by John Jackson: S Croley and J Jackson, 'WTO Dispute Procedures, Standard of Review, and Deference to National Governments', (1996) 90(2) *American Journal of International Law* 193, 194–5.

[155] On *Chevron* deference: n. 63 and accompanying text.

[156] S Croley and J Jackson, 'WTO Dispute Procedures, Standard of Review, and Deference to National Governments', n. 154, 194–5.

[157] On the negotiating history of Art. 11 DSU: M Oesch, *Standards of Review in WTO Dispute Resolution* (Oxford, Oxford University Press 2003) 72–80.

Agreement.[158] The wording of Art. 11 DSU has encouraged panels to view their role as defined by the text of the Agreement, with the focus on fact-finding particularly relevant.[159] Focussing on its role as fact-finder and assessor of facts produces a far closer fit with the position set forward by the US vis-à-vis regulation and review of decision-making. Thus in trying to legitimize itself, the panels are, in this instance, more inclined to support a restrictive view of what constituted risk assessment.

b. The Appellate Body's response: The careful court

When deciding on the distinction between risk assessment and risk management, the Appellate Body chose the model that would permit variation within a legal space (the WTO legal order). Though the Appellate Body did not go so far as to review the European decisions along the EU's own lines, it did accept the proposed paradigm as one that fulfils the requirements of the SPS Agreement. Its priority, therefore, is not to prefer one approach to another in a neutral fashion but instead, to select the approach that allows it to ensure its own legitimacy as it sees it. The contestation between the litigating parties feeds into the options available to the Appellate Body as it examines them as an autonomous globalized actor itself. While the panel focussed on a model that coincided with its own understanding of its constituted role as fact-finder and assessor of fact, the Appellate Body encouraged an approach that fits its conception of its role. Conscious of behaving appropriately and within the bounds of the DSU and its Working Procedures, the Appellate Body marries its own priority to self-legitimize with the available paradigms developed within the jurisdictions of the members before it. The result here is a focus on textual fidelity compounded by deference to the details in national agency determinations.

The outcome of the *EC–Hormones* cases owes as much to the way the Appellate Body and panels understand their own roles as dispute settlors and the constraints of the DSU as to the challenges between the primary litigants. The dispute itself is at the nexus of interacting influences: the pursuit by the litigants to use the rights available to them under WTO law to fulfil their objectives;

[158] Article 17.6, Agreement on implementation of Art. VI of the General Agreement on Tariffs and Trade 1994: '[I]n its assessment of the facts of the matter, the Panel shall determine whether the authorities' establishment of the facts was proper and whether their evaluation of those facts was unbiased and objective. If the establishment of the facts was proper and the evaluation was unbiased and objective, even though the Panel might have reached a different conclusion, the evaluation shall not be overturned; (ii) the Panel shall interpret the relevant provisions of the Agreement in accordance with customary rules of interpretation of public international law. Where the Panel finds that a relevant provision of the Agreement admits of more than one permissible interpretation, the Panel shall find the authorities' measure to be in conformity with the Agreement if it rests upon one of those permissible interpretations.' See further, G Messenger, 'Reforming the Law and Institutions of the WTO: the Dangers of Unexpected Consequences', in A Segura (ed.), *The Reform of International Economic Governance* (Farnham, Ashgate 2016).

[159] See generally, M Grando, *Evidence, Proof, and Fact-Finding in WTO Dispute Settlement* (Oxford, Oxford University Press 2009) Chapter 5.

the interplay between the Codex and the WTO in determining the content of risk regulation concepts as part of their mutually supportive relationship; and the need for institutions exercising delegated authority such as the panels and Appellate Body to legitimate themselves, in different ways given the constraints on their ability to act.

While the identity of the panels and the Appellate Body is a strong factor, over-emphasizing the agency of these bodies to the detriment of other legal influences fails to account for the same institution arriving at different conclusions in other areas such as technical barriers to trade. Note, under the TBT Agreement, the Appellate Body has focussed on legitimate objectives as a central element: aims rather than the process, unlike under the SPS Agreement where the requirements have strongly emphasized the need to conduct investigations in a determined fashion.[160] The distinct influence of the legal texts themselves thus spur the institutions to respond in alternative ways.

Instrumental accounts understand the development of the risk assessment/risk management distinction at the WTO as one of competing offers between litigants, without sufficient consideration for the importance of the legal constitution of the relevant actors (including the dispute settlement institutions themselves). Systemic accounts identify the correct interpretation of the legal rule as embodied under the applicable law, without sufficient consideration for the cross-cutting meaning given to these terms (such as the Codex influence on how risk is conceptualized). Constitutive accounts identify the importance of how legal rules determine the way in which the WTO distinguishes between the legitimate and illegitimate production of knowledge, with a far-reaching impact on how WTO law can then be used by members, yet they do not give sufficient weight to the mechanics of the settlement of this specific dispute.

D. Private Standards: Competing Conceptions of International Public Authority

Private standards present a challenge to the WTO in a number of ways. The first is the inability of the institution to respond to new circumstances through primary rule-making as the principal legislative arm of the WTO is paralysed. The systemic influence of the WTO Agreement in constraining the creation of new rules does not exclude the need for their creation. Rather, other sites are found: we note how the dispute settlement system has had to respond in filling gaps and clarifying the covered agreements, in this instance, it is the SPS Committee that is the battleground for the discussions over regulating private SPS standards.

[160] *United States—Measures Concerning the Importation, Marketing and Sale of Tuna and Tuna Products*, report of the Appellate Body (16 May 2012) WT/DS381/AB/R, para. 313; *United States—Certain Country of Origin Labelling (COOL) Requirements*, report of the Appellate Body (29 June 2012) WT/DS384-386/AB/R, para. 444.

1. Description and rationale

Private standards are non-governmental measures; they are neither mandated nor directly regulated by governmental authorities.[161] They are widespread and their numbers are increasing.[162] A draft definition of the SPS Committee defines SPS-related private standards as '[voluntary] requirements which are [formulated, applied, certified and controlled] [established and/or adopted and applied] by non-governmental entities [related to] [to fulfil] one of the four objectives stated in Annex A, paragraph 1 of the SPS Agreement and which may [directly or indirectly] affect international trade ...'.[163] Private standards serve a range of purposes and 'cover, safety, quality, labour, social and environmental issues'.[164] Private standards potentially affect numerous products, setting requirements for certification that is desirable to consumers and thus producers and suppliers.

SPS-related private standards have developed as a result of consumer concerns on one hand, and producer concerns on the other. For some consumers (within the European Union most notably), the public failings of governments to prevent, and in some instances respond to, food crises undermined trust in the ability of public authorities to protect the health of the citizenry in this regard.[165] Even within States where consumers did not experience such failings, they demonstrate an increased interest in food production methods whether for their impact on personal health or for social or environmental reasons.[166] Producers and retailers can take advantage of such concerns by differentiating their products within the market on the basis of certification that demonstrates commitment to one or more priorities of consumers.[167] Furthermore, the globalization of supply chains (and the use of vertical integration to minimize costs) as well as the increasing international reach of supermarkets and restaurant chains adds an incentive for these industries to minimize costs by creating harmonized standards across their businesses.[168] In

161 Though there may be indirect legal regulation through competition law or consumer protection law, for example.

162 At last count, in 2007, the International Task Force on Harmonization and Equivalency in Organic Agriculture ('ITF') identified 400 certification schemes for the classification of 'organic' produce alone: ITF (Joint Initiative International Federation of Organic Agriculture Movements, Food and Agriculture Organization, UN Conference on Trade And Development) 'Requirements for certification bodies—situation and scope for harmonization' (October 2005) 55.

163 Note by the Secretariat, 'Proposed Working Definition On SPS-Related Private Standards' (6 March 2012) G/SPS/W/265, 1–2.

164 Decision of the Committee on Sanitary and Phytosanitary Measures, 'Actions Regarding SPS-Related Private Standards' (6 April 2011) G/SPS/55, para. 4.

165 See n. 30 and accompanying text.

166 J Wouters and D Garaets, 'Private Food Standards and the World Trade Organization: Some Legal Considerations', (2012) 11(3) *World Trade Review* 479, 480.

167 For example, The Marine Stewardship Council 'Certified Sustainable Seafood' label requires compliance with standards on sustainable fishing practices and traceability (<www.msc.org>) and is recommended as a minimum standard by popular campaigners for sustainable fishing (e.g. 'Fish Fight' <http://www.fishfight.net/sustainable-tips>) (accessed 1 August 2015).

168 Note by the Secretariat, 'Private Standards and the SPS Agreement' (24 January 2007) G/SPS/GEN/746, 2.

some instances, adherence to private standards can also demonstrate due diligence for the purposes of food safety regulations within certain jurisdictions.[169]

Some private standards are developed within a global framework such as the GLOBALG.A.P system that provides certification for farmers that comply with certain 'Good Agricultural Practices'.[170] Other private standards are member-specific such as the UK-specific 'Freedom Food' certification monitored by the Royal Society for the Prevention of Cruelty to Animals,[171] or firm-specific such as Waitrose's 'Select Farm' label. All of these standards share a key characteristic: they are developed and maintained by private interests rather than public ones. The private interests involved are not necessarily producers or retailers (though this is the most common arrangement) but also consumer groups and NGOs. Their private nature does, however, create a serious difficulty for regulating the potential effects of such standards on international trade.

The trade impact of private standards can be serious. For producers who are required to comply with numerous different firm-specific or member-specific certification processes in order to access foreign markets, private standards may undermine economies of scale and add cumulative burdens in compliance costs.[172] Indeed, for some members (particularly those with large tourist industries) private standards can limit the access of domestic producers to buyers such as multinational hotels within the territory of that very member.[173] While private standards can offer producers the opportunity to market their own products distinctly (and potentially adding value),[174] the use of these standards is increasingly being seen as a one-sided process with powerful retailers in developed countries setting down further requirements (over and above governmental SPS requirements) for producers in the developing world.[175] The complexity of the standards further adds burdens to the producers and contributes to the impression that such requirements are unnecessary and constitute an arbitrary exercise of power.[176]

At the SPS Committee, in debates over SPS-related private standards, the government of Uruguay expressed its frustration, shared by many developing members:

[169] Ibid.

[170] On the legitimacy of GLOBALG.A.P in particular: N Hachez and J Wouters, 'A Glimpse at the Democratic Legitimacy of Private Standards: Assessing the Public Accountability of GLOBALG.A.P.', (2011) 14(3) *Journal of International Economic Law* 677.

[171] See <http://www.rspca.org.uk/freedomfood> (accessed 1 August 2015).

[172] WTO World Trade Report 2012, 'Trade And Public Policies: A Closer Look At Non-Tariff Measures In The 21st Century' (WTO 2012) 86.

[173] Communication from the Bahamas, 'Report By the Commonwealth of the Bahamas to the WTO-SPS Committee on Private Standards and the SPS Agreement: The Bahamas Experience' (28 February 2007) G/SPS/GEN/764, para. 2.

[174] WTO World Trade Report 2012, 'Trade And Public Policies: A Closer Look At Non-Tariff Measures In The 21st Century' (WTO 2012) 86.

[175] Ibid.

[176] '[Private standards] may be light-years more detailed and complicated than what is required nationally, therefore they may appear whimsical and capricious with little scientific basis.' Communication from the Bahamas, 'Report By The Commonwealth Of The Bahamas To The WTO-SPS Committee On Private Standards And The SPS Agreement: The Bahamas Experience' (28 February 2007) G/SPS/GEN/764, para. 6.

3. Our export sectors have been successful in gaining access to the demanding import markets of many developed countries. This has been made possible over the years by the tireless and persistent joint efforts of the competent national authorities and the private actors concerned. But since the requirements of importers and the sanitary and phytosanitary situations in the different countries tend to evolve extremely rapidly, remaining in the markets is a full-time job for exporters. And so far, we are referring only to official sanitary and phytosanitary import requirements.
4. However, the situation has become even more complex with the appearance in recent years of so-called 'private standards', which impose additional requirements. *So that in practice, to enter an importing country where there are companies that impose private standards, many export products have to meet both official and private requirements. Otherwise, there simply is no trade.*[177]

It is the contribution of private regulation to the more traditional burden of public regulation that is causing such concern. The shift from a site of public governance to private governance for some areas of SPS regulation stem from the failures of public administration in food crises by some members and the globalization of supply chains amongst others. However, it presents a serious problem for the WTO system that, though a site for continual processes of contestation over the appropriate levels of regulation and their nature in trade, did not contemplate the extension of SPS matters into the private sphere.

The next section briefly outlines the legal difficulty with regulating SPS-related private standards at the WTO. While the WTO cannot regulate them directly, the institutions of the WTO still serve as a site of contestation for globalized actors who can then use the committee structures to encourage adoption of their own preferences amongst the membership. Just as the constituted institutions of the dispute settlement system influenced the interpretation of Art. 5 SPS Agreement, the SPS Committee is playing an increasing role in the regulation of private standards as an autonomous actor.

2. The legal difficulties with regulating private standards at the WTO

At the heart of the debate surrounding SPS-related private standards is the proper scope of Art. 13 SPS Agreement that sets out the scope of members' obligations under the SPS Agreement:

Members are fully responsible under this Agreement for the observance of all obligations set forth herein. Members shall formulate and implement positive measures and mechanisms in support of the observance of the provisions of this Agreement by other than central government bodies. Members shall take such reasonable measures as may be available to them to ensure that non-governmental entities within their territories, as well as regional bodies in which relevant entities within their territories are members, comply with the relevant provisions of this Agreement. In addition, Members shall not take measures which have the

[177] Statement by Uruguay at the Meeting of 2–3 April 2008 'Private Standards' (21 May 2008) G/SPS/GEN/843, paras 3–4 (emphasis added).

effect of, directly or indirectly, requiring or encouraging such regional or non-governmental entities, or local governmental bodies, to act in a manner inconsistent with the provisions of this Agreement. Members shall ensure that they rely on the services of non-governmental entities for implementing sanitary or phytosanitary measures only if these entities comply with the provisions of this Agreement.[178]

Members are responsible, therefore, for their own actions through governmental bodies but must also 'take such reasonable measures as may be available to them' to ensure compliance by regional and non-governmental entities within their territory. Further, they shall not 'take measures which have the effect of directly or indirectly, requiring or encouraging' those bodies to act inconsistently with the SPS Agreement and where they use the services of these bodies to implement SPS measures they can do so 'only if these entities comply' with the SPS Agreement.[179]

The interpretation given to 'non-governmental entities', 'regional bodies', and 'local government bodies' was likely intended to be a narrow one from the drafters' perspective.[180] Importantly this would not have been meant to include, for example, a large supermarket chain in most instances. Rather, the priority appears to have been to resolve potential issues with members that have federated structures where certain SPS competences are at a regional or local level. This is an unusual stipulation as the responsibility on the part of the State for the actions of sub-State bodies is largely uncontested.[181] Similarly, the requirement that where members 'rely on the services of non-governmental entities for implementing sanitary or phytosanitary measures' such entities must comply with the provisions of this Agreement is already covered under the rules on State responsibility: specifically, either Art. 5 ASR ('Conduct of persons or entities exercising elements of governmental authority') or Art. 8 ASR ('Conduct directed or controlled by a State').[182]

An analogy has been drawn between the panel's approach in *Japan–Film*[183] (considering seemingly private acts to be governmental in nature) and attributing the actions of private actors in SPS measures to members.[184] However, for the act

[178] Article 13 SPS Agreement. [179] Ibid.

[180] J Wouters and D Garaets, 'Private Food Standards and the World Trade Organization: Some Legal Considerations', (2012) 11(3) *World Trade Review* 479, 484.

[181] Article 4(1) Articles on Responsibility of States of Internationally Wrongful Acts (2001) GAOR 56th Session Supp 10, 43 ('ASR'): 'The conduct of any State organ shall be considered an act of that State under international law, whether the organ exercises legislative, executive, judicial or any other functions, whatever position it holds in the organization of the State, and *whatever its character as an organ of the central Government or of a territorial unit of the State*' (emphasis added). See also, *LaGrand* (*Germany v United States of America*) (Provisional Measures) [1999] ICJ Rep 9, 16, para. 28.

[182] The inclusion of such provisions in Art 13 in spite of this may reflect the nature of the negotiators (i.e. largely diplomatic rather than legal) or alternatively, foreseeing potential concerns with the European Union or other regional groupings that do not fit into the traditional rules of State responsibility: hence the need for the development of, and difficulties in concluding the ILC 'Draft Articles on the Responsibility of International Organizations' (2011) UN Doc A/66/10.

[183] *Japan—Measures Affecting Consumer Photographic Film and Paper*, Panel Report (31 March 1998) WT/DS44/R, 10.328.

[184] J Wouters and D Garaets, 'Private Food Standards and the World Trade Organization: Some Legal Considerations', (2012) 11(3) *World Trade Review* 479, 485.

to be governmental in some way, the level of involvement by the member is sufficient that it would already fall within Art. 13 SPS Agreement.[185] This is the case as in *Japan–Film* the focus was on measures that were governmental in all but form to escape scrutiny. This is not the case here where private standards are not necessarily encouraged by government (indeed, one can imagine circumstances where governments would prefer private standards not to exist so as not to create disputes with trading partners).

Members thus incur responsibility for their own acts, or what they authorize or direct others (including private bodies) to do in their name. An alternative approach for including private standards within the remit of the SPS Agreement is the more general obligation under Art. 13: the obligation to 'not take measures which have the effect of, directly or indirectly, requiring or encouraging' such bodies to breach the agreement. The prohibition on measures that might 'encourage' non-governmental bodies to breach the SPS Agreement is potentially broad, however, there again an analogy could be drawn to non-violation complaints that are similarly broad in potential yet have been interpreted narrowly.[186]

The problem faced in regulating SPS-related private standards at the WTO is not unlike the problems faced in an attempt to regulate new voluntary export restraints identified in the previous chapter. The shift from public actors to private actors, or from the public sphere to the private sphere has created difficulties for those that wish for regulation to be centred at the WTO and opportunities for those who see greater possibilities in moving measures away from WTO oversight, with the response by some members to turn to the committee system.

3. The SPS Committee as a forum for globalized interests

First raised at the SPS Committee in 2005 by St Vincent and the Grenadines,[187] private standards have been a regular point of contention at the Committee.[188] In 2011, however, tentative agreement was reached over five 'actions' to be taken by the Committee and members in relation to SPS-related private standards.[189] A sixth 'action' was not adopted and is currently subject to further negotiation.[190] Further negotiations have stalled, highlighting the constraints on the use of the WTO institutions for norm-elaboration. Nonetheless, the process thus far offers

[185] And/or: Arts 4, 5, and 8 ASR n. 181.

[186] Article XXIII:1(b) GATT 1994. On the limited application of non-violation complaints: *India—Patent Protection for Pharmaceutical and Agricultural Chemical Products*, Report of the Appellate Body (19 December 1997) WT/DS50/AB/R, 14–18.

[187] Committee on Sanitary and Phytosanitary Measures, Summary of Meeting held 29–30 June 2005, G/SPS/R/37, paras 16–20.

[188] For example 'Private Standards, Mediation Cause Conflict at WTO Committee Meeting', Bridges Weekly Trade News Digest (7 July 2010) Vol. 14 No. 25.

[189] Decision of the Committee on Sanitary and Phytosanitary Measures, 'Actions Regarding SPS-Related Private Standards' (6 April 2011) G/SPS/55 ('Private Standards Decision').

[190] Committee on Sanitary and Phytosanitary Measures, 'Proposed Revisions to Action Six of the Report of the Ad Hoc Working Group on SPS-Related Private Standards' (20 June 2011) G/SPS/W/256.

insights into the mechanisms of legal change at the WTO, and the actors that seek to use them.

This section will examine the content of these proposed actions and highlight their purpose in refocusing the debate within the institutions of the WTO. Whereas private standards escaped WTO oversight by shifting to the private sphere, the acts of some within the SPS Committee have attempted to bring them back into the WTO fold and thus subject them to WTO regulation. Due to their inherently private nature, however, this takes place not through traditional legislative/judicial oversight institutions but rather through two complementary mechanisms: alternative, 'softer' quasi-legislative/adjudicative processes constraining and enabling actors; and by maximizing the opportunities to 'educate' those involved in SPS-related private standards in the outlook and priorities of the WTO institutions.[191]

The content of the five adopted actions within the Private Standards Decision[192] and their difference to the sixth all point to a new approach to engaging with SPS-related private standards. While the discussion had previously focussed on the competence of the WTO to regulate such measures,[193] these actions concentrate on taking subtle consensual measures that take care not to impinge on sovereignty concerns.[194]

The five actions in the Private Standards Decision are as follows: first, the SPS Committee is to develop a working definition of 'SPS-related private standards';[195] second, the SPS Committee should inform the Three Sisters of developments in discussions over SPS-related private standards and encourage them to do the same;[196] third, the SPS Committee is to invite the Secretariat to inform it on relevant developments in other WTO bodies;[197] fourth, members are to communicate with relevant actors involved in private standard-setting within their territory and 'underline the importance' of the Three Sisters' standards and the concerns of others with regard to private standards;[198] and finally, fifth, the SPS Committee is to 'explore the possibility' of working with the Three Sisters to develop and disseminate materials highlighting the importance of international SPS standards (i.e. public standards).[199]

The purpose of the five actions is to establish the SPS Committee as the centrepoint for debates surrounding SPS-related private standards. By ensuring that it sets the framework of the debate by defining the contours of what constitutes 'SPS-related private standards' (Action 1), acting as a meeting point for the

[191] J Scott, *The WTO Agreement on Sanitary and Phytosanitary Measures: A Commentary* (Oxford, Oxford University Press 2009) 45–8.

[192] Private Standards Decision, n. 189.

[193] For example T Epps, 'Demanding Perfection: Private Food Standards and the SPS Agreement', in M Lewis and S Frankel (eds), *International Economic Law and National Autonomy* (Cambridge, Cambridge University Press 2009); J Wouters and D Garaets, 'Private Food Standards and the World Trade Organization: Some Legal Considerations', (2012) 11(3) *World Trade Review* 479.

[194] For example, in the actions, the phrase 'given its mandate' is used to indicate the limitations on the SPS Committee's freedom to act given its limited legal competence (Private Standards Decision, n. 189, paras 6, 7).

[195] Private Standards Decision, n. 189, paras 5–7.

[196] Ibid., paras 8–9.

[197] Ibid., para. 10.

[198] Ibid., paras 11–12.

[199] Ibid., paras 13–14.

relevant public international bodies in the field (Action 2), as well as other WTO institutions (Action 3), and initiating a publicity campaign to encourage the use of (public) international standards (Action 5), the SPS Committee sets itself as the nexus for debates in the field. The role of the SPS Committee in carrying out transparency and reporting functions within the SPS legal regime is already documented,[200] allowing the Committee to perform a rule generating role as well as fulfil a compliance function. The traditional legislative/adjudicative approach is shifting for a 'softer' form of governance that allows the WTO to remain the principal site for contestations. This is a particular priority for those actors who are privileged by the WTO system: governmental representatives and (public) international standard setters.

The SPS Committee also enhances its position by co-opting members to carry out its functions within their own territory (Action 4). While the other actions focus on horizontal challenges to the WTO's primacy (i.e. amongst international actors), this action uses the members to pursue the objectives set by the SPS Committee without raising the sorts of sovereignty concerns that might be expressed in instances of more overt and formal vertical integration of governance structures.[201]

It is telling that the sixth proposed action that was not adopted is the only action that would (in one version) have potentially undermined the SPS Committee's role as institutional centre-point. The sixth action encourages members 'to exchange, outside the formal and informal sessions of the SPS Committee, relevant information regarding SPS-related private standards to enhance understanding and awareness on how these compare or relate to international standards and governmental regulations ...'.[202] While this would achieve the goal of bringing private standards back into public regulation it would have done so away from the SPS Committee. Without this action, fora used to encourage particular ways of thinking about SPS-related private standards and institutional learning take place under the aegis of the SPS Committee.

One example of the SPS Committee serving as the focal point for institutional learning and the 'teaching' of appropriate behaviour is a workshop on co-ordination between national and regional bodies in SPS regulation.[203] The workshop was primarily targeted at improving regional and national co-ordination, not between or at the WTO:

> The objective of the workshop was to bring together officials responsible for participation in and implementation of the SPS Agreement . . . [and] the "Three Sisters". . . for an in depth

[200] J Scott, *The WTO Agreement on Sanitary and Phytosanitary Measures: A Commentary* (Oxford, Oxford University Press 2009) Chapter 2.

[201] cf. the EU model that turns national courts into EU courts by virtue of the doctrines of direct effect and indirect effect.

[202] Emphasis in original: Committee on Sanitary and Phytosanitary Measures, 'Proposed Revisions to Action Six of the Report of the Ad Hoc Working Group on SPS-Related Private Standards' (20 June 2011) G/SPS/W/256, 1.

[203] Note by the Secretariat, 'Summary Report of the Workshop on SPS Coordination at the National and Regional Levels—17 October 2011' (17 January 2012) G/SPS/R/65.

discussion, at a technical level, *on best practices in coordination at national and regional levels.* The WTO Secretariat, through the Global Trust Fund (GTF), sponsored the participation of fifty officials from least-developed and developing countries to the workshop and the subsequent meetings of the SPS Committee.[204]

The SPS Committee serves as the primary site for attracting interested actors in the development of SPS-related private standards. Instead of the blunt and more obvious methods of incorporating preferences in provisions of the covered agreements or prioritizing judicial decision-making, in this instance potential legal development takes place through the SPS Committee. In spite of the different location, the Committee (like the dispute settlement system) still functions as a nexus where the same three causes play a role.[205]

E. Concluding Remarks

The process of value contestation in private standards differs only slightly from the debate surrounding the appropriate distinctions between risk assessment and risk management. Both demonstrate the ways in which different actors pursue objectives under different legal constraints, and take advantage of where the law enables their activity, thus the particular interest in *where* decision-making takes place. In the case of the *EU–Hormones* litigation we saw how the different concerns of commentators, and the ways in which the actors themselves engaged with the dispute highlighted the competing influences at play. As was the case in the previous chapter, the less emphasized point was here the principal focus: the importance of identities as understood and transmitted through legal instruments.

In the case of private standards the questions were in part also related to the identity and approach of the regulator, only here the question is whether this should be a private matter or a public one. It is a theme that reappears: as public regulation at the international level becomes more effective or demanding, some actors seek to shift the battlefield to the private sphere with the expectation or hope that members will not involve themselves at an international level.[206] It is not only governments that are involved with these debates: one of the key points raised

[204] Ibid., para. 3 (emphasis added).

[205] Contrast with the way in which the matter of private standards is accommodated within the TBT Agreement where 'standardizing bodies' are encouraged to accept and comply with the Code of Good Practice that includes provisions on non-discrimination and minimizing trade barriers (Art. 4 and Annex 3 TBT Agreement). Members are required to ensure that 'non-governmental standardizing bodies within their territories' comply with the Code (Art. 4.1 TBT Agreement). The TBT Committee has further adopted 'Decision of the Committee on Principles for the Development of International Standards, Guides and Recommendations with Relation to Articles 2, 5 and Annex 3 of the Agreement' (13 November 2001) G/TBT/9 on setting out a number of principles in standard setting including transparency, impartiality, and access (Annex 4). It should be noted, however, that the application of Art. 4 TBT Agreement to the private standard setting bodies identified here is not clear as the TBT Agreement foresees that a 'non-governmental body' has 'legal power to enforce a technical regulation' (Annex 1, 8).

[206] We can see parallels with the regulation of safeguard measures and the potential expansion of new voluntary export restraints: Chapter 4.E.

in this chapter was the importance of actors other than the parties to a dispute. Whether it is the Appellate Body, Codex, the EU, or the SPS Committee, these institutions are both sites of contestation themselves as well as actors in their own right with their own priorities.

It is tempting to approach debates as between two sides, each putting forward their own interpretation of the facts and law with the judicial organs acting as neutral arbiters. The version put forward here is more complex, indicating numerous actors competing within a globalized space. We have also seen a move, from the previous chapter where the focus was strongly on the US and its engagement with the WTO, to a principally transatlantic dialogue, though with the involvement of institutions that the powerful traders have customarily engaged with such as Codex.[207] The following chapter moves again, this time to what may become the standard form: a globalized dispute of subsidies that has moved from traditional transatlantic concerns to a new challenger, China.

[207] In spite of the seeming parochialism involved in examining the EU and US, transatlantic disputes have formed the context for world trade law for a long time. See generally: EU Petersmann and M Pollack, *Transatlantic Economic Disputes: The EU, the US, and the WTO* (Oxford, Oxford University Press 2003).

6

Subsidies

A. Introduction

Governments act to benefit private actors frequently and in many different ways. From tax cuts to investment in general infrastructure, government support for business is common. When this support is labelled as subsidization, however, it entails a number of legal and political consequences. Distinguishing governmental activity from subsidization is a difficult task, as it necessarily requires limiting the scope of government autonomy in supporting its citizens. It is thus a highly contentious area of trade law, influencing the way in which the State is structured and setting the limits between public and private activity. This chapter looks at the role of law (specifically subsidies regulation) in constituting fundamental structures of the State, and the contestations that have taken place in this area. Specifically, it looks to the increasing role of China in challenging what was a previously trans-atlantic settlement. The chapter then turns to the regulation of subsidies in services as an example of a failure in traditional WTO rule-making. Contrasting the progress at the WTO on this topic with the EU's internal system of state aid, this section seeks to identify reasons for the divergent outcomes, suggesting that we can understand the lack of development of WTO law here through the different ideational bases of legitimacy of each institution, as understood through their constitutive legal frameworks.

This chapter first examines (in Section B) the underlying logic of subsidies regulation, their role in the historical development of world trade law, and their regulation at the WTO today. Section C looks to the way in which subsidies regulation at the WTO has been used by globalized actors as a basis from which to propagate a specific State structure that encompasses assumptions regarding the relationship between market and State (including the existence of such a duality). In particular, this section examines the recent debate over the definition of a 'government or public body' under the SCM Agreement, and the shifts in how these terms are understood as a result of China's arrival at the WTO, moving from a test based on control to one focussed on the exercise of governmental authority.[1]

[1] Article 1.1(a)(1) Agreement on Subsidies and Countervailing Measures (15 April 1994) LT/UR/A-1A/9 <http://docsonline.wto.org> ('SCM Agreement').

The chapter turns (in Section D) to the question of subsidies and services. Whereas the discussions thus far have been on trade in goods, this part examines the way in which members sought, and subsequently failed to transpose subsidies rules to the GATS.[2] Specifically, this section argues that the impasse relates not to the institutional deadlock at the WTO in the systemic sense but rather as a result of the WTO's limited constitutive framework *for itself* unlike another trade liberalizing project, the EU. As with the previous chapters, it is argued here that many accounts of how subsidies have developed suffer from an over-emphasis on certain types of causal influence at the expense of others.

B. The Regulation of Subsidies: Context and Methods

Subsidies are a central part of WTO law, and play a key role in the history of world trade law.[3] As we will see in this chapter, the law on subsidies has played a part in the development of the early IT industry, the large scale privatizations of the 1980s, research and production of materials for renewable energy sources, and the quest for a new wave of liberalization in services.

Though the effect of subsidies on international trade has long been the subject of attention, the way in which the scope and effect of subsidies are understood has shifted over time. As ideas about what subsidies are and how they influence trade changed, so did the law that sought to regulate behaviour in light of these new understandings. What follows is a brief examination of the development of subsidies regulation to the WTO era, and the changes in the underlying logic and values in their use. This is an important exercise as it begins to identify the relationship between changing ideas, the role of law in entrenching them, and the ability of law to stimulate further shifts by interested actors.[4]

1. Regulating subsidies in international trade

Anxiety over the impact of subsidies on trade in the modern age has existed from the earliest days of the world economy in the nineteenth century.[5] As more efficient trade and communication networks were established more widely, and industrialization took hold, global trade in potentially subsidized

[2] General Agreement on Trade in Services (15 April 1994) LT/UR/A-1B/S/1 <http://docsonline.wto.org> ('GATS').

[3] A large proportion of WTO disputes now relate to the SCM Agreement or the Agreement on Implementation of Article VI (Anti-dumping) (15 April 1994) LT/UR/A-1A/3 <http://docsonline.wto.org> ('AD Agreement'). Compare disputes citing: SCM Agreement (109), AD Agreement (110), GATS (23), Agreement on the Application of Sanitary and Phytosanitary Measures (15 April 1994) LT/UR/A-1A/12 <http://docsonline.wto.org> ('SPS Agreement') (43).

[4] The following section (Section C) offers a specific example of this in the interpretation of 'public body' under the SCM Agreement.

[5] The beginnings of a truly global economy, if not its fruition: E Hobsbawm, *The Age of Capital: 1848–1875* (London, Abacus 1975) 86.

goods increased.[6] Subsidies ('bounties' in the terminology of the day) in primary commodities such as sugar, wheat, and later, steel were of particular concern.[7] When European sugar beet producers were subsidized by their respective States, for example, the sugar cane producers in the British West Indies raised the unfairness of what was seen as the harmful spill-over effect of domestic policies on international trade in sugar.[8] In order to respond to these subsidies, States introduced countervailing duties—tariffs which penalized subsidized imports. Thus the 1902 Brussels Convention was born, heralding 'arguably the earliest modern international trade treaty that established a multilateral institution'.[9] The model encouraged the use of unilateral measures to respond to subsidies rather than prohibited subsidies per se.[10] Thus, States were discouraged from subsidizing as should they wish to access the markets of the States parties, they were potentially subject to countervailing duties ('CVDs').[11]

The model of using countervailing duties to offset the impact of subsidized goods was common, and until recently, the primary tool for States to protect themselves from the effects of foreign subsidies in their market.[12] By the time of the Havana Charter,[13] in spite of previous debates over the extent of the commitments, the Charter made provision for subsidies.[14] The focus was principally on the impact of subsidies only where potentially harmful in international trade: that is not where domestic subsidies closed off the market to foreign entrants whose goods would be disadvantaged, but where the subsidy encouraged producers to export to foreign markets, thereby disrupting competitive opportunities for others. These 'export subsidies' were prohibited.[15] Other subsidies which members felt would have an effect were to be subject to notification and negotiations either

[6] The 'success' of many of these products was dependent on State support through military conquest and legal systems entrenching slavery and bonded labour: S Beckert, *Empires of Cotton: A New History of Global Capitalism* (New York, Random House 2014) 98–135.

[7] The impact of subsidized Canadian iron and steel was raised in the UK House of Commons as early as 1902: HC Deb 4 November 1902 vol. 114 cc8–9.

[8] M Fakhri, *Sugar and the Making of International Trade Law* (Cambridge, Cambridge University Press 2014) 21.

[9] Ibid.

[10] International Convention Relative to Bounties on Sugar (5 March 1902) Cd. 1535, 191 Parry 56.

[11] Note the fundamental difference with safeguard measures which are a creation of a trade agreement (constituting an exception) whereas subsidies pre-exist any liberalizing intention.

[12] There are questions as to the exact consequence of subsidies, some may well be beneficial for importing markets as they lower costs for consumers and the expense of foreign States: Matsushita et al., *The World Trade Organization: Law, Practice, and Policy* (2nd edn, Oxford, Oxford University Press 2006) 332.

[13] Final Act of the United Nations Conference on Trade and Employment (April 1948) UN Docs E/Conf. 2/78 ('Havana Charter').

[14] The disagreement hinged on whether domestic subsidies should be prohibited as well as export subsidies. The US was of the view that they both were to be tackled together, while others such as the United Kingdom were less concerned with domestic subsidies: B Steil, *The Battle of Bretton Woods* (Princeton, Princeton University Press 2013) 153. D Irwin et al., *The Genesis of the GATT* (Cambridge, Cambridge University Press 2009) 40.

[15] Article 26.1 Havana Charter.

with affected members or the institution itself.[16] Alternative systems were to be in place for primary commodities,[17] and for responding to subsidization by non-members.[18] Countervailing duties were permitted, though limited to the value of the subsidy, and where a determination of material injury or threat thereof to an 'established domestic industry' had taken place, or that the effect of the subsidy was sufficient 'as to retard materially the establishment of a domestic industry'.[19]

The GATT 1947 inherited these rules in a large part, maintaining the balance between limiting the use of export subsidies and those which caused harmful effects,[20] and permitting the Contracting Parties to use subsidies as part of their policy toolkit.[21] It is important to note that whereas the Havana Charter explicitly prohibited export subsidies, the GATT 1947 obligations did not contain the same clear language, 'contracting parties *should seek to avoid* the use of subsidies' and even then only 'on the export of primary products'.[22]

The Tokyo Round (1973–79) produced a subsequent agreement on subsidies which helped to clarify a number of points regarding the conduct of investigations for the imposition of countervailing duties, and finally prohibited export subsidies for non-primary products.[23] However, the Tokyo SCM Code, like the GATT 1947 did not contain a definition of a subsidy, and like the other Codes, was a plurilateral agreement and only bound the GATT Contracting Parties which were signatories.[24]

Over the 1980s, the regulation of subsidies became an important feature of transatlantic relations in two areas. First, in the realm of agricultural subsidies (which were transferred to the negotiations on agriculture and the subsequent Agreement on Agriculture).[25] The second related to the wave of privatizations

[16] Article 25 Havana Charter: '... the Member granting the subsidy shall, upon request, discuss with the other member or members concerned, or with the Organization, the possibility of limiting the subsidization.'

[17] Articles 27–8 Havana Charter.

[18] Article 26.4 Havana Charter.

[19] Articles 34.3 and 34.6 Havana Charter respectively.

[20] Article XVI General Agreement on Tariffs and Trade (30 October 1947) 55 UNTS 194 ('GATT 1947').

[21] Note the later Agreement on Interpretation and Application of Arts VI, XVI, and XXIII of the General Agreement on Tariffs and Trade ('Tokyo SCM Code'), second recital: 'Recognizing that subsidies are used by governments to promote important objectives of national policy.'

[22] Article XVI.3 GATT 1947 (emphasis added). cf., Article 26.1 Havana Charter: 'No Member shall grant, directly or indirectly, any subsidy on the export of any product, or establish or maintain any other system, which subsidy or system results in the sale of such product for export at a price lower than the comparable price charged for the like product to buyers in the domestic market, due allowance being made for differences in the conditions and terms of sale, for differences in taxation, and for other differences affecting price comparability.'

[23] Article 9.1 Tokyo SCM Code.

[24] Hence the pre-WTO problem of the 'GATT à la carte' where Contracting Parties could pick and choose obligations. The 'single undertaking' of the WTO covered agreements was due to end this state of affairs, though the recent increase in plurilateral agreements such as the Information Technology Agreement may challenge this assumption (though the concessions granted under the Agreement are on an MFN basis): Ministerial Declaration on Trade in Information Technology Products (13 December 1996) WT/MIN(96)/16.

[25] Agreement on Agriculture (15 April 1994) LT/UR/A-1A/2 <http://docsonline.wto.org>. Subsidies in agriculture present another set of challenges, and are subject to a separate set of disciplines. For this reason, though overlap exists, the focus of this chapter is on non-agricultural goods.

that took place in previously State-owned industries in Western Europe. As tariffs reduced and the US continued to face competitive pressures from both Japan and the EC, attention was drawn to other forms of behaviour which explained this imbalance, thus shifting attention to other forms of government action, now understood in terms of 'protection' or 'trade distortion'.[26]

Part of this movement involved a protracted dispute over European steel manufacturing: specifically UK, German, French, and later Italian, steel companies that had been privatized. The US investigated the previous support that the companies had received while State-owned and found that they had benefitted from subsidies and so introduced CVDs which were subsequently challenged by the EC during the GATT era,[27] and then at the WTO.[28] These disputes offer an insight into how interested actors can stimulate contestations instrumentally and thus encourage others to adapt to the changed systemic pressures of the reappraised legal obligation.

In spite of having been privatized, the US considered that the previous provisions of equity infusions to pre-privatized entities in a number of European States should have been factored into an estimation of whether or not a benefit had been conferred on the steel industry.[29] The European position was that where a sale is conducted at arms-length and for a fair price, any benefit granted previously is thus extinguished. The US, pushing further into the potential effects of subsidization argued that these benefits 'passed through' and continued to support the successor (private) entities: they were entitled to introduce appropriate countervailing duties on steel products from Europe.

Sarooshi has given a clear account of how this dispute over the transit of benefit under subsidies regulation points to a deeper preoccupation over State forms, deeper indeed than the desire to constrain European States' ability to advantage businesses through a privatization and claim that no government support had been provided. This case, he states, has a deeper (here we would say constitutive) meaning relating to an aspect of sovereignty, the value of 'corporate economic autonomy': the position that holds to the belief that government's involvement in the market should be restrained, only regulating or involving itself where necessary (for example, impending market failure) and incurring a political cost when it does so.[30] Thus Sarooshi states:

> It seems clear that the US rationale for the imposition of countervailing duties in this case flows from its opposition to the original subsidization of the steel industry, the initial

[26] A Lang, *World Trade Law After Neoliberalism* (Oxford, Oxford University Press 2011) 224–8.

[27] *United States—Imposition of Countervailing Duties on Certain Hot-Rolled Lead and Bismuth Carbon Steel Products Originating in France, Germany and the United Kingdom*, GATT Panel Report (15 November 1994), SCM/185, unadopted.

[28] *United States—Imposition of Countervailing Duties on Certain Hot-Rolled Lead and Bismuth Carbon Steel Products Originating in the United Kingdom*, dispute DS138; and *United States—Countervailing Measures Concerning Certain Products from the European Communities*, dispute DS212.

[29] For an illustrative argument: *United States—Imposition of Countervailing Duties on Certain Hot-Rolled Lead and Bismuth Carbon Steel Products Originating in the United Kingdom*, Panel report (23 December 1999) WT/DS138/R, 6.39–44.

[30] D Sarooshi, 'Sovereignty, Economic Autonomy, the United States, and the International Trading System', (2004) 15(4) *European Journal of International Law* 651, 656–8.

non-observance of the value of corporate economic autonomy. As such, the subsequent sale of the steel company for fair market value, after the government intervention had already taken place to establish the steel company as a viable entity, did not affect the value judgment by the US of the original government intervention in the market *nor indeed its view that such interventions should be discouraged by penalising the successor (privatized) corporations.*[31]

By introducing CVDs, and then responding on the basis of the SCM Agreement in these terms, the US sought not only to defend itself and its industry, but also to change the way in which the United Kingdom and other European states treated future privatizations. The success of such a gambit depends on the systemic strength of the WTO dispute settlement system and institutions to ensure compliance (something the GATT-era institutions had limited success in). Though the US failed in its reasoning in this dispute, the objectives remained the same: to use the SCM Agreement to shape the way in which States engaged in the process of privatization.

The steel dispute is one such example where subsidies stimulated a long battle during the GATT years that continued under the WTO. The negotiation of clearer rules on subsidies and an extension of the coverage of such disciplines was thus a priority for the Uruguay Round.[32]

2. Regulating subsidies at the WTO

As with so many areas in world trade law, the transatlantic dynamic in the regulation of subsidies was central. Until this point, questions over how subsidies were to be regulated had been conducted in part through a transatlantic lens; the US versus Europe, with the economic challenge of Japan close behind.[33] Over time, however, and with the increasing ambition of the Uruguay Round taking shape, it became clear that the US and EU had more in common with each other over industrial policy than they did with the developing world which presented both opportunities for exports, and barriers for access with much of the industry in developing members State-owned. This was most especially the case in light of a dramatic turn in the US's position on subsidies from an atavistic rejection of subsidies to a more variegated stance taken by the Clinton administration,[34] acknowledging the potential viability of certain subsidies (such as those for research and development) within limited circumstances.[35]

It was in this context that a more detailed set of rules restricting the use of subsidies previously developed during the Tokyo Round were refined and

[31] Ibid., 665–6 (emphasis added).

[32] T Stewart, *The GATT Uruguay Round: A Negotiating History Vol I* (Boston MA, Kluwer Law International 1993) 860ff.

[33] See the discussion on declinism: Chapter 3.C(1).

[34] G Horlick and P Clarke, 'The 1994 WTO Subsidies Agreement', (1993) 17(4) *World Competition* 46; D Sarooshi, *International Organizations and Their Exercise of Sovereign Powers* (Oxford, Oxford University Press 2007) 89–91.

[35] Article 8.2(a) SCM Agreement.

introduced in the form of the SCM Agreement. The SCM Agreement was unequivocal in its treatment of those subsidies considered the most harmful: export subsidies (those 'contingent, in law or in fact ... upon export performance') and local-content subsidies (those 'contingent ... upon the use of domestic over imported goods') were prohibited.[36] We recall how during the Havana Charter, export subsidies were to be prohibited, though there had been a debate over the need to prohibit local-content subsidies.[37] By the conclusion of the Uruguay Round, it was clear, subsidies were to be regulated to a degree hitherto unseen.

Further, members are not to cause 'adverse effects to the interests of other Members' through the use of a subsidy.[38] The SCM Agreement was successful in another respect: it provided a definition of what a 'subsidy' was to be for WTO law. This is analysed further in the next section, though here it is important to note that the definition of 'subsidy' for the purposes of the SCM Agreement is a framing tool, determining the scope of the Agreement and how far it applies. A number of other 'non-actionable subsidies' were also included. These provided exemptions for specific subsidies relating to research and development, supporting disadvantaged regions, or adapting to new environmental requirements.[39] These non-actionable 'green light' subsidies have not been renewed beyond their original five-year provisional application.

The WTO rules on subsidies marked a considerable shift from the GATT 1947 (and indeed the Havana Charter), accepting the view that subsidies were in principle harmful, with limited, narrow, and time-restricted exceptions. The SCM Agreement also changed the way in which subsidies were regulated from a defensive unilateral mechanism (CVDs) to the possibility of pursuing subsidization elsewhere. Note the US Department of Commerce's assessment of the SCM Agreement:

> Previously, the only effective U.S. remedy against foreign subsidization was application of the U.S. countervailing duty (CVD) law. While that law is effective in addressing the effects of subsidized merchandise in the U.S. market, it is not designed to address the effects of subsidies in other markets. The Subsidies Agreement, together with the WTO dispute settlement procedures, provides the substantive and procedural tools for addressing the problems faced by U.S. companies confronting subsidized competition anywhere in the world, while enabling the United States to retain strong and effective legal remedies against subsidized imports that injure domestic industries in the United States.[40]

[36] Article 3.1(a) and (b) SCM Agreement respectively (footnotes omitted).

[37] n. 14.

[38] Article 5 SCM Agreement. Adverse effects include: 'injury to the domestic industry of another Member', 'nullification or impairment of benefits', or 'serious prejudice to the interests of another Member'. Article 5(a), (b), and (c) respectively.

[39] Article 8.2(a), (b), and (c) SCM Agreement respectively.

[40] Report of the US Department of Commerce, 'Report to the Congress: Review and Operation of the WTO Subsidies Agreement' (June 1999) available at <http://enforcement.trade.gov/esel/reports/scm0699/scm-0699.htm> (accessed 25 May 2015).

The instrumental and systemic opportunities of WTO law are clear to see: the new SCM Agreement allowed the US for the first time to address problems 'anywhere in the world', changing the previous defensive subsidies settlement.

Even more ambitiously, members also had a specific obligation to negotiate over how to extend the disciplines on subsidies to trade in services.[41] Like the other covered agreements that form the 'single undertaking', the SCM Agreement binds the entire membership and is subject to compulsory dispute settlement.

These rules embodied a new (largely transatlantic) settlement on the appropriate role of the State in the market. As we have seen, however, the processes that develop and constitute legal systems do not stop, the law develops continually as those who seek to use it, who are constrained and constituted by it, are continually affected. Thus the ambiguities that remain in the text—whether for political reasons (the need to maintain ambiguity where agreement could not be found) or for linguistic reasons (and the inherent limitations in precision of language)—become sites of contestation where competing conceptions over the law's role and application are subsequently being fought. The meaning of 'public body' under the SCM Agreement has been one such battleground where transatlantic conceptions of subsidy regulation have been challenged by new approaches developed in China and (to a lesser degree) India.

C. Subsidies Regulation and the Structure of the State

We have seen how the preoccupation with subsidies in international trade moved from a focus on the effect that subsidization of one good could have for other States, to a deeper concern over the distortive effects that subsidies have in trade both externally and internally. The regulation of subsidies has turned from a unilateral instrument in the form of CVDs sought for by specific producers to be able to compete 'fairly' with foreign competitors, to a more profound influence on how States are structured. This section examines how the law on subsidies can exercise this constitutive influence on States, first in general terms, and then taking a recent example over the interpretation of the term 'government or public body' under the SCM Agreement. It is a particularly useful example as it demonstrates the importance that such legal changes can have, but also the increasing influence that China and other emerging economies are having on the development of WTO law.

1. The constitutive and systemic influences of the law on subsidies

Successfully including a definition of a subsidy was a particular achievement of the SCM Agreement under which its application is limited by the definitional

[41] Article XVI.1 GATS.

scope of the subsidy. A subsidy is defined by Art. 1.1 of the Agreement in the following terms:

For the purpose of this Agreement, a subsidy shall be deemed to exist if:

(a)(1) there is a financial contribution by a government or any public body within the territory of a Member (referred to in this Agreement as 'government'), i.e. where:
- (i) a government practice involves a direct transfer of funds (e.g. grants, loans, and equity infusion), potential direct transfers of funds or liabilities (e.g. loan guarantees);
- (ii) government revenue that is otherwise due is foregone or not collected (e.g. fiscal incentives such as tax credits);
- (iii) a government provides goods or services other than general infrastructure, or purchases goods;
- (iv) a government makes payments to a funding mechanism, or entrusts or directs a private body to carry out one or more of the type of functions illustrated in (i) to (iii) above which would normally be vested in the government and the practice, in no real sense, differs from practices normally followed by governments;

or

(a)(2) there is any form of income or price support in the sense of Article XVI of GATT 1994;

and

(b) a benefit is thereby conferred.

The definition of a subsidy contains three key elements: a 'financial contribution' by 'government or public body' which confers a 'benefit'.[42] Note that the financial contribution must be made 'by a government or any public body', or failing that, by a private body that the government 'entrusts or directs ... to carry out' the types of function previously listed in the Article.

This requirement distinguishes the scope of application of the SCM Agreement from what would otherwise potentially constitute a broader agreement that would extend into competition law. It is only public (i.e. governmental behaviour) that the SCM Agreement (and the WTO) is intended to regulate. Exactly what type of body falls within the scope of Art. 1.1(a)(1) is subject to debate.

The law here seeks to encourage certain types of State form by disciplining the involvement of governmental bodies in the market. The constitutive influence of law is dependent on the strength of the systemic influence of the WTO Agreement and DSU so that it might have effect. The SCM Agreement carves a line between government and public bodies on one hand, and private bodies on another, and in doing so, both restrict the scope of State structures but also seed a concept of the State born on certain assumptions relating to the limits of governmental authority in the efficient management of the market. It does this by providing the normative and institutional framework that influence the domestic structures of the State.

[42] The requirement that a subsidy be 'specific' (i.e. to an industry or enterprise) under Art. 2 is not a definitional component of the subsidy but rather necessary for the subsidy to be either prohibited, actionable, or subject to CVDs. *Contra*: Matsushita et al., n. 12, 336.

The 'structures of governance and rule in society'[43] inform and influence the priorities of actors and help define how they perceive certain issues (i.e. whether they matter for government or the market, private, or public). The legal structures that influence this relationship help to constitute the ideas and interests of the actors involved.

The 'domestic structures' paradigm is a useful one in understanding the internal arrangements of States in economic policy.[44] Katzenstein defines domestic structures as the 'domestic policy networks which link state and society'.[45] This definition is somewhat vague and the literature on domestic structures rarely expands on a specific definition.[46] Instead, the domestic structures approach is to focus on specific social structures and examine their influence on policy making. These domestic structures have a variety of facets; they include the political arrangements of the State, the structure of its economy and the mechanisms for social groups to engage with organs of the State. These are broad categories and include the level of centralization of government administration, plurality within the market place, and the strength of different interest groups.

Structures are historically conditioned and reflect the biases of those who were involved with their creation.[47] They provide a space for the determination of the 'correct' balancing of trade and non-trade values, understanding the role of trade law and determining who may speak for the State and influence trade policy. In this way, domestic structures reflect prior value judgments.

In trade policy the focus has traditionally been on examining how the market and society within the State interact and on what terms.[48] In these studies, States are distinguished by their constitutional settlement relating to their approach to the market. The State may be highly centralized or not, while the society within that State may be highly centralized or not.[49] Molyneux has adapted this model by interpreting 'State' as 'Government' and 'Society' as 'Market'.[50] The domestic structures approach, as modified by Molyneux, leads to the typology of States as either having strong governments or weak governments, and organized markets or plural markets. This characterization is then used to help determine the State's foreign policy by virtue of the domestic structures in place. These structures are distinct from policy, instead of determining the State's policy per se, they constrain and encourage its development. This approach helps to explain why States react differently to a single international event or situation; for example, how the oil

[43] R Benjamin and R Duvall, 'The Capitalist State in Context' (1985) cited by A Wendt, *Social Theory of International Politics* (Cambridge, Cambridge University Press 1999) 200.

[44] P Katzenstein, 'International Relations and Domestic Structures: Foreign Economic Policies of Advanced Industrial States', (1976) 30(1) *International Organization* 2.

[45] Ibid., 4.

[46] Though on the need to distinguish between types of structure: GJ Ikenberry, 'Conclusion: An Institutional Approach to Foreign Economic Policy', in GJ Ikenberry, D Lake, and M Mastanduno (eds), *The State and American Foreign Economic Policy* (New York, Cornell University Press 1988) 226.

[47] J Goldstein, 'Ideas, Institutions, and American Trade Policy', in GJ Ikenberry et al., n. 46, 180.

[48] P Katzenstein, 'Conclusion', in P Katzenstein (ed.), *Between Power and Plenty: Foreign Economic Policies of Advanced Industrial States* (Madison, University of Wisconsin Press 1978) 324.

[49] Ibid.

[50] C Molyneux, *Domestic Structures and International Trade* (Oxford, Hart Publishing, 2001) 7.

shocks of the 1970s led to a wide range of responses from developed nations in the face of a single crisis.[51]

This approach implies a constraint on the economic policy of the State (as the government incurs a political cost where it behaves contrary to its values) but also provides a motivation for certain systems to project themselves externally. This results from having a series of distinct ways for States to interact with their markets, leading to potential conflicts over divergent methods. For example, we saw how the United States responded to the steel dispute with Europe. Here, where another State subsidizes a domestic industry which is in competition with the US non-subsidized industry, the principle of corporate economic autonomy limits the actions of the US in aiding its unfairly challenged industry. This explains the need to structure international rules so as to minimize potential conflict with those who would not otherwise enforce it and in doing so, maximizing domestic benefits.[52]

Instead of coercing or co-opting other States (so called 'carrots and sticks'), in this example, the US might instead attempt to influence the structure and activity of the WTO.[53] In the case of subsidies at the WTO, the SCM Agreement seeks to condition the ways in which States make choices by limiting their ability to 'interfere' in the market.

We recall how policy-makers expected China to change its economic system and thereby political system through accession to the WTO.[54] Though China's Accession Protocol refers to the 'right to trade' as related to the import and export of goods,[55] in practice the extension of obligations to non-discriminatory and non-discretionary treatment extends the obligation from mere border measures.[56] Further, the scope of the obligation is wide, applying to 'all enterprises' whether private, State-owned, or joint-ventures.[57] While the 'right to trade' committed to under China's Accession Protocol applies in an international sense (i.e. trading with an international dimension),[58] the restrictive interpretation given to the Protocol in limiting China's ability to use exception provisions found in the GATT unless specifically referred to by the Accession Protocol further strengthens this influence.[59]

[51] P Katzenstein, 'Conclusion', n. 48, 295–6. [52] D Sarooshi, n. 30, 659.

[53] J Nye, *Soft Power: The Means to Success in World Politics* (New York, PublicAffairs 2004), 10–11.

[54] Chapter 3.B(4).

[55] Article 5.1, Accession of the People's Republic of China, Decision of 10 November 2001, WT/L/432 (23 November 2001). See also, China's Accession Working Party Report, paras 83(d) and 84(a).

[56] Article 5.2, Accession of the People's Republic of China, n. 55. See also, China's Accession Working Party Report, para. 84(b).

[57] *China—Measures Affecting Trading Rights and Distribution Services For Certain Publications and Audiovisual Entertainment Products*, Report of the Panel (12 August 2009) WT/DS363/R ('*China–AV* (panel)') 7.249, 7.251, and 7.252. The panels' determination of the scope of China's obligations in this regard was not appealed by either party: *China—Measures Affecting Trading Rights and Distribution Services For Certain Publications and Audiovisual Entertainment Products*, report of the Appellate Body (21 December 2009) WT/DS363/AB/R, para. 140.

[58] *China–AV* (panel), 7.257.

[59] *China—Measures Related to the Exportation of Various Raw Materials*, Report of the Appellate Body (30 January 2012) WT/DS394-5-8/AB/R, 293, excluding the possibility of China's recourse to Art. XX GATT for its obligation to eliminate export duties under Art. 11.3 of the Accession Protocol

The disputes over the interpretation of this provision are an example of how members have sought to use WTO law instrumentally to stimulate contestations over the content of the term in question (here, 'government or public body') sensitive to its constitutive effects and dependent on the strength of its systemic influence.

2. Borderline cases in classifying public action

International law is accustomed to having to deal with unclear areas between those acts which we consider attributable to a State and those which are not. The International Law Commission Articles on State Responsibility[60] offer a number of alternative scenarios for attributing conduct to the State (*inter alia*): those where the State acts, those where others act in the exercise of governmental authority, those placed at the disposal of the State, where the State controls or directs the conduct of another, or where the State acknowledges and adopts the act of another as its own.[61]

WTO law is not different in this regard as it is dependent on regulating public (i.e. State or customs union) rather than private behaviour. As earlier GATT cases were often concerned with either taxation or regulation, the distinction was not necessarily a pressing one.[62] However, during the *Japan–Film* dispute,[63] it became necessary to clarify whether the formal status of a measure (i.e. whether a binding governmental act) was not determinative. In this case, the US alleged that Japanese 'officials and Japanese manufacturers … jointly devised a plan to streamline Japan's distribution system while at the same time bringing it under the control of domestic producers'.[64]

That the measure imposed by the government was not binding did not stop it from falling under the GATT as the panel held: '… it is clear that non-binding actions, which include sufficient incentives or disincentives for private parties to act in a particular manner, can potentially have adverse effects on competitive conditions of market access.'[65] The covered agreements also contain a number of references to, or definitions of relevant terms: 'government',[66] 'governmental action',[67] 'public entity',[68] 'governmental authority',[69] 'governmental purposes',[70]

as (unlike Art. 5.1 referred to above), there was no *specific* reference to 'China's right to regulate in a manner consistent with the WTO Agreement'.

[60] Articles on Responsibility of States of Internationally Wrongful Acts (2001) GAOR 56th Session Supp 10, 43.

[61] Ibid., Arts 4.1, 5, 6, 8, and 11 respectively.

[62] Concerns on this point had been raised in the GATT-period *Japan—Trade in Semiconductors*, Report of the Panel, (4 May 1988) L/6309—35S/116, adopted.

[63] *Japan—Measures Affecting Consumer Photographic Film and Paper*, Panel Report (31 March 1998) WT/DS44/R.

[64] Ibid., 4.3.

[65] Ibid., 10.49.

[66] Agreement on Government Procurement (15 April 1994) LT/UR/A-4/PLURI/2 <http://docsonline.wto.org>, footnote 8.

[67] Article 9.1(c) AoA.

[68] Annex, Financial Services, para. 5(c) GATS.

[69] Article 1.1(a)(i) SCM Agreement.

[70] Article III.8(a) GATT.

'public body',[71] and so on. Though similarities may be shared, the logic for each agreement can differ, and thus each term is to be interpreted in its context.[72]

For example, under the GATS, a service is one 'in any sector except services supplied in the exercise of governmental authority'.[73] Here the question of governmental functions is used to ensure that members do not unintentionally schedule greater commitments than intended. The GATS is based on a 'positive listing' system where members only commit to liberalize those sectors they wish (unlike the GATT).[74] Governmental action in the GATS context is, therefore, a shield from WTO scrutiny.[75]

The SCM Agreement, however, specifically regulates the provision of a financial contribution by 'government or public body' which subsequently confers a benefit. How far should the 'government or public body' provision extend? Ought it to include autonomous yet State-owned entities? Or government funded finance initiatives? Should what one member considers governmental be recognized as such by others? And what is the relationship between 'government' and the separate 'public body'?

A number of cases have arisen on the scope of the 'government or public body' provision in which panels applied a test that would offer greater clarity to members and their investigating authorities, while at once potentially increasing the scope of the SCM Agreement's application. Specifically they focussed on control as the key determining factor.

For example, in the case of *Korea–Commercial Vessels*,[76] the Korean export–import bank (KEXIM) offered financing and loan guarantees to support domestic businesses grow and expand.[77] Here the panel considered the issue to be clear. Rather than examining whether a commercial or governmental purpose was pursued,[78] or whether the entity acted on the basis of governmental authority:

> [t]he *SCM Agreement* envisages a more straightforward approach, based on a clear distinction between public and private bodies. On the basis of this clear distinction, one may

[71] Article 1.1(a)(iii) SCM Agreement.

[72] On the 'internal logic' of each individual commitment: *China—Measures Affecting Trading Rights* (12 August 2009), n. 57, para. 7.1210. This is further complicated as an agreement will likely have more than one object or purpose: R Gardiner, *Treaty Interpretation* (Oxford, Oxford University Press 2008) 194–5.

[73] Article I.3(b) GATS.

[74] Market access and national treatment obligations only apply to scheduled commitments: Arts XVI.2 and XVII.1 GATS.

[75] Further highlighting the unusual place of services in the machinery of liberalization.

[76] *Korea—Measures Affecting Trade in Commercial Vessels*, Panel Report (7 March 2005) WT/DS273/R, ('*Korea–Commercial Vessels* (panel)') para. 7.50.

[77] An added layer of involvement existed through the support to KEXIM of State-owned Korean banks. *Korea–Commercial Vessels* (panel), para. 7.35.

[78] In a curious turn, the Korean argument was in part that KEXIM was not a public body as it pursued a commercial interest (i.e. was acting as a bank offering loans and loan guarantees). By contrast, in the US the equivalent institution, EXIM, insists that it does not compete in the market as financing is only available where private lenders are unwilling or unable to lend. This argument is made, in part, as a defence against the criticism that EXIM constitutes 'corporate welfare' and distorts the market. As of writing, EXIM's authority has yet to be renewed.

establish with relative certainty whether or not an entity is a public body whose financial contributions fall within the scope of the *SCM Agreement*.

. . .

In our view, an entity will constitute a 'public body' if it is controlled by the government (or other public bodies). If an entity is controlled by the government (or other public bodies), then any action by that entity is attributable to the government, and should therefore fall within the scope of Article 1.1(a)(1) of the *SCM Agreement*.[79]

The test was thus whether the entity was controlled by the government or other public bodies. The problem here is obvious: how are we to know whether the body that controls the entity is a public body if it is unclear? The facts in *Korea–Commercial Vessels* did not require further elaboration, and this line of reasoning was taken up later by the *EC–Large Civil Aircraft*[80] panel where control was again the focus.[81]

Panels were not the only dispute settlement actors prioritizing control: the Appellate Body too (though under the Agreement on Agriculture) looked to direction more specifically, and control in a wider sense, through a legal framework. An earlier Appellate Body report arose concerning the interpretation of 'governments and their agencies' under Art. 9.1(a) Agreement on Agriculture in the *Canada–Dairy* dispute.[82] Here the Appellate Body upheld the panel's position that provincial milk marketing boards could constitute government agencies as they both performed governmental functions and were delegated the powers to do so by a governmental authority.[83] There is an advantage here, as it provides a more nuanced approach than that taken by the panels in *Korea–Commercial Vessels* and *EC–Large Civil Aircraft*.

This seemingly clear solution, however, presents challenges. With regard to the requirement that powers must have been delegated, it was considered relevant that the provincial milk marketing boards 'operate within a framework set up by federal and provincial legislation'.[84] Under English law, however, contracting private parties operate within a legal framework determined by Parliament and the common law. We would not consider contracting private parties to exercise any form of governmental authority, however. The Appellate Body's definition of a government agency when examining the functional requirement (that is, exercising governmental authority) is similarly problematic: 'A "government agency" is, in our view, an entity which exercises powers vested in it by a "government" for the purpose of performing functions of a "governmental" character, that is, to "regulate", "restrain", "supervise" or "control" the conduct of private

[79] *Korea–Commercial Vessels* (panel), paras 7.49–50. Footnotes omitted.

[80] *European Communities and Certain Member States—Measures Affecting Trade in Large Civil Aircraft* (30 June 2010) WT/DS316/R.

[81] Ibid., para. 7.1359.

[82] In particular: *Canada—Measures Affecting the Importation of Milk and the Exportation of Dairy Products*, Report of the Appellate Body (13 October 1999) WT/DS103-113/AB/R.

[83] Ibid., para. 98.

[84] *Canada—Measures Affecting the Importation of Milk and the Exportation of Dairy Products*, Panel Report (17 May 1999) WT/DS103-113/R, para. 7.76.

citizens.'[85] Many government functions do not depend on regulating, restraining, supervising, or controlling the conduct of private citizens: the provision of healthcare, education, transport services, general infrastructure, or welfare to name but a few. While elements of governmental oversight or control of these services may be understood through a supervision/regulation lens, the commitment can extend to provide and enable or empower citizens to act.[86]

While the Appellate Body's analysis opened up alternative perspectives to the issues (albeit under the Agreement on Agriculture), the panels' subsequent interpretation of 'public body' under the SCM Agreement appeared to have settled on control as the principal criterion.[87]

3. The entry of China: A new bout of contestations

The importance of China's entry to the WTO is only now increasingly appreciated. While it was felt that WTO membership moved China in the direction that developed economies wanted, the assumption was that China would adapt, restrained by the new rules to which it agreed to and, in time, changed by the culture of trading rights and independent markets that would spread throughout its territory.[88]

China has not been a passive recipient of norms, however, in the sense of 'importing' norms without engagement. China has instead actively and vigorously engaged with the WTO and in particular the dispute settlement system to challenge the assumptions of some members at the WTO. The 'public body' interpretation is one such case.

Contrary to the expectations of some, China's economic reform has not pursued a previously established model.[89] Though a large number of former State-owned enterprises (SOEs) have been privatized, the government has retained ownership of a number of large and strategically important companies.[90] And running against the conventional wisdom, these companies have performed very well, indeed, better than domestic private companies (though worse than foreign companies in China).[91] One reason has been the advantages that large SOEs enjoy in relation to governmental support generally, and access to financing from State-owned

[85] *Canada—Measures Affecting the Importation of Milk and the Exportation of Dairy Products*, Report of the Appellate Body (13 October 1999) WT/DS103-113/AB/R, para. 97. Note also the systemic assumptions of how government functions, constraining actors.

[86] The opposite is also the case: an absence of authority to direct private actors does not *necessarily* exclude these bodies from being considered governmental: see the arguments of the US in *United States—Countervailing Measures on Certain Hot-Rolled Carbon Steel Flat Products from India*, Report of the Appellate Body (8 December 2014) WT/DS436/AB/R, para. 4.23.

[87] The *EC—CVDs on DRAMS* (*Korea*) dispute related to support through SOCBs yet here the analysis was on the basis of Art. 1.1(a)(iv) SCM Agreement, the direction of private bodies provision.

[88] See Chapter 3.B(4).

[89] M Du, 'China's State Capitalism and World Trade Law', (2014) 63 *International and Comparative Law Quarterly* 409, 411.

[90] See generally: P Nolan, 'Globalisation and Industrial Policy: the Case of China', (2014) *The World Economy* 747.

[91] R Elliott and Y Zhou, 'State-owned Enterprises, Exporting and Productivity in China: A Stochastic Dominance Approach', (2013) *The World Economy* 1000, 1023.

Commercial Banks (SOCBs) specifically. This has led to criticism that there exists a two-tier system, those companies within the political system and favoured by it, and those outwith. From an external perspective, the ability of SOEs to access cheap financing and preferential arrangements on materials, gives them an unfair advantage.[92] Many SOEs and SOCBs constitute, from the perspective of US petitioners and subsequent Department of Commerce investigations, a 'public body' for the purposes of Art. 1.1(a)(1) SCM Agreement and should, therefore, (in conjunction with other requirements under the SCM Agreement) be subject to WTO law (and, of course, CVDs). This led to the introduction of countervailing (and anti-dumping) duties on a large number of goods from China.[93]

The *US–AD/CVDs* (*China*) dispute presented an opportunity for the WTO to re-engage with the concept of a 'public body'. One of the key disputes was the extent to which SOEs or SOCBs constituted public bodies for the purposes of Art. 1.1(a)(1) SCM Agreement. If they are not public bodies, then the SOEs that provide raw materials to businesses, and the SOCBs that provide them with loans are merely other private actors engaged in the market place. However, if not, then these bodies constitute public bodies and the loans and raw materials become potential subsidies and the goods exported by the businesses become potential targets for protective measures (specifically countervailing duties, and in this instance, also anti-dumping duties).

The US's investigating authority, the Department of Commerce, had determined that a number of SOEs and SOCBs constituted public bodies, a finding upheld by the panel. The panel acknowledged that there was no clear definition for the term 'public body'[94] and identified the core challenge with such a term: namely, that different jurisdictions define what constitutes a 'public body' under their own law in numerous different ways. They pointed out that '[s]ome of these go well beyond government agencies or similar organs of government, and include, inter alia, government-owned or -controlled corporations providing goods and/or services'.[95]

Having examined the relevant provisions in French and Spanish, the panel felt that the question that needed to be answered was whether SOEs or SOCBs were public or private bodies specifically for the purposes of the SCM Agreement.[96] The focus was on the relationship between public and private, rather than between 'public body' and 'government'. In drawing the division in this manner, the panel framed the discussion in terms of the public–private relationship rather than, as

[92] P Nolan, n. 90, 762.

[93] Marking a change in established practice at the Department of Commerce which did not conduct investigations into non-market economies. See: US DOC, 'Countervailing Duty Investigation of Coated Free Sheet Paper from the People's Republic of China—Whether the Analytical Elements of the Georgetown Steel Opinion are Applicable to China's Present-Day Economy' (29 May 2007) and discussion in M Du, n. 89, 434–5.

[94] *United States—Definitive Anti-Dumping and Countervailing Duties on Certain Products from China*, Panel Report (22 October 2010) WT/DS379/R, para. 8.59.

[95] Ibid., para. 8.60. The panel also examined municipal law of numerous jurisdictions including Scots law and the law of Quebec.

[96] Ibid., para. 8.68.

the Appellate Body had done in *Canada–Dairy*, between governmental and non-governmental functions. In this instance it led the panel to an interpretation centred on control as the key distinguishing factor: the 'public sector' as part of the economy though under State control, 'private enterprise' as part of the economy though privately controlled.[97]

By identifying control as the standard, the panel excluded the need for the body to exercise governmental functions. It concluded on this point: '[W]e consider that interpreting 'any public body' to mean any entity that is controlled by the government best serves the object and purpose of the SCM Agreement.'[98] The Appellate Body did not reject the panel's approach in its entirety: it accepted that there are times when governmental control could indicate that the body in question was to be viewed as a 'public body' for the purposes of the SCM Agreement.[99] It did this with caution, identifying that this was relevant insofar as it demonstrated that there was a governmental function being exercised. Control was needed but was not sufficient; control was important where necessary to exercise a governmental function.[100] Like the panel before it, the Appellate Body also sought guidance from dictionary definitions, though in this case the composite term 'public body' led to a focus on the exercise of functions that would be considered governmental in nature.[101]

Clearly, a definition that depends on defining governmental authority presents considerable difficulties for administrative investigators, policy makers, and judicial bodies. The Appellate Body expressed this challenge as follows: '[J]ust as no two governments are exactly alike, the precise contours and characteristics of a public body are bound to differ from entity to entity, State to State, and case to case.'[102] Unlike the panel which sought to provide a clearer rule that would offer greater certainty, the Appellate Body offered an alternative test that is, by its very nature, flexible and indeterminate.[103] At a superficial level, the Appellate Body's interpretation[104] is deeply influenced by its understanding of the Articles on State Responsibility,[105] in particular Art. 5.[106] This is a contentious

[97] Ibid., para. 8.69, asserting that '[t]his is fully in keeping with the everyday notions of "private" meaning unrelated to the government, and "public" meaning governmental in some sense'.

[98] Ibid., para. 8.94.

[99] *United States—Definitive Anti-Dumping and Countervailing Duties on Certain Products from China*, Report of the Appellate Body (11 March 2011) WT/DS379/AB/R, ('*US–AD/CVDs* (*China*), Appellate Body') para. 318.

[100] Reaffirmed in *United States—Countervailing Measures on Certain Hot-Rolled Carbon Steel Flat Products from India*, Report of the Appellate Body (8 December 2014) WT/DS436/AB/R, para. 4.37.

[101] *US–AD/CVDs* (*China*), Appellate Body, para. 285.

[102] Ibid., para. 317.

[103] Note the US request for clarity on this test and its relation to the 'control' criterion: *United States—Countervailing Measures on Certain Hot-Rolled Carbon Steel Flat Products from India*, Report of the Appellate Body (8 December 2014) WT/DS436/AB/R, para. 4.6.

[104] *United States—Definitive Anti-Dumping and Countervailing Duties on Certain Products from China*, Report of the Appellate Body (11 March 2011) WT/DS379/AB/R, para. 310.

[105] Articles on Responsibility of States of Internationally Wrongful Acts (2001) n. 60. For a short comment on the Appellate Body's use of the ASR in the *US–AD/CVDs* (*China*) dispute: J Pauwelyn, 'Treaty Interpretation or Activism? Comment on the AB Report on *United States—ADs and CVDs on Certain Products from China*', (2013) 12(2) *World Trade Review* 235, 235–7.

[106] 'The conduct of a person or entity which is not an organ of the State under article 4 but which is empowered by the law of that State to exercise elements of the governmental authority shall be

turn,[107] especially in light of the lack of clarity that this test offers compared to the simpler (though broader) control test. Note how Art. 5 ASR:

> does not attempt to identify precisely the scope of 'governmental authority' for the purpose of attribution of the conduct of an entity to the State. Beyond a certain limit, what is regarded as 'governmental' depends on the particular society, its history and traditions. Of particular importance will be not just the content of the powers, but the way they are conferred on an entity, the purposes for which they are to be exercised and the extent to which the entity is accountable to government for their exercise. These are essentially questions of the application of a general standard to varied circumstances.[108]

There is no guidance on how to determine what we are to consider 'governmental'. Instead, '[b]eyond a certain limit', it depends on each case. This 'certain limit' is still unclear though, with the Commentary suggesting that there is an element of predetermination involved: there are types of action or authority that are per se governmental. The purpose of Art. 5, according to the Commentary, is to deal with entities 'which exercise elements of governmental authority in place of State organs, as well as situations where former State corporations have been privatized but retain certain public or regulatory functions'.[109]

The implication is that the core nature of the power is self-evident, only the nature of its delivery or provision changes. Thus, though the entity may be private, it now exercises functions that were public and are, therefore, 'governmental'. Conversely, where an entity is private, though majority owned and headed by government officials, it may well be free from oversight where it does not exercise authority considered to be governmental.[110]

There are difficulties with such an approach, as it is dependent on a case-by-case analysis of what is governmental—a contentious discussion to be had *within* States, let alone when conducted by international organizations. In spite of this challenge, this is an instance where none of the tests on offer are entirely helpful, as each presents problems. Thus, if we use a test on the basis of ownership (i.e. whether majority, fully owned, or other) the scope of 'public body' becomes too wide, potentially capturing a number of bodies that it may not mean to, such as banks which have received bailouts, automotive manufacturers which have the government as a shareholder, or legacy industries that have been privatized and are in transition to full market ownership.

The control test presented by the earlier *Korea–Commercial Vessels* and *EC–Large Civil Aircraft* creates an overlap between Art. 1.1(a)(i) and Art. 1.1(a)(1)(iv) SCM which makes provision for private bodies which have been entrusted or directed

considered an act of the State under international law, provided the person or entity is acting in that capacity in the particular instance.'

[107] J Pauwelyn n. 105.

[108] General Commentary to Articles on Responsibility of States of Internationally Wrongful Acts (2001), p. 43.

[109] Ibid., p. 42.

[110] The relevant test at this point then concerning itself with the level of control of the State over the entity under Art. 8, Articles of State Responsibility.

to carry out the functions that constitute potential subsidies (such as transfer of funds). This provision performs the 'anti-circumvention' aim that would otherwise be attributed to the 'public body' definition.[111] Meanwhile, a test based on the source of the entities' authority is similarly problematic. As the US identified during the *US–Carbon Steel* (*India*) dispute,[112] as not all public acts are the result of specific legal frameworks, while many private acts are.[113] Finally, a test on the basis of the exercise of governmental *functions* is inadequate as it overlaps with 'government' in the narrow sense (i.e. the first half of Art. 1.1(a)(1): 'government or any public body') and creates additional challenges as this examination would necessarily mean that some entities are public at one point but not another.[114]

What we are left with is a range of choices, and a transition from one choice (the control test) to another (the exercise of governmental authority test). The control test benefitted members which do not maintain extensive financial interests in the market, and in this way supported an interpretation of the SCM Agreement which coincided with the underlying rationale of the Agreement as a tool to structure the private–public relationship and discourage members from engaging in the market. The choice taken by the Appellate Body in *US–AD/CVDs* (*China*), one focussed on the examination of a number of factors which demonstrate the exercise of governmental authority, offers less clarity and certainty for members (in particular those wishing to introduce countervailing duties). Yet this choice accommodates a wider range of State forms. This approach accepts the underlying proposition that governmental involvement in the market is not *ipso facto* harmful.

China's instrumental use of the dispute settlement system in challenging US investigations has sparked a change in the way in which WTO law regulates the public–private relationship. Emboldened by its own success on the basis of a model that does not coincide with the received wisdom developed by the transatlantic relationship, and supported by other emerging members such as India, what we see is a dispute over the scope of the SCM Agreement along a new axis, rather than transatlantic, instead globalized, part transatlantic, part transpacific, an expression of the continually shifting demands placed on WTO law.

4. Actors' responses: Clarifications and legitimacy claims

We have seen how the interpretation of 'public body' has shifted in response to the objectives of the participants from a control test that had more general application, gave greater autonomy to members, and potentially caught a number of SOEs, to a test that incorporates control but avoids deferring full authority to the members' investigating authorities to decide, and accommodates a wider range of models of State form than would otherwise be the case. This has had special resonance

[111] *US—Countervailing Duty Investigation on DRAMS from Korea*, Report of the Appellate Body (27 June 2005) WT/DS296/AB/R, para. 113.

[112] n. 86.

[113] Ibid. and accompanying text.

[114] *Korea–Commercial Vessels* (*panel*) 7.45.

not only for China but also India where the State is involved in a number of national entities for the provision of raw materials such as the National Mineral Development Corporation.

Following the *US–AD/CVDs* (*China*) dispute, China once again challenged US countervailing duties, as did India.[115] In these subsequent disputes the Appellate Body maintained its position though, in each, insisted on drawing attention to the ways in which members could comply with the investigative requirements and still introduce countervailing duties:

> a government's exercise of 'meaningful control' over an entity and its conduct, including control such that the government can use the entity's resources as its own, may certainly be relevant evidence for purposes of determining whether a particular entity constitutes a public body. Similarly, government ownership of an entity, while not a decisive criterion, may serve, in conjunction with other elements, as evidence. Significantly, however, in its consideration of evidence, an investigating authority must 'avoid focusing exclusively or unduly on any single characteristic without affording due consideration to others that may be relevant'.[116]

In part, the increased detail offered in *US–Carbon Steel* (*India*) has been a response to the criticism placed on the Appellate Body by the US, but it is also in keeping with the Appellate Body's vision of itself as a world trade court and not merely a reviewing body. In each of these disputes, the Appellate Body has refused to act as a mechanistic review body that confirms investigations on the basis of presumptions relating to technical details (such as government ownership in percentage shares), yet nor has it closed the door to members to examine a number of factors as they produce a coherent and considered report. The balance between procedural deference and substantive review is a hallmark of the Appellate Body's interpretation of its role under the DSU.

As the law has changed, so has the US's response: much like in safeguards measures, where the interpretation has gone against the image of the WTO community that the US sought, it first repeated the same legal arguments, and then moved the debate to a wider systemic ground, questioning the legitimacy of the decision-making process of the Appellate Body, fully cognizant that the Appellate Body is concerned with ensuring its own status within the constellation of WTO institutions. In challenging the more recent *US–Countervailing Measures* (*China*) Appellate Body report, the US went to the heart of the Appellate Body's outlook:

> the Appellate Body Report suggested a view of dispute settlement that departed markedly from that set out in the DSU and reflected in numerous prior reports. As the United States understood it, the fundamental role of a panel was to consider the evidence and arguments put forward by the complaining party and the responses by the responding party, to make an objective assessment of the matter before it, and to issue a report

[115] *US—Countervailing Duty Measures on Certain Products from China*, dispute DS437; and *United States—Countervailing Measures on Certain Hot-Rolled Carbon Steel Flat Products from India*, dispute DS436.

[116] *United States—Countervailing Measures on Certain Hot-Rolled Carbon Steel Flat Products from India*, Report of the Appellate Body (8 December 2014) WT/DS436/AB/R, 4.20.

explaining the basis of its findings. The Appellate Body Report had suggested that panels and the Appellate Body had a different role: namely, to conduct independent investigations and apply new legal standards, regardless of what either party actually argues to the panel.

. . .

Namely, it had developed legal interpretations of the SCM Agreement, and had then sought to apply those interpretations to the US measures—without regard to the case made by China through the evidence and arguments it had actually submitted to the Panel. In doing so, the Appellate Body had assumed a role more like an investigative authority. This was not a role provided for in the DSU.[117]

It is tempting to interpret this response as the frustration of a party that has lost a series of legal disputes yet it is more subtle. It speaks to the frustrated expectations of how the law (in the speaker's mind) *ought* to work. As part of the process of legal development, these challenges can influence other actors as they contest the exercise of authority of others—the retreat of the Appellate Body on the matter of *amicus* briefs in the face of pointed criticism from members is testament to this.[118]

The heat with which the debate has developed draws attention to the profound consequences that such an interpretation has for the WTO and its members. This effects the identity of the WTO and the forms of governance that it encourages. The debate over the role of SOEs and SOCBs is just another instance where the changing dynamics of the WTO find expression in the competing contestations and patterns of legal challenge that in turn shape the law in different ways.

The following section examines a different form of legal development: in essence, a failure to create or elaborate rules. In spite of the failings of the rule-making bodies at the WTO, the question of subsidies in services nonetheless offers fertile ground to examine the process of legal development at the WTO.

D. Subsidies in Services

The subsidization of goods has been a subject of regulation since the earliest days of world trade law.[119] The subsidization of services, however, presents an entirely separate challenge. In this section, the aim is to examine the way in which the law has sought to respond to the change in subject-matter of liberalization. As the way in which members and institutions interpret subsidization has expanded, along with the expansion of the liberalization agenda to services, the law has had to catch up to these changes. The failure of the WTO to grapple with this area serves as a helpful example which along with other key areas in WTO law, the expected law-making bodies have failed to fulfil the goals set for them in the covered agreements.

The failure to complete (even partially) the 'incomplete' bargain of services liberalization has been principally understood in either systemic or instrumental

[117] Minutes of Meeting, Dispute Settlement Body (16 January 2015) WT/DSB/M/355, 1.11–13.
[118] Chapter 3.B(2). [119] Section B(1).

terms.[120] That is, in systemic terms that decision-making bodies are deadlocked due to the tradition of consensus at the WTO (an account based on viewing the WTO Agreement as a constraint on members), and/or, in instrumental terms, that developing members are no longer willing to agree to further liberalization in areas in which developed members enjoy a comparative advantage without movement on issues which matter for them, such as agriculture (an account based on the use of legal structures to pursue specific interests).[121]

Here the focus will be on how these influences (both correct in their way) offer partial accounts of the failure of the WTO to agree on services rule negotiations, and in particular subsidies regulation. Distinguishing the WTO from the European Union, where subsidies in services *are* regulated, it will be argued that the difference lies in the constitutive role that law plays in each institution: at the WTO, legitimacy of the legal order rests on economic claims which in turn produce outcomes for members, while at the EU economic liberalization is seen as directly related to the political communitarian project of 'ever closer union'.[122]

1. Treating services as goods

Understanding trade in goods is comparatively easy: goods are made on the territory of one member, and exported to the territory of another. True, increasingly complex global value chains challenge this simple picture[123]—most notably in trade defence instruments and ensuring that a member targets goods appropriately and does not punish producers in other members for the acts of their trading partners.[124]

Services are often related to goods, and in many cases are supportive of the trade in goods,[125] yet they are different. The exact nature of the service, how it is to be traded and how the existing logic of trade rules fits with services raise a number of difficulties.[126] Nonetheless, the Uruguay Round expanded to include the liberalization of

[120] There are both political and economic reasons for 'incomplete contracts' in international trade. See P Mavroidis, 'Free Lunches? WTO as Public Good, and the WTO's View of Public Goods', (2012) 23(3) *European Journal of International Law* 731, 736.

[121] See: T Hale, D Held, and K Young, *Gridlock: Why Global Cooperation is Failing When We Need It Most* (Oxford, Polity Press 2013) 152–61; P Collier, 'Why the WTO is Deadlocked: And What Can be Done About It', (2006) 29(10) *The World Economy* 1423; Warwick Commission, 'The Multilateral Trade Regime: Which Way Forward?' (2007) 29–32. Available at <http://www2.warwick.ac.uk/research/warwickcommission/worldtrade/report/uw_warcomm_tradereport_07.pdf>.

[122] Preamble, 13th recital, Treaty on European Union [2010] OJ C83/15 ('TEU'); 1st recital, Treaty on the Functioning of the European Union [2010] OJ C83/47 ('TFEU').

[123] See generally: UNCTAD World Investment Report, 'Global Value Chains: Investment and Trade for Development' (2013).

[124] Note the need to prevent circumvention of anti-dumping duties by some members, something not foreseen in the Anti-Dumping Agreement. For example, 19 USC §1677j; Article 13 Council Regulation (EC) No 1225/2009 of 30 November 2009 *on protection against dumped imports from countries not members of the European Community* [2009] OJ L343/51.

[125] For example, *European Communities—Regime for the Importation, Sale and Distribution of Bananas* (22 May 1997) WT/DS27/R, para. 7.285.

[126] Note, the GATS does not provide a definition of a service. Under EU law a service is defined negatively, indicating the difficulty with providing a clear definition: 'Services shall be considered to

services as it became clear that it was in the interest of the North to encourage liberalization in an area where great gains could be made. Interests in the US had sought to include services liberalization within the Tokyo Round, though there had been insufficient traction to achieve any meaningful progress on this front.[127]

During the Uruguay Round negotiators extended the general principles of the GATT to services, making alterations where necessary (in particular understanding how 'protection' can be thought of in trade in services). In doing so it sought to apply the general principles of trade law that applied to goods, to services. In some areas, negotiators sought to go further even than the new disciplines on goods. Note the proposal reported by the Secretariat on applying the rules on subsidies to services: '[O]thers, however, take the position that implicit forms of subsidization *where there may be no financial contribution by government*, but where government action results in benefits for the domestic producers should in principle also be countervailable.'[128] This marks a considerable shift from the accepted position that a financial contribution was required for a subsidy to exist. Though the final text did not include this change, it is telling that the environment was such that it was felt a legitimate proposal at the time.[129]

Concepts used in the GATT were thus extended to the GATS: most favoured nation, national treatment, schedules where members made commitments and thus bound themselves, are all part of the GATS.[130] As a result of the unclear effect of the rules, and the wary commitment of developing members to make commitments in services, the GATS was drafted with a number of key differences. The principal difference was the introduction of 'positive listing', the system whereby members are only bound by the national treatment and market access provisions in sectors where they have made commitments, unlike the GATT where such obligations apply to all goods.[131] Thus the importance of understanding the exact scope of the commitment scheduled by a member.[132]

Extending the logic of trade in goods to services has a further complication as trade in services can take form in a range of different ways. The GATS accommodated these different 'modes' of trade in service by distinguishing four forms:

(a) from the territory of one Member into the territory of any other Member;

(b) in the territory of one Member to the service consumer of any other Member;

be "services" within the meaning of the Treaties where they are normally provided for remuneration, in so far as they are not governed by the provisions relating to freedom of movement for goods, capital and persons', Art. 57 TFEU.

[127] A Lang, n. 26, 274–5.

[128] Note by the Secretariat, 'Subsidies and International Trade in Services' (20 April 1990) MTN. GNS/W/98, para. 8.

[129] This line has been pursued by Chile: Communication from Chile, 'The Subsidies Issue' (2 April 1996) S/WPGR/W/10. See G Horlick and P Clarke, 'WTO Subsidies Discipline During and After the Crisis', (2010) 13(3) *Journal of International Economic Law* 859, 873.

[130] Articles II, XVII, and XVI GATS respectively.

[131] Guidelines were developed to aid in clarifying the process: Scheduling Guidelines (28 March 2001) S/L/92.

[132] For example *United States—Measures Affecting the Cross-Border Supply of Gambling and Betting Services*, Report of the Appellate Body (7 April 2005) WT/DS285/AB/R.

(c) by a service supplier of one Member, through commercial presence in the territory of any other Member;

(d) by a service supplier of one Member, through presence of natural persons of a Member in the territory of any other Member.[133]

These are not self-evident categories. They are a choice, a choice to include (for example) foreign investment within the ambit of the WTO, even if only in the manner set out by the GATS. The expansion of the GATT machinery to trade in services was incomplete, however, and a number of provisions required further elaboration. The three provisions are in domestic regulation, emergency safeguards, and subsidies.[134] It is not surprising that given the general state of negotiations at the WTO, these obligations have not been met.[135] The argument here is that this is more closely related to the role that law plays in creating the identity of the WTO community and its basis of legitimacy than a problem of either institutional design or political will alone.

2. Extending subsidies regulation to services

We have seen how the logic underlying subsidies regulation in goods is that where members subsidize the production of goods they may cause harm to other members and distort markets. This is in turn premised on a distinction between the public and private spheres, including a conception of the appropriate role of government in the market.[136] By attempting to expand the regulation of subsidies to services, it became necessary to transfer the same logic to trade in services, premised on the belief that eliminating such distortions would have benefits for welfare gains. Law was the tool to change the views of the membership on this point.

Subsidies are a common feature of the services sector in many States. Whether through the grant of monopolies, direct transfers, or more commonly, tax incentives, members provide support for politically and strategically important service sectors such as banking, transport, healthcare, and education. The recent banking crisis amongst many Western economies has drawn attention to the large-scale transfers that can take place to protect national champions.[137]

133 Article I(2) GATS.

134 Article VI(4), Art. X(1), Art. XV(1) GATS respectively. On the difference between the negotiating mandates under these provisions: P Sauvé and M Soprana, 'Learning by Not Doing: Subsidy Disciplines in Services Trade', (ICTSD 2015) 6. Available at: <www.e15initiative.org/> (accessed 1 August 2015).

135 The three areas are interrelated, making it difficult to make progress is one and not another. See R Adlung, 'Negotiations on Safeguards and Subsidies in Services: A Never-Ending Story?', (2007) 10(2) *Journal of International Economic Law* 235, 264.

136 Section C.1.

137 See generally: P Delimatis and P Sauvé, 'Financial Services Trade After the Crisis: Policy and Legal Conjuectures', (2010) 13(3) *Journal of International Economic Law* 837; B de Meester, 'The Global Financial Crisis and Government Support For Banks: What Role For The GATS?', (2010) 13(1) *Journal of International Economic Law* 27.

Unlike goods, however, it is not clear how subsidies of services can have a cross-border effect, or better put, how we are to understand where the effect takes place.[138] Does a subsidised bank effect the market where it provides financing? Or where it attracts consumers from other territories? This leads to a related difficulty: even where we accept that a definition of a subsidy (including a benefit analysis) could be agreed upon, how would members respond to them? Countervailing duties function (politically at least) as they can target goods as they enter a member's territory.[139] Yet, with services, it is unclear how this would work in practice.

Members have proposed different solutions or responses to the deadlock in the services negotiations. Some have suggested that the regulation of subsidies should be put to one side until members have scheduled greater commitments under the GATS.[140] Under this logic, it makes sense for members to be able to liberalize without concern over potential litigation under a developed Art. XV GATS. Not concluding the negotiations on this topic would encourage members to schedule commitments as they would still be free to subsidize their own services. This position has not enjoyed support for a number of reasons. First, developing members in particular see services liberalization as an area of benefit principally to developed members who are seeing their comparative advantage in goods production eroded.[141] Second, the negotiations on subsidies regulations are also related to the negotiations over the ability to introduce emergency safeguards measures under Art. X GATS, similar to those under Art. XIX GATT. Not clarifying the scope of the safeguard provision potentially reduces the desirability to schedule further concessions if there is no 'escape clause' as under the GATT.[142]

For those concerned that the lack of liberalization in services might lead to slow down or indicate a reduced commitment to free trade, more worrying is the position taken by a number of members who are unconvinced of the trade effects of subsidies in services.[143] It is of course perfectly possible that such a position is a political gambit, designed to halt negotiations until further studies are completed. Yet, underpinning this position is an expression of doubt in the formerly established belief in the benefits in free trade and the expansion of liberalization beyond more traditional trade barriers.

3. Explaining differing outcomes: The WTO and the EU

On the basis of the preceding analysis, one might conclude that subsidies in services are not amenable to regulation. This need not be the case, however. The EU

[138] For some illustrative examples: M Benitah, 'Subsidies, Services and Sustainable Development', *ICTSD Issue Paper 1* (2004), 17.

[139] Though their economic effects may well be harmful: A Sykes, 'Trade Remedy Laws', *John M. Olin Program in Law and Economics Working Paper* No. 240 (2005).

[140] Identifying the asymmetric progress between minimal movement on disciplines, and minor movement on market access: Report by the Chairman to the Trade Negotiations Committee (21 April 2011) TN/S/36, para. 2.

[141] Ibid., para. 6.

[142] See Chapter 4.B.

[143] Report by the Chairperson of the Working Party on GATS Rules (14 April 2011) S/WPGR/21, para. 11.

has developed a sophisticated system to regulate government support in services under its law on state aid which applies to both goods and services. Indeed, one of the arguments in favour of permitting preferential trade agreements (which necessarily discriminate against third parties) in a multilateral non-discriminatory trading system is that they can function as greenhouses for liberalization, testing new models to open trade.[144]

Under the EU, the regulation of state aid is seen as one of two principal tools to ensure the effective functioning of the internal market. This has an economic dimension clearly, but also a political one, fearful of the 'political damage to economic integration that subsidy races would create, rather than their economic efficiency'.[145]

DG Competition oversees acts which may distort the market by private actors (under competition law), and by governments (under state aid law).[146] Where Member States seek to support a service, they require Commission authorization to agree. The Commission examines the effect on the market, taking into account potential positive outcomes relating to values considered to be of EU importance such as (*inter alia*) 'aid having a social character' and 'aid to promote culture and heritage conservation'.[147] The UK government recently received authorization to support the UK video-games industry through tax relief on production of a game, not on the basis of correcting market failure (which the Commission was unconvinced was a feature of the industry)[148] but on the basis of cultural support.[149] The impact of the subsidy on the internal market was considered, the worry was that it might spark a 'subsidies race' within the EU, and especially with France (the only other Member State to grant state aid to the video-games industry). The potential response from *international* competitors was not of primary concern.[150]

The community focus on the regulation of subsidies within the EU in this instance begins to illuminate the differences with the WTO as we ask why has the EU developed a system to regulate the subsidization of services whereas the WTO has failed to agree on a definition of what constitutes a subsidy in this area?

[144] C Damro, 'The Political Economic of Regional Trade Agreements', in L Bartels and F Ortino (eds), *Regional Trade Agreements and the WTO Legal System* (Oxford, Oxford University Press 2006) 25–6; V Zahrnt, 'How Regionalization can be a Pillar of a More Effective World Trade Organization', (2005) 39(4) *Journal of World Trade* 671.

[145] K Bacon, *European Union Law of State Aid* (Oxford, Oxford University Press 2013) 1.04.

[146] Articles 101–9 TFEU.

[147] Articles 107(2)(a) and 3(d) TFEU. Note, restrictions are placed on the grant of aid, including a 'common interest' test in the case of Art. 107(3).

[148] European Commission Press Release, 'State aid: UK video games tax relief faces Commission scrutiny' (16 April 2013): 'The market for developing video games is dynamic and commercially promising. It is not clear whether the taxpayer should be subsidising this activity. Such subsidies could even distort competition.'

[149] Commission Decision (27 March 2014) On State Aid Scheme SA.36139 (2013/C) (ex 2013/N).

[150] Ibid., 32–4.

A number of suggestions have been put forward for the failure of the WTO to make progress on the subsidization of services. They are largely divided into two camps: systemic explanations based on the constraints of the WTO decision-making rules and the difficulty in coming to consensus;[151] and instrumental explanations based on using the decision-making rules to the advantage of an interested group, whether developing members seeking to assert their position as equal negotiating powers, or rent-seeking sectors which do not want the benefits they receive from governments challenged.[152]

Both of these factors play a role, yet they do not explain the success of subsidy regulation within another trade agreement. The EU has developed a regulatory system for subsidies of services in part because of the smaller grouping of Member States with more closely aligned interests and more effective decision-making structures. Yet, the inclusion of state aid in the constituent Treaties required unanimity, and though EU economies may share many commonalities, they are still varied: France and Slovakia, the United Kingdom and Portugal, Spain and Malta—the services in which EU Member States have interests are not necessary similar, let alone the effect or structure of their domestic economic settlements.

We thus return to the core difference: the constitutive influence of law in each system. At the WTO, the law that constitutes the institution and embodies the value judgments of the successful interested actors (the covered agreements, principally the WTO Agreement) is based on a legitimating premise: the promise that economic liberalization offers the most effective route for welfare gains for participants.[153] It is an economic argument that then in turn seeks to offer more general gains. The EU differs in that the law that constitutes it seeks to use economic liberalization as part of a communitarian project.[154] Note the role that the Commission plays as the community arbiter in deciding on state aid grants,[155] the role of individuals within the EU legal order as rights holders in state aid matters,[156] and the more general overlap between economic and rights considerations within the EU legal order.[157]

The identity of the WTO that the law on services liberalization and in particular the regulation of subsidies in this area seeks to constitute is not one shared by

[151] Section C.1. [152] Chapter 4.B.1(b).

[153] For some accounts in trade law: R Baldwin, 'The Case for a Multilateral Trade Organization', in A Narlikar, M Daunton, and R Stern (eds), *The Oxford Handbook on the World Trade Organization* (Oxford, Oxford University Press 2012), M Trebilcock and R Howse, *The Regulation of International Trade* (3rd edn, London, Routledge 2005) Chapter 1, A Lowenfeld, *International Economic Law* (2nd edn, Oxford, Oxford University Press 2008) Chapter 1, S Lester, B Mercurio, and A Davies, *World Trade Law: Texts, Materials and Commentary* (2nd edn, Oxford, Hart Publishing 2012) Chapter 1, P Van den Bossche and W Zdouc, *The Law and Policy of the World Trade Organization* (3rd edn, Cambridge, Cambridge University Press 2013) Chapter 1.

[154] Its exercise of 'civilian' power: K Nicolaïdis and R Howse, '"This is my EUtopia ...": Narrative as Power', (2002) 40(4) *Journal of Common Market Studies* 767, 770ff.

[155] Article 108 TFEU and Council Regulation (EC) No 659/1999 [1999] OJ L83/1.

[156] Article 108(3) enjoys direct effect and thus can be invoked before national courts: Case 6/64 *Costa v ENEL* [1964] ECR 58.

[157] Case C-112/00 *Schmidberger, Internationale Transporte und Planzüge v Republik Österreich* [2003] ECR I-5659, accepting a limitation on the fundamental freedoms in light of human rights concerns.

all members. It is the product of a specific time and specific group of interests, based on a premise which not all members accept: that it is possible to treat services like goods, to apply rules to the subsidies of services as we do of goods, and that liberalization of services (including a conception of liberalization that requires restrictions on governmental involvement in service sectors) offers welfare gains.[158] Instead, the current settlement expressed through the goods-related agreements accepts more modest claims: liberalization and limited protection, trade facilitation, and controlled regulation.[159]

Attempts to move services liberalization forward in other economic agreements whether preferential trade agreements or plurilateral agreements such as the Trade in Services Agreement ('TiSA'), which do not share the same communitarian outlook of the European Union, have met similar problems in attempting to develop rules for the regulation of subsidies of services. The EU–Korea Free Trade Agreement[160] commits the parties to negotiate further on subsidies of services, without concretizing any details,[161] while TiSA in its current form does not appear to include subsidy regulation at all.[162]

E. Concluding Remarks

The regulation of subsidies cuts to the heart of how we understand the role of the State and its relationship to the market. Both the State and the market are legal constructs, dependent on legal systems to provide authority, legitimacy, and effectivity.[163] The law that regulates how the State interacts with the market is thus deeply influential and embedded in the way in which we understand the role of the State.

This chapter has drawn attention to two areas, acknowledging the different types of influence on how the law is understood and how it develops within the WTO. In the case of the 'public body' cases, we can see how shifting conceptions of what constitutes a subsidy alter the law, finding greater detail first in the Tokyo Subsidies Code, and then later in the SCM Agreement. Yet, the continual development of law does not end there, as new players with different views on the structure of the State challenge the fundamental terms that underpin the legal text. The law responds, adapting under the impetus of litigation but influenced by the constraints placed on the decision-making dispute settlement institutions and the impact that the law has had on their own identities.

158 A Lang, n. 26, 242–7.

159 On the balances found in the agreements, and their interacting components: C Charmody, 'A Theory of WTO Law', (2008) 11(3) *Journal of International Economic Law* 527. There is a sense in which this is a return to the 'embedded liberalism' of the post-war period: J Ruggie, 'International Regimes, Transactions, and Change: Embedded Liberalism and the Postwar Economic Order', (1982) 36(2) *International Organization* 379.

160 EU–Korea Free Trade Agreement [2011] OJ L127 (14 May 2011).

161 Ibid., Art. 11.5(2): 'The Parties shall use their best endeavours to develop rules applicable to subsidies to services, taking into account developments at the multilateral level, and to exchange information upon the request of either Party.'

162 On the basis of leaked drafts thus far.

163 Chapter 3.B.

In the second example, the (attempted) expansion of subsidies regulation to trade in services, we have seen how a failure to agree on legal rules can tell us as much as agreement. The inability of the WTO to conclude the negotiations of services speaks to a deeper challenge resulting from contrasting ideologies underpinning the covered agreements. It is not only that the decision-making system of the WTO is not functioning as intended or that interested parties are manipulating the system for their own ends (though each of these is correct) but it is also, and more importantly, the disconnect between the premise underlying the WTO Agreement and the premise embodied in the GATS. The continual and continuing contestations over the core values expressed through the law of the WTO open the door to eventual agreement, though given the systemic weaknesses of the institutions, the likelihood may be slim.

7
Conclusion

A. Introduction

This book set out to examine how WTO law develops. By viewing WTO law as part of a globalized legal process, the analysis expanded to include different types of influences on the development of WTO law. These instrumental, systemic, and constitutive influences not only played a role in understanding how the law developed, but also helped identify why it was that some actors (policy-makers or scholars) felt that the law had not developed according to plan.

More specifically, the examination of the WTO's institutional and normative framework, and the subject-areas of regulation, has produced a number of insights that, it is hoped, merit discussion and further investigation.

B. Law as a Multi-Causal Construct

If there is one point to be taken from the analysis here in general terms, it is that emphasizing how law functions in one way (say instrumentally) at the expense of others, will lead to unexpected outcomes. This is not to say that the approach taken here is predictive, it clearly is not, but it does suggest an agnostic stance in relation to how we think the law should play out in a given instance.

In each example, whether in the case of institutional design and the role of the Appellate Body, or how rules on trade defence instruments are to be interpreted and applied, outcomes have confounded those who were central to their creation. Nor is it fair to equate criticism with simple frustration—the frustration of, for example the US, is not blind or without reason. Though we may offer more comprehensive explanations for the development of the law, this is not to say that the expectation was unreasonable. Rather, that the expectation of the party in question is the fruit of having prioritized certain ways of thinking about the law.

Beyond the actor-centric elements of the plural causes, the interrelation between the casual influences is noteworthy. Where actors seek to use the law to challenge the fundamental constitutive structure of a legal instrument (on subsidies, for example), the success of the instrumental use to stimulate a shift in the constitutive effect of the law is dependent on the strength of the systemic influence. Without an effective edifice on which to rest, the law cannot be used instrumentally and has a weaker influence on actors. Equally, without the will to use the law instrumentally (determined by the actor's interests), there is no realization of the law's potential as an empowerer or stimulator of change. It is this fluid interrelationship between causes that stresses the need to look outside of Humean perspectives to more open conceptions of influence and cause.

C. Globalized Actors: Institutions and Individuals

One of the recurring themes has been the importance of institutions as autonomous actors. States, international organizations, and the bodies within them such as administrative agencies, committees, and dispute settlement institutions all play a role in the development of WTO law, not only as forums but also as actors in their own right. The interesting issues here arise by virtue of their autonomy from the aims of those that create them or attempt to control them. How are we to know when an institution will interpret its constitutive legal framework in one way or another? The contestations involved are continual and never-ending, and yet, we can trace certain ideas, pressures, and interests that encourage the choices that are made.

A purely instrumental view of the law would suggest that institutions behave as they are told to. However, institutions do not do exactly as instructed for various different reasons, principally that it is not clear what it is that they are instructed to do, as their mandate requires some form of interpretation. Further, there is a necessary margin of discretion and independence for all institutions as they carry out their roles. The legal framework that these institutions are constituted by 'is not a straightjacket which leaves no room for an imaginative interpretation'.[1] Instead the law gives them guidance but this is to be interpreted by the institution in pursuing its objectives.

A purely systemic view of the law would suggest that the institution, however constituted, follows certain parameters and that these encourage it towards some form of predictability.[2] While predictability is often considered a virtue by judicial decision-makers it is still held in tension with the need to be 'responsive to the legitimate needs and aspirations of the international community'.[3] By prioritizing predictability, a systemic view caricatures the way in which (particularly judicial) institutions behave. The criticisms cited over the Appellate Body's interpretation of the 'unforeseen developments' clause is a clear example of this. Such a criticism fails to accept the other types of cause that influence the institution at the same time.

[1] P Kooijmans, 'The ICJ in the 21st Century: Judicial Restraint, Judicial Activism, or Proactive Judicial Policy', (2007) 56 *International and Comparative Law Quarterly* 741, 742.

[2] 'We must continue to provide that *core predictability* that distinguishes law from politics ...' (emphasis added). R Higgins, 'Speech by HE Judge Rosalyn Higgins, President of the International Court of Justice, at the solemn sitting on the occasion of the sixtieth anniversary of the inaugural sitting of the Court' Press Release (12 April 2006).

[3] Ibid.

A purely constitutive examination of the role of law with regard to these institutions is equally limited, failing to explain the institution's existence, why it was constituted, and how. The constitutive influence of the law helps to explain why the institution (here the Appellate Body) acts in the way it does by identifying its interests and objectives. It does not explain *how* the institution pursues those interests or in what way. Instead the three causal influences together offer an explanation that identifies how the law has developed, motivated by actors yet influencing them at the same time.

A multi-causal account brings together these insights and offers a different picture, a worryingly unpredictable one to be sure, yet, it is hoped, one that furnishes a more complete explanation than might otherwise be the case.

D. The Private Sphere and WTO Scrutiny

It would seem that the WTO represents an advance on previous institutions: more democratic voting, an effective dispute settlement system, and engagement by members across the North-South divide (insofar as such a distinction is useful). The WTO is, therefore, a step forward, part of the evolution of international organizations. A challenge to this premise is the behaviour of some actors identified in both safeguard measures and SPS measures are shifting their activities from the public to the private sphere—a distinction that as we saw, is also contentious within the regulation of subsidies.

By concluding voluntary export restraints and other such 'gentlemen's agreements' the locus of the trade restriction is moved away from the scrutiny of the WTO. In SPS measures, by setting standards privately, the WTO's authority to oversee and restrict such measures is limited.

If we suggest that actors are interested in institutions such as the WTO because they allow them to establish their preferences over others via the normative influence of the system, it would seem counterintuitive that they would then seek to undermine the process. In the case of safeguard measures it is perhaps more understandable than others: members may prefer to use the WTO but in the light of a particularly restrictive set of Appellate Body reports, it may be felt that the second-best solution is preferable. Alternatively one might suggest that a member prefers the less trade-enhancing yet more predictable advantages that voluntary export restraints offer in the trade of commercially sensitive materials such as primary commodities. Concerns over market stability could be increased by the perceived lack of predictability of reports of the Appellate Body (a particularly systemic view of its function).

In the case of SPS measures, the move to the private sphere from the public has not been led by members or institutions exercising public authority but rather by private globalized actors. Here, whether responding to the increasing demands and concerns of consumers, or exerting their power in an attempt to protect certain elements in their chain of production, the move is for greater activity in the private sphere. The SPS Committee, as an interested actor, has responded by attempting to ensure its monopoly (or at least central position) in the debates over this issue and, it is presumably hoped, the regulation of SPS-related private standards though, of course, the outcome is still unsettled.

This trend (if it is one) could also indicate a broader challenge to WTO law, with warnings for international governance more broadly. As we progress from an era of international institution building, actors are responding to the increasing effectiveness of these international institutions. International organizations have become more effective in constraining and enabling behaviour (with the normative strength of these influences increasing through more effective compliance mechanisms such as those at the WTO). They offer more opportunities for actors to use the law instrumentally at domestic, regional, and international levels, developing norms within forums or initiating litigation in ways that were previously unforeseeable. Actors have responded by using these institutions but also by trying to protect themselves from the behaviour of others. It may be that as the international community progresses in its attempt to regulate matters more effectively, actors will increasingly find ways to behave outside of the spheres of influence of these institutions that took such a great effort to create.

Whereas debates over international regulation were previously over States transferring sovereign powers to international organizations, or other institutional frameworks, as actors have become globalized they have become more adept at acting across jurisdictional borders. As a consequence the concern might instead be over the autonomy of actors at the international level seeking to carve out a greater private sphere from encroaching international organizations rather than between the division of governmental authority between States and international organizations. This would have more in common with debates at the domestic level over the proper role of the State and the Market. Such debates could pose a serious challenge to the WTO that has until now been preoccupied with the relationship between itself and its members or between itself and other legal regimes in international law. For international law it may challenge the cosy narrative we tell of 'epochs' and the improvement of international governance over time.

E. A Multipolar WTO: The Challenges of Complexity Multiplied?

The case studies examined in this book have moved their focus: from the US; to the US, EU, and Codex; and then finally the US, EU, China, and India. The attention given to the US and the EU may seem parochial, however, as key players in the development of the GATT system and the constitution of the WTO, it is impossible not to identify their influence on the development of WTO law. However, as time passes, we can question whether increasing attention will be given to other 'big players' such as China. The approach taken here is not undermined by an increasing number of actors on the stage: the purpose of the use of causal language has been to respond to a cacophony of influences and attempt to construct reasoned explanations on this basis. If anything, the increasing involvement of members with different views on the direction of WTO law and their economic settlements will only expand the need to identify not only narrow interests, but also the identities that constitute them.

Further, the deadlock of the Doha Round does not stop the development of WTO law; rather it moves the focus from members negotiating over the covered agreements to the role of institutions. Indeed, they can be expected to become more relevant as judicial decision-making bodies and the committees are required to respond to changing circumstances in the face of quasi-legislative arms of the WTO that are incapable of reaching a consensus. Understanding the confluence of instrumental, systemic, and constitutive influences on the development of law is even more important in such instances than prioritizing the examination of obligations under the covered agreements alone.

F. Final Remarks

Though this book has focussed on WTO law, the questions raised, challenges identified, and insights offered are relevant for international law across the board. The WTO is a representation, a laboratory for the rest of international law. If we are to examine what takes place in the maelstrom of competing interests and normative structures, we must clarify how WTO law and international law develop in the face of perpetual change. The study of international law is no longer the sole domain of international lawyers; nor is the study of law's effect on the world the sole domain of social-scientists. As increasing numbers of scholars seek to encourage engagement between these groups, there is much to gain. Insights from liberal institutionalism, constructivism, and realism have all informed international legal scholarship, while international relations scholarship has developed interesting new ways of appreciating the special character of international law as distinct from other non-legal norms. There is a danger, however, that our superficially similar roles disguise the fundamental epistemological differences in the disciplines and their objectives. Empirical analysis is incapable of telling us what the law is, or how the law develops *qua* law. Similarly, legal analysis alone cannot tell us what the material effects of law are. This book has attempted to offer a way in which a constructive engagement between methodological traditions can aid us to analyse the way in which international law develops as part of a complex and complicated system.

This task is more relevant now than ever before. The certainties of the post-war settlement (such as they were) have been challenged, and other voices on the international stage expect to be heard. We will have to see what effect this will have on the development of WTO law, or international law more widely.

Bibliography

Abbott, K et al. - 'The Concept of Legalization', (2000) 54(3) *International Organization* 401

Abbott, K and Snidal, D - 'Values and Interests: International Legalization in the Fight Against Corruption', (2002) XXXI *Journal of Legal Studies* 141

Ackerman, B and Golove, D - 'Is NAFTA Constitutional?', (1995) 108(4) *Harvard Law Review* 799

Adler, E - 'Seizing the Middle Ground: Constructivism in World Politics', (1997) 3 *European Journal of International Relations* 319

Adlung, R - 'Negotiations on Safeguards and Subsidies in Services: A Never-Ending Story?', (2007) 10(2) *Journal of International Economic Law* 235

Allott, P - *Eunomia: A New World Order For a New World* (Oxford, Oxford University Press 1990)

Allott, P - 'The Concept of International Law', (1999) 10 *European Journal of International Law* 31

Alschner, W - 'Amicable Settlements of WTO Disputes: Bilateral Solutions in a Multilateral System', (2014) 13(1) *World Trade Review* 65

Alvarez-Jiménez, A - 'Mutually Agreed Solutions under the WTO Dispute Settlement Understanding: An Analytical Framework after the Softwood Lumber Arbitration', (2011) 10(3) *World Trade Review* 343

Alvarez, J - *International Organizations as Law-makers* (Oxford, Oxford University Press 2005)

Anghie, A - *Imperialism, Sovereignty and the Making of International Law* (Cambridge, Cambridge University Press 2005)

Anscombe, GEM - *Causality and Determination* (Cambridge, Cambridge University Press 1971)

Arcuri, A - 'Food Safety at the WTO after "Continued Suspension": a Paradigm Shift?', in A Antoniadis, R Schütze, and E Spaventa (eds), *The European Union and Global Emergencies: A Law and Policy Analysis* (Oxford, Hart Publishing 2011)

Arcuri, A - 'The TBT Agreement and private standards', in M Trebilcock and T Epps (eds), *Research Handbook on the TBT Agreement* (Cheltenham, Edward Elgar 2013)

Ashford, N - 'The Legacy of The Precautionary Principle In U.S. Law: The Rise of Cost-Benefit Analysis and Risk Assessment as Undermining Factors in Health, Safety and Environmental Protection', in N de Sadeleer (ed.), *Implementation of the Precautionary Principle: Approaches from the Nordic Countries, the EU and the United States* (London, Earthscan 2007)

Bacon, K - *European Union Law of State Aid* (Oxford, Oxford University Press 2013)

Bagwell, K and Staiger, R - 'An Economic Theory of GATT', (1999) 89(1) *The American Economic Review* 215

Bagwell, K and Staiger, R - 'GATT-Think', *Columbia University Economics Discussion Paper Series*, no. 0102-39 (March 2002)

Baldwin, R - 'The Case for a Multilateral Trade Organization', in A Narlikar, M Daunton, and R Stern (eds), *The Oxford Handbook on the World Trade Organization* (Oxford, Oxford University Press 2012)

Barnes, J (ed.) - *Complete Works of Aristotle Volume 1: Revised Oxford Translation* (Princeton, Princeton University Press 1984)

Barnes, J (ed.) - *Complete Works of Aristotle Volume II: Revised Oxford Translation* (Princeton, Princeton University Press 1985)

Bartels, L - 'Applicable Law in WTO Dispute Settlement Proceedings', (2001) 35 *Journal of World Trade* 499

Baumann, R, Mayer, P, and Zangl, B (eds), *International Relations: The Great Debates* (Cheltenham, Edward Elgar 2011)

Becker, GS - 'A Theory of Competition Among Pressure Groups for Political Influence', (1983) 98(3) *The Quarterly Journal of Economics* 371

Beckert, S - *Empire of Cotton: A New History of Global Capitalism* (London, Allen Lane 2014)

Becroft, R - *The Standard of Review in WTO Dispute Settlement: Critique and Development* (Cheltenham, Edward Elgar 2012)

Bello, J - 'Review: The Jurisprudence of the GATT and the WTO: Insights on Treaty Law and Economic Relations by John H. Jackson', (2001) 95(4) *American Journal of International Law* 984

Bello, J - 'The WTO Dispute Settlement Understanding: Less is More', (1996) 90 *American Journal of International Law* 416

Benitah, M - 'Subsidies, Services and Sustainable Development', *ICTSD Issue Paper 1* (2004), 17

Bergson, H - *An Introduction to Metaphysics* (London, Macmillan 1913)

Berman, F - 'What Does "Change" Mean? International Law vs. the International Legal System', (2003) 8 *Austrian Review of International and European Law* 11

Bhagwati, J - *In Defense of Globalization* (New York, Oxford University Press 2007)

Bhuyian, S - *National Law in the WTO* (Cambridge, Cambridge University Press 2007)

Bourdieu, P - 'The Force of Law: Toward a Sociology of the Juridical Field', (1987) 38 *Hastings Law Journal* 814

Bown, CP and McCulloch, R - 'Trade Adjustment in the WTO System: Are More Safeguards the Answer?', (2007) 23(3) *Oxford Review of Economic Policy* 415

Boyle, A and Chinkin, C - *The Making of International Law* (Oxford, Oxford University Press 2007)

Brewster, R - 'Rule-Based Dispute Resolution in International Trade Law', (2006) 92(2) *Virginia Law Review* 251

Brewster, R - 'The Domestic Origins of International Agreements', (2003) 44(2) *Virginia Journal of International Law* 1

Breyer, S - 'Judicial Review of Questions of Law and Policy', (1986) 38 *Administrative Law Review* 363

Breyer, S, Stewart, R, and Sunstein, C (eds) - *Administrative Law and Regulatory Policy* (6th edn, Aspen 2006)

Bronckers, M - 'From "Direct Effect" to "Muted Dialogue": Recent Developments in the European Courts' Case Law on the WTO and Beyond', (2008) 11(4) *Journal of International Economic Law* 885

Bronckers, M - 'Nondiscrimination in the World Trade Organization Safeguards Agreement: A European Perspective', in K Bagwell, G Bermann, and P Mavroidis (eds), *Law and Economics of Contingent Protection in International Trade* (Cambridge, Cambridge University Press 2014)

Broude, T and Shany, Y (eds) - *Multi-Sourced Equivalent Norms in International Law* (Oxford, Hart Publishing 2011)

Bull, H - 'International Theory: The Case for a Classical Approach', (1966) 18(3) *World Politics* 361

Burkard, M - 'The Ractopamine Dispute in the Codex Alimentarius Commission', (2012) 4 *European Journal of Risk Regulation* 610

Calabresi, G - 'Concerning Cause and the Law of Torts', (1975) 43 *University of Chicago Law Review* 69

Cass, D - 'The "Constitutionalization" of International Trade Law: Judicial Norm-Generation as an Engine of Constitutional Development in International Trade', (2001) 12(1) *European Journal of International Law* 39

Charmody, C - 'A Theory of WTO Law', (2008) 11(3) *Journal of International Economic Law* 527

Charmody, C - 'International Decisions - Softwood Lumber Dispute (2001-2006)', (2006) 100 *American Journal of International Law* 664

Charmody, C - 'WTO Obligations as Collective', (2006) 17(2) *European Journal of International Law* 419

Chayes, A and Chayes, AH - *The New Sovereignty: Compliance with New Regulatory Agreements* (Cambridge Mass, Harvard University Press 1995)

Cho, S - *The Social Foundations of World Trade: Norms, Community and Constitution* (Cambridge, Cambridge University Press 2014).

Cho, S - 'United States: Continued Suspension of Obligations in the EC-Hormones Dispute', (2009) 103(2) *American Journal of International Law* 299

Clark, I - *Globalization and International Relations Theory* (Oxford, Oxford University Press 1999)

Codex Alimentarius Commission, *Procedural Manual* (17th edn, FAO 2007)

Codex Secretariat, *Understanding the Codex Alimentarius* (3rd edn, FAO 2006), 6–9;

Collier, P - 'Why the WTO is Deadlocked: And What Can be Done About It', (2006) 29(10) *The World Economy* 1423

Cooper, A - *Internet Gambling Offshore: Caribbean Struggles over Casino Capitalism* (Basingstoke, Palgrave Macmillan 2011)

Cortell, A and Davis, J - 'When Norms Clash: International Norms, Domestic Practices and Japan's Internalisation of the GATT/WTO', (2005) 31(3) *Review of International Studies*

Cottier, T - 'The Common Law of International Trade and the Future of the World Trade Organization', (2015) 18(1) *Journal of International Economic Law* 3

Craven, M, Marks, S, Simpson, G, and Wilde, R - 'We Are Teachers of International Law', (2004) 17 *Leiden Journal of International Law* 363

Crawford, J - 'Chance, Order, Change: The Course of International Law', (2013) 365 *Recueil des Cours de l'Académie de Droit International*

Crawford, J - 'Continuity and Discontinuity in International Dispute Settlement: An Inaugural Lecture', (2010) 1(1) *Journal of International Dispute Settlement* 4

Croley, S and Jackson, J - 'WTO Dispute Procedures, Standard of Review, and Deference to National Governments', (1996) 90(2) *American Journal of International Law* 193

d'Aspremont, J - *Formalism and the Sources of International Law: A Theory of Ascertainment of Legal Rules* (Oxford, Oxford University Press 2011)

Damro, C - 'The Political Economic of Regional Trade Agreements', in L Bartels and F Ortino (eds), *Regional Trade Agreements and the WTO Legal System* (Oxford, Oxford University Press 2006)

de Bellis, M - 'Public Law and Private Regulators in the Global Legal Space', (2011) 9(2) *ICON* 425 de Meester, B - 'The Global Financial Crisis and Government Support For Banks: What Role For The GATS?', (2010) 13(1) *Journal of International Economic Law* 27

Delimatis, P and Sauvé, P - 'Financial Services Trade After the Crisis: Policy and Legal Conjuectures', (2010) 13(3) *Journal of International Economic Law* 837

Destler, IM - *American Trade Politics* (4th edn, Washington DC, Institute for International Economics 2005) 14

Drezner, D - *All Politics is Global: Explaining International Regulatory Regimes* (Princeton, Princeton University Press 2007)

Du, M - 'China's State Capitalism and World Trade Law', (2014) 63 *International and Comparative Law Quarterly* 409

Du, M - 'Standard of Review Under the SPS Agreement After EC-Hormones II', (2010) 59 *International and Comparative Law Quarterly* 441

Dunnoff, J and Pollack, M (eds) - *Interdisciplinary Perspectives on International Law and International Relations: The State of the Art* (Cambridge, Cambridge University Press 2013)

Dworkin, R - 'How Law is Like Literature', in *A Matter of Principle* (Oxford, Clarendon Press 1986)

Echols, M - *Food Safety and the WTO: The Interplay of Culture, Science and Technology* (London, Kluwer Law International 2001)

Ehlermann, CD - 'Six Years on the Bench of the "World Trade Court": Some Personal Experiences as Member of the Appellate Body of the WTO', (2002) 36(4) *Journal of World Trade* 605

Elliott, R and Zhou, Y - 'State-owned Enterprises, Exporting and Productivity in China: A Stochastic Dominance Approach', (2013) 36(8) *The World Economy* 1000

Elsig, M - 'The World Trade Organization's Legitimacy Crisis: What Does the Beast Look Like?', (2007) 41 *Journal of World Trade* 1

Endicott, T - *Vagueness in the Law* (Oxford, Oxford University Press 2000)

Epps, T - 'Demanding Perfection: Private Food Standards and the SPS Agreement', in M Lewis and S Frankel (eds), *International Economic Law and National Autonomy* (Cambridge, Cambridge University Press 2009)

Fakhri, M - *Sugar and the Making of International Trade Law* (Cambridge, Cambridge University Press 2014)

Finch, G - 'The Progressive Development of International Law', (1947) 41 *American Journal of International Law* 611

Fish, S - *Is There a Text in This Class? The Authority of Interpretative Communities* (Cambridge MA, Harvard University Press 1980)

Fisher, E - 'Beyond the Science/Democracy Dichotomy: The World Trade Organization Sanitary and PhytoSanitary Agreement and Administrative Constitutionalism', in C. Joerges & E. Petersmann (eds), *Constitutionalism, Multilevel Trade Governance and Social Regulation* (Oxford, Hart Publishing 2006)

Fisher, E - 'Food Safety Crises as Crises in Administrative Constitutionalism', (2010) 20 *Health Matrix* 55

Fisher, E - *Risk Regulation and Administrative Constitutionalism* (Oxford, Hart Publishing 2010)

Fitzmaurice, G - 'The General Principles of International Law Considered From the Standpoint of the Rule of Law', (1957) 92 *Recueil des Cours de l'Académie de Droit International* 38

Fitzmaurice, M - 'Third Parties and the Law of Treaties', (2002) 6 *Max Planck UN Yearbook* 37

Follesdal, A and Hix, S - 'Why There is a Democratic Deficit in the EU: A Response to Majone and Moravscik', (2006) 44(3) *Journal of Common Market Studies* 533

Food and Agriculture Organization & World Health Organization, *Food Safety Risk Analysis: A Guide for National Food Safety Authorities* (FAO 2006)

Footer, ME - 'Post-normal Science in the Multilateral Trading System: Social Science Expertise and the EC–Biotech Panel', (2007) 6(2) *World Trade Review* 281

Footer, ME - 'Some Theoretical and Legal Perspectives on WTO Compliance', (2007) 38 *Netherlands Yearbook of International Law* 61.

Footer, ME - 'The WTO as a 'Living Instrument', in T Cottier and M Elsig (eds), *Governing the World Trade Organization: Past, present and beyond Doha* (Cambridge, Cambridge University Press 2011)

Franck, T - *Fairness in International Law and Institutions* (Oxford, Oxford University Press 1997)

Franck, T - 'Legitimacy in the International System', 82 *American Journal of International Law* (1988) 705

Franck, T - *The Power of Legitimacy Among Nations* (Oxford, Oxford University Press 1990)

Gallie, WB - *Philosophy and the Historical Understanding* (London, Chatto & Windus 1964)

Gardiner, R - *Treaty Interpretation* (Oxford, Oxford University Press 2008)

Gardner, J - 'Legal Positivism: 5½ Myths', (2001) 46(1) *American Journal of Jurisprudence* 199

Geboye Desta, M - 'GATT/WTO law and international standards: an example of soft law instruments hardening up?', in A Bjorklund and A Reinisch, *International Investment Law and Soft Law* (Cheltenham, Edward Elgar 2012) 148

Gilpin, R - *Global Political Economy* (Princeton, Princeton University Press 2001)

Godfrey-Smith, P - 'Causal Pluralism', in H Beebee, C Hitchock, and P Menzies (eds), *The Oxford Handbook of Causation* (Oxford, Oxford University Press 2012)

Goldsmith, J and Vermeule, A - 'Empirical Methodology and Legal Scholarship', (2002) 69(1) *University of Chicago Law Review* 153

Goldstein, J - 'Ideas, Institutions, and American Trade Policy', in G.J Ikenberry, D Lake, and M Mastanduno (eds), *The State and American Foreign Economic Policy* (Ithaca, Cornell University Press 1988)

Goldstein, J and Martin, L - 'Legalization, Trade Liberalization and Domestic Politics: A Cautionary Note', (2000) 54(3) *International Organization* 603

Goodhart, CAE - 'Economics and the Law: Too Much One-Way Traffic?', (1997) 60 *Modern Law Review* 1

Grando, M - *Evidence, Proof, and Fact-Finding in WTO Dispute Settlement* (Oxford, Oxford University Press 2009)

Green, L - 'The Causal Relation Issue in Negligence Law', (1962) 60 *Michigan Law Review* 543

Greenwald, J - 'WTO Dispute Settlement: An Exercise in Trade Law Legislation?', (2003) 6(1) *Journal of International Economic Law* 113

Gruszcyzynski, L - 'Risk Management Policies under the WTO Agreement on the Application of Sanitary and Phytosanitary Measures', (2008) 3(1) *Asian Journal of WTO & International Health Law and Policy* 261

Grynberg, R et al. - 'Bilateral Commodity Agreements – New Generation Grey-Area Measures? A Scoping Study', in V Qalo (ed.), *Bilateralism and Development: Emerging Trade Patterns* (London, Cameron May 2008)

Guglya, L - 'The Interplay of International Dispute Resolution Mechanisms: The Softwood Lumber Controversy', (2011) 2(1) *Journal of International Dispute Settlement* 175

Gunitsky, S - 'Complexity and Theories of Change in International Politics', (2013) 5(1) *International Theory* 35

Guthrie, WKC - *A History of Greek Philosophy: Volume I* (Cambridge, Cambridge University Press 1962)

Guthrie, WKC - *The Greek Philosophers* (London, Methuen 1950)

Guzman, A - 'A Compliance-Based Theory of International Law', (2002) 90 *California Law Review* 1823

Guzman, A - *How International Law Works: A Rational Choice Theory* (Oxford, Oxford University Press 2008)

Hachez, N & Wouters, J - 'A Glimpse at the Democratic Legitimacy of Private Standards: Assessing the Public Accountability of GLOBALG.A.P.', (2011) 14(3) *Journal of International Economic Law* 677

Hafner-Burton, E, Victor, D, and Lupu, Y - 'Political Science on International Law: The State of the Field', (2012) 106(1) *American Journal of International Law* 47

Hale, R - 'Coercion and Distribution in a Supposedly Non-Coercive State', (1923) 38(3) *Political Science Quarterly* 470.

Hale, T, Held, D, and Young, K - *Gridlock: Why Global Cooperation is Failing when We Need It Most* (Cambridge, Polity Press 2013)

Halliday, T and Carruthers, B - 'The Recursivity of Law: Global Norm Making and National Law Making in the Globalization of Corporate Insolvency Regimes', (2007) 112(4) *American Journal of Sociology* 1135

Halpin, A and Roeben, V (eds) - *Theorising the Global Legal Order* (Oxford, Hart Publishing 2009)

Hanrahan, C - 'Agricultural Biotechnology: The US-EU Dispute', Congressional Research Service Reports (2010) Paper 69

Hart, HLA - *The Concept of Law* (2nd edn, Oxford, Oxford University Press 1994)

Hart, HLA and Honoré, T - *Causation in the Law* (2nd edn, Oxford, Clarendon Press 1985)

Held, D, McGrew, A, Goldblatt, D, and Perraton, J (eds) - *Global Transformations, Politics, Economics and Culture* (Cambridge, Polity Press 1999)

Henkin, L - *How Nations Behave* (2nd edn, New York, Columbia University Press 1979)

Herdegen, M - *Principles of International Economic Law* (Oxford, Oxford University Press 2013)

Hernández, G - *The International Court of Justice and the Judicial Function* (Oxford, Oxford University Press 2014)

Higgins, R - 'Policy Considerations and the International Judicial Process', (1968) 17 *International and Comparative Law Quarterly* 58

Higgins, R - *Problems and Process: International Law and How We Use It* (Oxford, Clarendon Press 1996)

Hirsch, M – 'The Sociology of International Economic Law: Sociological Analysis of the Regulation of Regional Agreements in the World Trading System', (2008) 19(2) *European Journal of International Law* 277.

Hizon, EM - 'The Safeguard Measure/VER Dilemma: The Jekyll and Hyde of Trade Protection', (1994–1995) 15 *Northwestern Journal of International Law & Business* 105

Horlick, G and Clarke, P - 'The 1994 WTO Subsidies Agreement', (1993) 17(4) *World Competition*

Horlick, G and Clarke, P - 'WTO Subsidies Discipline During and After the Crisis', (2010) 13(3) *Journal of International Economic Law* 859

Howse, D and Teitel, R - 'Beyond Compliance: Rethinking Why International Law Really Matters', *Public Law and Legal Theory Research Paper Series*, NYU School of Law, Working Paper No.10-08.

Howse, R - 'Adjudicative Legitimacy and Treaty Interpretation in International Trade Law: The Early Years of WTO Jurisprudence', in JHH Weiler (ed.), *The EU, the WTO, and the NAFTA: Towards a Common Law of International Trade?* (Oxford, Oxford University Press 2001)

Howse, R - 'Democracy, Science, and Free Trade: Risk Regulation on Trial at the WTO', (2000) 98 *Michigan Law Review* 2329

Hudec, R - 'GATT Dispute Settlement after the Tokyo Round: An Unfinished Business', (1980) 13 *Cornell Journal of International Law* 145

Hudec, R - 'The New Dispute Settlement System of the WTO: An Overview of the First Three Years', (1999) 8(1) *Minnesota Journal of Global Trade* 1

Hume, D - *A Treatise of Human Nature* (L Selby-Bigg (ed.)) (Oxford, Clarendon Press 1975)

Huntington, S - 'The US. – Decline or Renewal?', *Foreign Affairs* (Winter 1988/1989)

Hurrell, A - *On Global Order: Power, Values, and the Constitution of International Society* (Oxford, Oxford University Press 2007) 199.

Ikenberry, GJ - 'Conclusion: An Institutional Approach to Foreign Economic Policy', in G.J Ikenberry, D Lake, and M Mastanduno (eds), *The State and American Foreign Economic Policy* (Ithaca, Cornell University Press 1988)

Irwin, D et al. - *The Genesis of the GATT* (Cambridge, Cambridge University Press 2009)

Jackson, JH - 'International Law Status of WTO Dispute Settlement Reports: Obligation to Comply or Option to "Buy Out"', (2004) 98 *American Journal of International Law* 109

Jackson, JH - 'Status of Treaties in Domestic Legal Systems: A Policy Analysis', (1992) 86(2) *American Journal of International Law* 310

Jackson, JH - 'The Great 1994 Sovereignty Debate: United States Acceptance and Implementation of the Uruguay Round Results', (1997) 36 *Columbia Journal of Transnational Law* 157

Jackson, JH - *The Jurisprudence of GATT & the WTO* (Cambridge, Cambridge University Press 2000)

Jackson, JH - 'The Varied Policies of International Juridical Bodies – Reflections on Theory and Practice', (2004) 25 *Michigan Journal of International Law* 869

Jackson, JH - *The World Trading System* (2nd edn, London, MIT Press 1997)

Jackson, JH - 'The WTO Dispute Settlement Understanding – Misunderstandings on the Nature of Legal Obligation', (1997) 91 *American Journal of International Law* 63

Jackson, PT - 'Hegel's House, or "People are States Too"', (2004) 30 *Review of International Studies* 281

Jennings, RY - 'The Judiciary, International and National, and the Development of International Law', (1996) 45 *International and Comparative Law Quarterly* 1

Jessup, PC - 'Development of International Law by the United Nations', (1945) 39 *American Journal of International Law* 745

Jessup, PC - *Transnational Law* (New Haven, Yale University Press 1956)

Jones, K - 'The Safeguards Mess Revisited: the Fundamental Problem', (2004) 3 *World Trade Review* 83

Kammerhofer, J - 'International Legal Positivism', in F Hoffmann, A Orford (eds), *Oxford Handbook of International Legal Theory* (Oxford, Oxford University Press, forthcoming)

Katzenstein, P (ed.) - *Between Power and Plenty: Foreign Economic Policies of Advanced Industrial States* (Wisconsin, University of Wisconsin Press 1978)

Katzenstein, P - 'International Relations and Domestic Structures: Foreign Economic Policies of Advanced Industrial States', (1976) 30(1) *International Organization* 2

Kelsen, H – *General Theory of Law and State* (Cambridge MA, Harvard University Press 1945)

Kelsen, H - 'The Principle of Sovereign Equality of States as a Basis for International Organization', (1944) 53(2) *Yale Law Journal* 207

Kennedy, D - 'Legal Formality', (1973) 2 *Journal of Legal Studies* 351

Kennedy, D - 'Three Globalizations of Law and Legal Thought: 1850-2000', in D Trubek and A Santos (eds), *The New Law and Economic Development: A Critical Appraisal* (Cambridge, Cambridge University Press 2006)

Keohane, R - *Power and Governance in a Partially Globalized World* (London, Routledge 2002)

Keohane, R and Nye, J - *Power and Interdependence* (3rd edn, New York, Longman 2001)

Khan, KUR - *The Law and Organisation of International Commodity Agreements* (The Hague, Martinus Nijhoff 1982)

Kingsbury, B - 'The Concept of "Law" in Global Administrative Law', (2009) 20(1) *European Journal of International Law* 23

Kingsbury, B et al. - 'The Emergence of Global Administrative Law', (2005) 68 *Law and Contemporary Problems* 15

Klabbers, J - 'The Emergence of Functionalism in International Institutional Law: Colonial Aspirations', (2014) 25(3) *European Journal of International Law* 645

Knorr, K - *Power and Wealth – The Political Economy of International Power* (London, Macmillan 1973)

Koh, H - 'Jefferson Memorial Lecture: Transnational Legal Process After September 11th', (2004) 22 *Berkeley Journal of International Law* 337

Koh, H - '1994 Roscoe Pound Lecture: Transnational Legal Process', (1996) 75 *Nebraska Law Review* 181

Koh, H - 'The Globalization of Freedom', (2001) 26 *Yale Journal of International Law* 305

Koh, H - 'Why Do Nations Obey International Law?', (1997) 106 *Yale Law Journal* 2599

Koh, H - 'Why Transnational Law Matters', (2005–2006) 24 *Pennsylvania State International Law Review* 745

Kolakowski, L - *Bergson* (Oxford, Oxford University Press 1985)

Komuro, N - 'Japan's Safeguard Law and Practice', (2001) 35(5) *Journal of World Trade* 851

Kooijmans, P - 'The ICJ in the 21st Century: Judicial Restraint, Judicial Activism, or Proactive Judicial Policy', (2007) 56 *International and Comparative Law Quarterly* 741, 742

Koskenniemi, M - 'The Fate of Public International Law: Between Technique and Politics', (2007) *Modern Law Review* 1

Koskenniemi, M - *From Apology to Utopia: The Structure of International Legal Argument* (Cambridge, Cambridge University Press, 2005 reissue)

Koskenniemi, M - 'The Politics of International Law – 20 Years Later', (2009) 20 *European Journal of International Law* 1

Krajewski, M - 'Legitimising Global Governance Through Transnational Parliamentarisation: How Far Have We Come? How Much Further Must We Go?', in T Cottier and M Elsig (eds), *Governing the World Trade Organization: Past, present and beyond Doha* (Cambridge, Cambridge University Press 2011)

Krasner, S - 'Compromising Westphalia', (1995–1996) 20(3) *International Security* 115

Krasner, S - 'State Power and the Structure of International Trade', (1976) 28(3) *World Politics* 317

Kratochwil, F - *Rules, Norms and Decisions: On the Conditions of Practical and Legal Reasoning in International Relations and Domestic Affairs* (Cambridge, Cambridge University Press 1989)

Krisch, N - 'International Law in Times of Hegemony: Unequal Power and the Shaping of the International Legal Order', (2005) 16(3) *European Journal of International Law* 369

Krisch, N - *Beyond Constitutionalism: The Pluralist Structure of Postnational Law* (Oxford, Oxford University Press 2010)

Krüger, T - 'Shaping the WTO's institutional evolution: the EU as a strategic litigant in the WTO', in D Kochenov & F Amtenbrink (eds), *The European Union's Shaping of the International Legal Order* (Cambridge, Cambridge University Press 2013)

Kumm, M - 'The Legitimacy of International Law: A Constitutionalist Framework of Analysis', (2004) 15(5) *European Journal of International Law* 907

Kurki, M - *Causation in International Relations: Reclaiming Causal Analysis* (Cambridge, Cambridge University Press 2008)

Laird, S and Valdés, R - 'The Trade Policy Review Mechanism', in A Narlikar, M Daunton, and R Stern, *The Oxford Handbook on the World Trade Organization* (Oxford, Oxford University Press 2012)

Lamy, P - *The Geneva Consensus: Making Trade Work For All* (Cambridge, Cambridge University Press 2013)

Lang, A - 'Reflecting on "Linkage": Cognitive and Institutional Change in The International Trading System', (2007) 70(4) *Modern Law Review* 523

Lang, A - 'Rejoinder', (2014) 23(3) *Social & Legal Studies* 453

Lang, A - 'Some Sociological Perspectives on International Institutions and the Trading System', in C Picker, I Bunn, and D Arner (eds), *International Economic Law: The State and Future of the Discipline* (Oxford, Hart Publishing 2008)

Lang, A - *World Trade Law After Neoliberalism: Reimaging the Global Economic Order* (Oxford, Oxford University Press 2011)

Lang, A and Scott, J - 'The Hidden World of WTO Governance', (2009) 20 *European Journal of International Law* 575

Lang, A and Scott, J - 'The Hidden World of WTO Governance: A Rejoinder to Richard H. Steinberg', (2010) 20 *European Journal of International Law* 1073.

Laski, H - *Studies in Law and Politics* (London, Allen & Unwin 1932, 1969 reprint)

Lauterpacht, H - 'Codification and Development of International Law', (1955) 49 *American Journal of International Law* 16

Lauterpacht, H - *The Development of International Law by the International Court* (Cambridge, Cambridge University Press 2010 reissue, first published 1954)

Lee, YS - 'Destabilization of the Discipline on Safeguards', (2001) 35 *Journal of World Trade* 6

Lee, YS - 'Not Without a Clue: Commentary on "the Persistent Puzzles of Safeguards"', (2006) 40 *Journal of World Trade* 385

Lee, YS - 'Revival of Grey-Area Measures?', (2002) 36(1) *Journal of World Trade* 155

Lee, YS - *Safeguard Measures in World Trade: the Legal Analysis* (3rd edn, Cheltenham, Edward Elgar 2014)

Leebron, D - 'Implementation of the Uruguay Round Results in the United States', in J Jackson and A Sykes (eds), *Implementing the Uruguay Round* (Oxford, Clarendon Press 1997)

Legrand, P - 'What "Legal Transplants?"', in D Nelken and J Feest (eds), *Adapting Legal Culture* (Oxford, Hart Publishing 2001)

Leiter, B - 'Legal Formalism and Legal Realism: What is the Issue?', (2010) 16 *Legal Theory* 111

Lepard, B - *Customary International Law: A New Theory with Practical Applications* (Cambridge, Cambridge University Press 2010)

Lindsay, AD - *The Philosophy of Bergson* (London, J.M Dent & Sons 1911)

Lipton, P - 'Causation and Explanation', in H Beebee, C Hitchock, and P Menzies (eds), *The Oxford Handbook of Causation* (Oxford, Oxford University Press 2012)

Löfstedt, R - 'The Swing of the Regulatory Pendulum in Europe: From Precautionary Principle to (Regulatory) Impact Analysis', (2004) 28(3) *The Journal of Risk and Uncertainty* 237

Löfstedt, R and Vogel, D - 'The Changing Character of Regulation: a Comparison of Europe and the United States', (2001) 21 *Risk Analysis* 399.

Lowenfeld, A - 'Fair or Unfair Trade: Does it Matter?', (1980) 13 *Cornell International Law Journal* 205

MacCormick, N - *Institutions of Law: An Essay in Legal Theory* (Oxford, Oxford University Press 2007)

Manners, I - 'Normative Power Europe: A Contradiction in Terms?', (2002) 40 *Journal of Common Market Studies* 23

Marks, S - 'Human Rights and Root Causes', (2011) 74(1) *Modern Law Review* 57

Matsushita, M et al. - *The World Trade Organization: Law, Practice, and Policy* (2nd edn, Oxford, Oxford University Press 2006)

Mavroidis, P - 'Amicus Curiae Briefs Before the WTO: Much Ado About Nothing', Jean Monet Working Paper 2/01, 8

Mavroidis, P - 'Free Lunches? WTO as Public Good, and the WTO's View of Public Goods', (2012) 23(3) *European Journal of International Law* 731

Mavroidis, P - *The General Agreement on Tariffs and Trade: A Commentary* (Oxford, Oxford University Press 2009)

Mavroidis, P - *Trade in Goods* (Oxford, Oxford University Press 2007)

McCall Smith, J - 'WTO Dispute Settlement: The Politics of Appellate Body Rulings', (2003) 2 *World Trade Review* 65

McDougal, M et al. - *Studies in World Public Order* (New Haven, Yale University Press 1960)

McGuire, S - 'What Happened to the Influence of Business? Corporations and Organized Labour in the WTO', in A Narlikar, M Dauton, and R Stern (eds), *The Oxford Handbook on the World Trade Organization* (Oxford, Oxford University Press 2012)

McRae, D - 'What is the Future of WTO Dispute Settlement', (2004) 7(1) *Journal of International Economic Law* 3

Meron, T - 'War Crimes in Yugoslavia and the Development of International Law', (1994) 88 *American Journal of International Law* 76

Messenger, G - 'National Law As An Unpredictable Generator Of International Law: the Case of Norm Export at the World Trade Organization', *ESIL Conference Paper Series* 10/2014

Messenger, G – 'Reforming the Law and Institutions of the WTO: the Dangers of Unexpected Consequences', in A Segura (ed.), *The Reform of International Economic Governance* (Farnham, Ashgate 2016, forthcoming)

Meyer, CO and Strickmann, E - 'Solidifying Constructivism: How Material and Ideational Factors Interact in European Defence', (2011) 49(1) *Journal of Common Market Studies* 61

Molyneux, C - *Domestic Structures and International Trade* (Oxford, Hart Publishing 2001)

Moravcsik, A - 'Taking Preferences Seriously: A Liberal Theory of International Politics', (1997) 51(4) *International Organization* 513

Morgenthau, H - *Politics Among Nations* (New York, Knopf 1948)

Morgenthau, H - 'Positivism, Functionalism, and International Law', (1940) 34(2) *American Journal of International Law* 260

Mueller, F - 'Is the General Agreement on Tariffs and Trade Article XIX "Unforeseen Developments Clause" Still Effective Under the Agreement on Safeguards?', (2003) 37(6) *Journal of World Trade* 1119

Murayama, W - 'The Evolution of the Escape Clause – Section 201 of the Trade Act of 1974 as Amended by the Omnibus Trade and Competitiveness Act of 1988', (1989) *Brigham Young University Law Review* 393

Nicolaïdis, K and Howse, R - '"This is my EUtopia …": Narrative as Power', (2002) 40(4) *Journal of Common Market Studies* 767

Nolan, P - 'Globalisation and Industrial Policy: the Case of China', (2014) *The World Economy* 747

Nollen, SD and Quinn, DP - 'Free Trade, Fair Trade, Strategic Trade, and Protectionism in the U.S. Congress, 1987-1988', (1994) 48(3) *International Organization* 491

Nye, J - *Soft Power: The Means to Success in World Politics* (New York, PublicAffairs 2004)

O'Donoghue, A - *Constitutionalism in Global Constitutionalisation* (Cambridge, Cambridge University Press 2014)

Oesch, M - *Standards of Review in WTO Dispute Resolution* (Oxford, Oxford University Press 2003)

Onuma, Y - 'A Transcivilizational Perspective on International Law', (2010) 342 *Recueil des Cours de l'Académie de Droit International* 95

Oppenheim, L - 'The Science of International Law: Its Tasks and Method', (1908) 2 *American Journal of International Law* 313

Orford, A - 'Constituting Order', in J Crawford and M Koskenniemi (eds), *The Cambridge Companion to International Law* (Cambridge, Cambridge University Press 2012)

Orford, A - 'Scientific Reason and the Discipline of International Law', (2014) 25(2) *European Journal of International Law* 369

Osiander, A - 'Sovereignty, International Relations, and the Westphalian Myth', (2001) 55(2) *International Organization* 251

Panagariya, A - 'TRIPs and the WTO: An Uneasy Marriage', in K Maskus (ed.), *The WTO, Intellectual Property Rights And The Knowledge Economy* (Cheltenham, Edward Elgar 2004).

Pauwelyn, J - 'A Typology of Multilateral Treaty Obligations: Are WTO Obligations Bilateral or Collective in Nature?', (2003) 14(5) *European Journal of International Law* 907

Pauwelyn, J - 'At the Edge of Chaos? Foreign Investment Law as a Complex Adaptive System, How It Emerged and How It Can Be Reformed', (2014) 29(2) *ICSID Review* 372

Pauwelyn, J - *Conflict of Norms in Public International Law* (Cambridge, Cambridge University Press 2003)

Pauwelyn, J - 'Is It International Law or Not, and Does It Even Matter?', in J Pauwelyn, R Wessel, and J Wouters (eds), *Informal International Lawmaking* (Oxford, Oxford University Press 2012)

Pauwelyn, J - 'The Role of Public International Law in the WTO: How Far Can We Go?', (2001) 95 *American Journal of International Law* 595

Pauwelyn, J - 'Treaty Interpretation or Activism? Comment on the AB Report on *United States – ADs and CVDs on Certain Products from China*', (2013) 12(2) *World Trade Review* 235

Peel, J - 'A GMO by Any Other Name ... Might Be an SPS Risk!: Implications of Expanding the Scope of the WTO Sanitary and Phytosanitary Measures Agreement', (2007) 17(5) *European Journal of International Law* 1009

Peel, J - 'Risk Regulation Under the WTO SPS Agreement: Science as an International Normative Yardstick?', Jean Monet Working Paper 02/04, June 2004

Petersmann, EU - 'The WTO Constitution and Human Rights', (2000) 3(1) *Journal of International Economic Law* 19

Petersmann, EU and Pollack, M - *Transatlantic Economic Disputes: The EU, the US, and the WTO* (Oxford, Oxford University Press 2003)

Picciotto, S - 'The WTO's Appellate Body: Legal Formalism as a Legitimation of Global Governance', (2005) 18 *Governance* 3

Piérola, F - *The Challenge of Safeguards in the WTO* (Cambridge, Cambridge University Press 2014)

Pollack, M and Shaffer, G - *When Cooperation Fails: The International Law and Politics of Genetically Modified Foods* (Oxford, Oxford University Press 2009)

Pound, R - *Interpretations of Legal History* (Cambridge, Cambridge University Press 1930)

Puig, S - 'International Regime Complexity and Economic Law Enforcement', (2014) 17(3) *Journal of International Economic Law* 491

Putnam, R - 'Diplomacy and Domestic Politics: The Logic of Two-Level Games', (1998) 42(3) *International Organization* 427

Quick, R and Blüthner, A - 'Has the Appellate Body Erred? An Appraisal and Criticism of the Ruling in the WTO Hormones Case', (1999) *Journal of International Economic Law* 603

Raz, J - *Between Authority and Interpretation* (Oxford, Oxford University Press 2009)

Raz, J - *The Authority of Law: Essays on Law and Morality* (Oxford, Clarendon Press 1979)

Reed, P - 'Relationship of WTO Obligations to US International Trade Law: Internationalist Vision Meets Domestic Reality', (2006) 38 *Georgetown Journal of International Law* 209

Reid, E - 'Risk Assessment, Science and Deliberation: Managing Regulatory Diversity under the SPS Agreement?', (2012) *European Journal of Risk Regulation* 535

Resnik, J - 'Globalization(s), Privatization(s), Constitutionalization, and Statization: Icons and Experiences of Sovereignty in the 21st Century', (2013) 11(1) *International Journal of Constitutional Law* 162

Roberts, A and Sivakumaran, A - 'Lawmaking by Nonstate Actors: Engaging Armed Groups in the Creation of International Humanitarian Law', (2012) 37(1) *Yale Journal of International Law* 107

Rolland, S - *Development at the WTO* (Oxford, Oxford University Press 2012)

Ross, D - *Aristotle* (6th edn, London, Routledge 1995)

Ross, D - *Aristotle Physics* (Oxford, Clarendon Press 1936)

Roughan, N - *Authorities: Conflicts, Cooperation, and Transnational Legal Theory* (Oxford, Oxford University Press 2013)

Ruggie, J - 'International Regimes, Transactions, and Change: Embedded Liberalism and the Postwar Economic Order', (1982) 36(2) *International Organization* 379
Ruiz Fabri, H - 'Is There a Case – Legally and Politically – for Direct Effect of WTO Obligations?', (2014) 25 *European Journal of International Law* 151.
Ryan, D - 'The Effects of Section 201 Safeguards on US Industries', (2013) 44 *Georgetown Journal of International Law* 249
Sarooshi, D - *International Organizations and their Exercise of Sovereign Powers* (Oxford, Oxford University Press 2005)
Sarooshi, D - 'Sovereignty, Economic Autonomy, the United States, and the International Trading System', (2004) 15(4) *European Journal of International Law* 651
Scalia, A - 'Judicial Deference to Agency Interpretations of Law', (1989) *Duke Law Journal* 511
Schauer, F - 'Formalism', (1988) 97(4) *Yale Law Journal* 509
Schwartz, W and Sykes, A - 'The Economic Structure of Renegotiation and Dispute Resolution in the World Trade Organization', (2002) 31 *Journal of Legal Studies* 179
Schwarzenberger, G - 'The Principles and Standards of International Economic Law', I *Recueil des Cours* (1966)
Scott, C - '"Transnational Law" as a Proto-Concept: Three Conceptions', (2009) 10(7) *German Law Journal* 859
Scott, J - *The WTO Agreement on Sanitary and Phytosanitary Measures: A Commentary* (Oxford, Oxford University Press 2009)
Shaffer, G - *Defending Interests: Public- Private Partnerships in WTO Litigation* (Minneapolis MN, Brookings Institution Press 2003)
Shaffer, G - 'Globalization and Social Protection: The Impact of EU and International Rules in the Ratcheting Up of U.S. Privacy Standards', (2000) 25(1) *Yale Journal of International Law* 1
Shaffer, G - 'Transnational Legal Ordering and State Change', in G Shaffer (ed.), *Transnational Legal Ordering and State Change* (Cambridge, Cambridge University Press 2012)
Shaffer, G and Ginsburg, T - 'The Empirical Turn in International Legal Scholarship', (2012) 106(1) *American Journal of International Law* 1
Shaffer, G and Meléndez-Ortiz, R - *Dispute Settlement at the WTO: The Developing Country Experience* (Cambridge, Cambridge University Press 2010)
Shaffer, G and Trachtman, J - 'Interpretation and Institutional Choice at the WTO', (2012) 52(1) *Virginia Journal of International Law* 103
Sikkink, K - *The Justice Cascade: How Human Rights Prosecutions are Changing World Politics* (New York, WW Norton & Co 2011)
Simma, B - 'Of Planets and the Universe: Self-Contained Regimes in International Law', (2006) 17(3) *European Journal of International Law* 483
Simmons, B and Breidenbach, A - 'The Empirical Turn in International Economic Law', (2011) 20 *Minnesota Journal of International Law* 198
Skinner, Q - 'The Limits of Historical Explanations', (1966) 157 XLI *The Journal of the Royal Institute of Philosophy* 199
Skogstad, G - 'Contested Accountability Claims and GMO Regulation in the European Union', (2011) 49(4) *Journal of Common Market Studies* 895
Slaughter, AM - 'International Law and International Relations Theory', (2000) 285 *Recueil des Cours de l'Académie de Droit International* 9
Slaughter, AM and Ratner, SR - 'Symposium on Method in International Law', (1999) 93 *American Journal of International Law* 291

Smith, RD - 'Food Security and International Fisheries Policy in Japan's Postwar Planning', (2008) 11(2) *Social Science Japan Journal* 259
Stebbing, L - *A Modern Introduction to Logic* (2nd edn, London, Meuthen 1933)
Steffek, J - 'Awkward Partners: NGOs and Social Movements at the WTO', in A Narlikar, M Dauton and R Stern (eds), *The Oxford Handbook on the World Trade Organization* (Oxford, Oxford University Press 2012)
Steger, M - *Globalization: A Very Short Introduction* (3rd edn, Oxford, Oxford University Press 2013)
Steil, B - *The Battle of Bretton Woods* (Princeton, Princeton University Press 2013)
Stein, E - 'Lawyers, Judges, and the Making of a Transnational Constitution', (1981) 75(1) *American Journal of International Law* 1
Steinberg, R - 'Judicial Lawmaking at the WTO: Discursive, Constitutional, and Political Constraints', (2004) 98(2) *American Journal of International Law* 247
Steiner, H - 'Constructing and developing transnational law: the contribution of Detlev Vagts', in PHF Bekker, R Dolzer, and M Waibel (eds), *Making Transnational Law Work in the Global Economy: Essays in Honour of Detlev Vagts* (Cambridge, Cambridge University Press 2010)
Stewart, T - *The GATT Uruguay Round: A Negotiating History Vol I* (Deventer, The Netherlands, Kluwer Law International 1993)
Stewart, T - *The GATT Uruguay Round: A Negotiating History Vol II* (Deventer, The Netherlands, Kluwer Law International 1993)
Stiglitz, J - 'Dumping on Free Trade: The US Import Trade Laws', (1997) 64(2) *Southern Economic Journal* 402
Stiglitz, J - *Globalization and its Discontents* (London, Penguin 2002)
Strange, S - *The Retreat of the State* (Cambridge, Cambridge University Press 1996)
Suganami, H - 'Agents, Structures, Narratives', (1999) *European Journal of International Relations* 365
Suganami, H - *On the Causes of War* (Oxford, Oxford University Press 1996)
Sunstein, C - *Risk and Reason: Safety, Law, and the Environment* (Cambridge, Cambridge University Press 2002)
Supiot, A - 'The Public–Private Relation in the Context of Today's Refeudalization', (2013) 11(1) *International Journal of Constitutional Law* 129
Suranovic, S - 'A Positive Analysis of Fairness with Applications to International Trade', (2000) 23(3) *The World Economy* 294
Sykes, A - 'Protectionism as a "Safeguard": A Positive Analysis of the GATT "Escape Clause" with Normative Speculations', (1991) 58 *University of Chicago Law Review* 255
Sykes, A - 'The Fundamental Deficiencies of the Agreement on Safeguards: A Reply to Professor Lee', (2006) 40(5) *Journal of World Trade* 979
Sykes, A - 'The Persistent Puzzles of Safeguards: Lessons from the Steel Dispute', (2004) 7(3) *Journal of International Economic Law* 523
Sykes, A - 'The "Safeguards Mess" Revisited – A Reply to Professor Jones', (2004) 3(1) *World Trade Review* 93
Sykes, A - *The WTO Agreement on Safeguards: A Commentary* (Oxford, Oxford University Press 2006)
Sykes, A - 'Trade Remedy Laws', *John M. Olin Program in Law and Economics Working Paper* No. 240 (2005) 6
Talmon, S - 'The Constitutive versus the Declaratory Theory of Recognition: Tertium Non Datur?', (2005) 75 *British Year Book of International Law* 101

Talmon, S - 'The Security Council as World Legislature', (2005) 99 *American Journal of International Law* 175

Tamanaha, B - 'An Analytical Map of Social Scientific Approaches to the Concept of Law', (1995) 15(4) *Oxford Journal of Legal Studies* 501

Tamanaha, B - 'The Folly of the "Social-Scientific" Concept of Legal Pluralism', (1993) 20 *Journal of Law and Society* 192

Tamanaha, B - 'The Perils of Pervasive Legal Instrumentalism', Montesquieu Lecture Series, Tilburg University, (2005) Vol 1

Tams, CJ and Sloan, J (eds) - *The Development of International Law by the International Court of Justice* (Oxford, Oxford University Press 2013).

Teubner, G - *Constitutional Fragments: Societal Constitutionalism and Globalization* (Oxford, Oxford University Press 2012)

Trebilcock, M and Howse, R - *The Regulation of International Trade* (3rd edn, London, Routledge 2007)

Tunkin, G - *Theory of International Law* (Cambridge MA, Harvard University Press 1974)

Tzanakopoulos, A - 'Judicial Dialogue in Multi-level Governance: The Impact of the Solange Argument', in O Fauchald and A Nollkaemper (eds), *The Practice of International and National Courts and the (De-)fragmentation of International Law* (Oxford, Hart Publishing 2012)

Tzanakopoulos, A and Tams, CJ - 'Introduction: Domestic Courts as Agents of Development of International Law', (2013) 26 *Leiden Journal of International Law* 531

UNCTAD World Investment Report, 'Global Value Chains: Investment and Trade for Development' (2013)

Van Den Bossche, P - 'From Afterthought to Centerpiece: The WTO Appellate Body and its Rise to Prominence in the World Trading System', Maastricht Faculty of Law Working Paper 2005/1

Van Den Bossche, P - 'The Making of the "World Trade Court": the Origins and Development of the Appellate Body of the World Trade Organization', in R Yerxa and B Wilson, *Key Issues in WTO Dispute Settlement: The First Ten Years* (Cambridge, Cambridge University Press 2005)

Van Den Bossche, P - 'The WTO Appellate Body and Its Rise to Prominence', in G Sacerdoti, A Yanovich, and J Bohanes (eds), *The WTO at Ten: The Contribution of the Dispute Settlement System* (Cambridge, Cambridge University Press 2006)

Van den Bossche, P and Zdouc, W - *The Law and Policy of the World Trade Organization* (3rd edn, Cambridge, Cambridge University Press 2013)

Varella, M - *Internationalization of Law: Globalization, International Law and Complexity* (London, Springer 2014)

Venzke, I - *How Interpretation Makes International Law: On Semantic Change and Normative Twists* (Oxford, Oxford University Press 2012)

Vermulst, E Pernaute, M, and Lucenti, K - 'Recent EC Safeguards' Policy: "Kill Them All and Let God Sort Them Out"?', (2004) 38(6) *Journal of World Trade* 955

Vidmar, J - *Democratic Statehood in International Law* (Oxford, Hart Publishing 2013).

Vignarajah, K - 'Reconciling Free Trade and Safe Trade: New Paradigms for Regulating Imports in the Twenty-First Century', (2009) 43(4) *Journal of World Trade* 771

von Bogdandy, A, Wolfrum, R, von Bernstorff, J, Dann, P, and Goldmann, M (eds) - *The Exercise of Public Authority by International Institutions: Advancing International Institutional law* (London, Springer 2010)

Waltz, K - *Man, the State, and War: A Theoretical Analysis* (2nd edn, New York, Columbia University Press 2001)

Warwick Commission - 'The Multilateral Trade Regime: Which Way Forward?' (2007)

Weeramantry, C - 'Constitutional and Institutional Developments: The Function of the International Court of Justice in the Development of International Law', (1997) 10 *Leiden Journal of International Law* 309.

Weiler, JHH - 'The Rule of Lawyers and the Ethos of Diplomats: Reflections on the Internal and External Legitimacy of WTO Dispute Settlement', (2001) 35(2) *Journal of World Trade* 206

Wendt, A - *Social Theory of International Politics* (Cambridge, Cambridge University Press 1999)

Wheatley, S - 'The Security Council, Democratic Legitimacy and Regime Change in Iraq', (2006) 17(3) *European Journal of International Law* 531

Wight, C - 'State Agency: Social Action Without Human Activity?', (2004) 30 *Review of International Studies* 269

Wilson, B - 'Compliance by WTO Members With Adverse WTO Dispute Settlement Rulings: The Record to Date', (2007) 2(1) *Journal of International Economic Law* 398

Winickoff, DE, Jasanoff, S, Busch, L, Grove-White, R, and Wynne, B - 'Adjudicating the GM Food Wars: Science, Risk, and Democracy in World Trade Law', (2005) 30 *Yale Journal of International Law* 81

Winickoff, DE and Bushey, DM - 'Science and Power in Global Food Regulation: The Rise of the Codex Alimentarius', (2010) 35(3) *Science, Technology, & Human Values* 356

Wouters, J and Garaets, D - 'Private Food Standards and the World Trade Organization: Some Legal Considerations', (2012) 11(3) *World Trade Review* 479

Yamaguchi, T - 'Social Imaginary and Dilemmas of Policy Practice: The Food Safety Arena in Japan', (2014) 45 *Food Policy* 167

Yilmaz, M (ed.) - *Domestic Judicial Review of Trade Remedies* (Cambridge, Cambridge University Press 2013)

Young, M - 'The WTO's Use of Relevant Rules of International Law: An Analysis of the Biotech Case', (2007) 56 *International and Comparative Law Quarterly* 907

Zahrnt, V, - 'How Regionalization can be a Pillar of a More Effective World Trade Organization', (2005) 39(4) *Journal of World Trade* 671

Zimmermann, A, Tomuschat, C, Oellers-Frahm, K, and Tams, C - *The Statute of the International Court of Justice: A Commentary* (2nd edn, Oxford, Oxford University Press 2012)

Zimmermann, C - 'Rethinking the Right to Initiate WTO Dispute Settlement Proceedings', (2011) 45(5) *Journal of World Trade* 1057

Zorrilla, L - *Historia de las Relaciones entre México y los Estados Unidos de América 1800-1958* (Mexico, Porrua 1965)

Index

Milton Keynes UK
Ingram Content Group UK Ltd.
UKHW010011030224
437180UK00005B/150